Memoir:
A Charged Life

MEMOIR: A CHARGED LIFE

How A Woman Became an Electrician
(plus other things)

*To Dr. Mingle
My favorite Doctor
Pat*

PAT STANLEY-BEALS

COVER ILLUSTRATION BY THE AUTHOR

890-5739
73 Durgin Rd
S. Paris, ME
04281

authorHOUSE

AuthorHouse™
1663 Liberty Drive
Bloomington, IN 47403
www.authorhouse.com
Phone: 1-800-839-8640

© 2013 by Pat Stanley-Beals. All rights reserved.

No part of this book may be reproduced, stored in a retrieval system, or transmitted by any means without the written permission of the author.

Published by AuthorHouse   02/21/2013

ISBN: 978-1-4817-1780-9 (sc)
ISBN: 978-1-4817-1778-6 (hc)
ISBN: 978-1-4817-1779-3 (e)

Library of Congress Control Number: 2013902893

Any people depicted in stock imagery provided by Thinkstock are models, and such images are being used for illustrative purposes only.
Certain stock imagery © Thinkstock.

This book is printed on acid-free paper.

Because of the dynamic nature of the Internet, any web addresses or links contained in this book may have changed since publication and may no longer be valid. The views expressed in this work are solely those of the author and do not necessarily reflect the views of the publisher, and the publisher hereby disclaims any responsibility for them.

CONTENTS

Acknowledgements vii
Introduction ix
Foreword xi

Chapter One	Germination 1
Chapter Two	Primary Leaf 12
Chapter Three	Secondary Leaf 21
Chapter Four	Stunting 34
Chapter Five	New Growth (Michael) 50
Chapter Six	Lightning Strike 64
Chapter Seven	Branching 91
Chapter Eight	Rooting: (Harry) 106
Chapter Nine	Shaping (Wear And Tear) 122
Chapter Ten	Grafting (New Branch On Wild Root) 132
Chapter Eleven	Rampant Growth: (Stewart) 150
Chapter Twelve	Part I Stewardship At The Little Red House—Small Animals 171
	Part II Stewardship At The Little Red House—Large Animals 187
Chapter Thirteen	Stewardship At Chantrel 198
Chapter Fourteen	Harvest 212

ACKNOWLEDGEMENTS

A few years ago I received a notice that my high school class was going to have their fiftieth reunion. I realized this would be the way to get in touch with a friend I hadn't seen for almost that length of time. I had been wondering how his life had been over the years, but had been unsuccessful in finding his current address.

I called the reunion organizer and asked if my friend had signed up. She said he hadn't but she could give me his phone number. The number she gave me was for a fax, which looked like a dead end until I figured I could handwrite a note and send it as a fax.

Here's what I wrote: "Hey, Bill. This is Pat from High school. Do you remember me? Call me at the following number."

Well, I talked him into going to the reunion banquet, and we had a great time, but it was too short, so we started emailing. His first communication was, "Tell me about work, and I'll tell you about my life."

That statement opened a floodgate. I sent him two or three pages almost every night until I was somewhere over twenty pages. Bill was the ideal reader. He gave me the feedback I needed: laughter, horror, amazement. I realized I had been saving stories over the years and had a lot more to go, so I began writing them down. Some of it was difficult; most of it was a blast. Bill was always ready to read more. Without that encouragement, this book probably would never have been written. Thank you, Bill Wasserman.

Some other people I need to acknowledge are my younger sisters, Stephanie Swaney and Margo Torelli. They were invaluable with additions of other memories I had forgotten. Steph helped me edit, also.

My youngest daughter, Emma-Rose, was a great help, too. Her thoughts enabled me to write another eight pages.

Unfortunately, my older sister was horrified with the full disclosure, as was my oldest daughter.

My final thanks go to Jack Scow, whose professional opinion and numerous donated readings were greatly appreciated.

Oh, by the way, I never did get much of a life story from Bill. I think I might have somewhat overwhelmed him.

INTRODUCTION

This is my life story as the first female master electrician in the state of Maine. It describes what it was like to carry my own weight in a man's field: sometimes arduous, sometimes dangerous, but mostly interesting. The book begins with the burning death of my older brother, and the haven I sought in nature and books. It is the story of the overcoming of obstacles and the development of my character.

I acquired my master's electrical license in 1979 and have operated my own electrical company since 1986. I designed and, for two years, taught a course in house wiring for women under the auspices of Women Unlimited. Along the way, I had three husbands and four children, all without the loss of my sanity, humor or identity as a woman.

On this path, I gradually became aware of the reality of God's protective love and His intervention throughout my life. This memoir chronicles the transition from a self-absorbed realist to a faith-based child of God.

I have used the growth of a tree as the analogy of my life. Sometimes growth has been gradual, sometimes luxurious, or even stunted. I think branching off in new directions has been a constant factor, as has firm grounding and rooting. The harvest is still in progress and I hope it is more than meager.

I invite you to take a look at my life and share my discoveries of God's blessings.

FOREWORD

By Dr. Suzanne Best, Veterinarian

When my husband and I were first searching for a new home for our veterinary clinic, we heard from a building inspector about a woman electrician who was "top notch." He was clearly very impressed with her. We asked her to come and give an estimate on the job. I was surprised and pleased to hear of this woman electrician and looked forward to meeting her.

She arrived at the job and got out of her truck. She was wearing a blue visor with her straight white bangs on top of it. She looked stiff as she maneuvered her way around, like her knees were giving her some problems. Later I found out she was 70 years old!

She was honest, to the point, and affordable. We liked her very much. As we worked with her, we found her to be inquisitive, thoughtful, and interested in many facets of life. I thought she must be tough to have proven herself in a male dominated profession.

My profession, at one time was also male dominated, but that has changed in the last twenty years. Now there are more women than men as veterinarians. My older colleagues needed to prove themselves worthy and oftentimes were not accepted at all. That was probably true for Pat, also.

Pat struck me as a woman who was doing what came naturally to her. Her ability to be analytical and problem solve, as well as being able to see the big picture, fit her chosen profession. To have succeeded at her profession also took toughness and perseverance that not many possess, and I admire her for that.

After reading her book, I now realize that she had to surmount numerous obstacles in her life, and she has exceeded the odds in many ways.

1 GERMINATION

It was a soft summer morning, almost idyllic. Helen and her three children were staying in the Wee House on her parents' farm. A fire was crackling in the fireplace because of the early chill. The two older children, Barbara and Budgie were downstairs by the fire, getting out of their nightclothes. Four-year-old Budgie stirred the fire with a poker causing some sparks to shoot out and land on his pajamas.

Suddenly the piercing sound of screaming shattered the summer air. Budgie was engulfed in flames. His screeches were blood-curdling, and the smell of burning flesh was overpowering. Six-year-old Barbara sobbed while she stumbled back and forth from the kitchen with saucepans full of water, but it was a futile effort. The flammable nylon clothing had already melted into his skin and not much remained of his genitals.

Because Helen was deaf she heard none of what was happening downstairs and was sleeping with the baby. Something startled her awake. Helen tore down the stairs, ran to Budgie, and knelt beside him. She scooped him up in her arms, and when she did his shrieking diminished to moaning as he slipped into unconsciousness. She held him tightly to her chest, tears pouring down her face.

Others from the next cottage over called the ambulance and then gently spoke to the young girl. "It wasn't your fault," they said, but Barbara was inconsolable.

They all waited tensely for the ambulance to arrive. When the paramedics got there and saw the mutilated little boy they gave him a hefty dose of morphine. Once he was admitted to the hospital he was given more. A day and a half later Budgie slipped away. The consensus was that this was better for Budgie. What kind of life would he have had with such brutal damage done to him?

This turned out to be one of the most formative events in my life, even though I was a baby and didn't really know anything about what had happened. I'd been born two years before (September 19, 1940) and my parents felt they had the perfect family; two girls and a boy. After Budgie died my parents kept having children to replace him. They said this jokingly, but my sisters and I knew it was really the truth. It was just their bad luck that we continued to be females. They finally gave up after Mom almost died giving birth to her fifth one. Mom had something called placenta previa, which occurs when the umbilical cord attaches to the uterine wall at the cervix. As labor begins and the cervix dilates, it rips and detaches the umbilical connection. There is bleeding and possible death for both child and mother. Because of this problem, Mom and Dad gave up on having a replacement for Budgie.

Why was the loss of my older brother so significant in shaping my life? Somehow, I got the idea that the missing male was of more value than all the rest of us females. Boys were more special than girls. As a result I regarded my own feminine qualities as weak. From then on, I worked to be their replacement son. It wasn't until I had my first child twenty years later that I realized how fantastic it was to be a woman.

My earliest memory was when I was about three. I had run away from home; all the way across the street to an unknown lady's house. I hid under her bed. I still have this image of her head upside down with her long black hair hanging in her face. She asked, "What are you doing there?"

I replied, "I am running away." I had complete confidence and resolution. I was not to recapture that feeling until I was almost in my thirties.

My next memory was when I was six. Dad was an officer in the Navy and there wasn't a good place to rent. Therefore, our housing at the time was at a very posh place called the United Nations Club in Long Island, New York.

Waiters served us dinner in the lavish dining room. One of them was Tomas (accent on the second syllable). He had long straight dark hair and smooth olive skin. His slight build was much smaller than Dad's, but there was elegance to it. He also had the most romantic accent. Once, when I came down the back hallway, he swooped down to my level, put his arm around my shoulder, and planted a wet kiss on my lips. He said, "You are so pretty." I was completely stunned. My lips burned for days afterward.

I, of course, was consumed with love for him.

A boy my age at the club named Michael G. became my playmate. Since my knowledge of male anatomy was nonexistent (as I had only sisters) I talked Michael into getting into a closet with me, so I could remedy that ignorance. I was well prepared with a flashlight for the darkness of the closet. However, before anything could happen, the door flew open and there stood my father roaring at me, "What are you doing!"

I shrank as I realized I was truly bad.

That feeling clung like a bad odor for many years.

Our family finally found a nice place to rent in Port Washington, Long Island, so we left the Club, (and Tomas, and Michael). I entered second grade in the new town.

The first day of school, during recess, all the boys lined up and said, "You need to pick who is going to be your boyfriend." I looked them over and was drawn to two boys. One was tall, dark, and skinny. His name was David. He had a brooding scowling look. The other one was shorter, with curly blond hair, and a sweet open countenance. Because he looked a lot like Michael, I picked him.

Unfortunately, I picked the wrong one. He was the class Dufuss. The other one was the leader of the boys. Because I had picked someone low on the totem pole, I was relegated to that position, also. I didn't know how to change the situation, so I just isolated myself from the group completely.

Solitude became a lifelong attitude, aggravated by the frequent moving of military life. I was always the 'new kid', awkward, uncomfortable, and not part of the group: And yet I didn't mind being alone. It seemed peaceful to me, without the necessity to make choices. They would only turn out to be the wrong ones, anyway.

Let me give you an example. We had a champion dog given to us. His name was Chief, (which is a rank in the Navy.) He was an atypical black and white Springer Spaniel, much larger than the ideal type, without the fancy feathered ears and legs you see in show dogs. He was my favorite companion, instead of children my own age.

I had decided I wanted to get up in the second story of the neighbor's garage. It looked like a good place for peace and quiet from the hubbub of the family. I wanted the company of Chief, though. So, I encouraged him to climb up the ladder, which he did quite easily. Going back down was a different story. No way was he going to do that. The only solution to that predicament was to tell my father. It took both my father and the neighbor to get Chief back down. I was in the dog house for weeks after that.

However, my parent's idea of punishment was completely ineffectual for me. Isolation was uncomfortable for them because they were so social. Therefore, that became the chosen method for discipline. Going to my room was not a problem for me. I actually preferred it.

David, the leader of the boys at school, briefly broke my isolation. It was he who showed me a shortcut to the elementary school. The way to go was through the forbidden bad section of town, where he came from. I greatly admired him by this time. He was tough and I wished I had picked him. But that was the only time he had any contact with me, since that fateful day in the school yard.

I had a great time cutting through people's yards and making discoveries, like a praying mantis I found. I collected her egg sac and hoped to see her babies hatch; didn't happen, though.

Another fruitful find was a cherry tree. It was of mythical hugeness, with great spreading branches that were quite within reach. I would eat handfuls of explosive sweetness; taking great pride in the distance I could spit the stones. These were Bing cherries which would indelibly stain my mouth and hands. I soon learned to eat them, without the giveaway of my disobedience.

Because of the horrible experience in the Wee House, my parents were researching where to buy a summer home away from my mother's family farm in New London, New Hampshire. The next idea was to visit Dad's parents at their summer home. This was on the Thousand Islands, in the Saint Lawrence River, in upper New York State. I was extremely impressed when my cousin Jim came to pick us up from land, driving an outboard motor boat—*all by himself*, and he was only my age (about six)!

My grandparents owned a small island on the river that was actually two islands hooked by a little walking bridge. They called it Spectacle Island because that was what it resembled from the air. There were no other residents on the island, so it was a little gem of privacy.

Grand Daddy B had suffered a stroke which paralyzed his left side, but that didn't put him down. He was a retired physician and to keep busy he wrote poetry and his autobiography. He also created lamps and other things out of copper; and—FISHED. Since he only had the use of one hand he rigged up a bench that he could sit on with a foot-operated pedal that clamped the fish tight. That way he could clean his own catch. It was quite an invention to my young eyes.

I guess my parents decided the St. Lawrence was too far away from Mom's family, because, in the summer of '46, they bought a summer home in Georges Mills, New Hampshire. It was just three miles from where Mom had grown up (and Budgie died.) Since Dad was stationed quite a distance away, he only came north to stay with us on the weekends. That left Mom alone to cope with things, but she didn't do a very good job of it.

We inherited an old coal furnace with the house. It was a huge rusty hulk of a thing that didn't look very safe. I would watch my father shovel coal into its gaping maw, amazed that heat could come from black rocks. While that old furnace did manage to heat the place, Mom couldn't bring herself to go anywhere near it. I thought it was because she didn't want to get dirty. It really *was* a dirty job. The coal dust would get all over you and inevitably be tracked back up into the house. I now realize the fire itself probably was the problem for Mom (memories of Budgie and all).

It didn't take long for the coal furnace to be abandoned. We didn't need much heat because it was for summer use only. Some mornings could be pretty cold though, so we got a kerosene heater for the kitchen. Again, Mom did not get involved. When it came time to set a full metal jug of kerosene on top of the little heater Dad would do it. If he wasn't there, then either Barbara or I would do that job.

The house was called Waterlily Cottage, although it wasn't a cottage at all. It was a rambling country farmhouse with a two-story attached barn. It was located on the outlet brook of Otter Pond and had several acres of woods and fields all around it. Between the brook and the lake was a small old-fashioned adjustable dam that could raise or lower the level of water on the lake.

I had many happy memories there, mostly of a naturalistic nature. The first thing was pretty grim. Our dog killed a mother mink that lived in the rock bank by the water. Soon her two babies crawled out of the bank. Dad made a large cage for them. I was fascinated with how his hands could take pieces of wood and steel net and then with just a saw, hammer and nails, create a home for them. My Father, the cerebral physician, working with tools, amazing!

In spite of our care, sadly, the babies died. We had much more success with animals when we adopted a stray black cat that actually adopted us. We called her Cinder, and when she had a litter of kittens we gave away all but her longhaired son. We named him Rumplestiltzkin. He lived almost twenty years.

Dad made a great wooden slide so we could get our big Old Town canoe down the stone embankment/wall into the water without damaging it. Another of his projects was the removable wooden deck that was placed over the stone and cement dock. It had long arms that ran along the length of the dock and were weighted down with heavy rocks. It also had two front uprights where we hooked the rowboat. This was where Dad taught me how to do a double-half hitch. It was so neat to do two quick turns around the post and not have it slip off. It took some practicing to get the flip over that made it secure. But once I did, it was almost magical.

The dock had another function besides mooring the boat. It was also where we could get a good run from the grassy lawn, thunder across the wood, and project ourselves a good five feet out into the water. Explosive cannonballs were the object here. Or maybe it was to see who could get to the big rock first.

Dad saw my interest in his handyman projects, and for my eighth birthday he gave me a set of children's tools. Unfortunately, they were designed as play things. The saw, itself, was so dull; it took me ten minutes to cut a board in half. I wasn't impressed with them at all. I wanted my own set of adult tools that I could actually build something with.

My interest in nature led me to spend long hours in our brook area below the dam. I constructed miniature dams and ponds for the bullfrogs I caught in the swamp across the bridge. I never understood why they didn't stay there. I guess they would somehow find their way back to their home in the swamp.

As we had once visited our cousin Jimmy on the St. Lawrence River, he came to visit us. He would stay for weeks on end so he was almost a summer brother. We were very alike in our interests.

One day when we were poking around the dam, I noticed a long bar half-buried in the grass beside the dam. It was shaped like a fire poker with a big hook on the end, but much longer (about eight feet long). It was immediately apparent to me the purpose of this hook. It was obviously the tool for lifting the wooden pieces of the dam up and out of their channels. I had no idea who was responsible for the water level in the lake, and had never seen anyone using the hook.

An irresistible idea occurred to me. Why not change the puny dribble that was now going over the dam into something more impressive? I took the hook and rubbed it along the top of the dam. Sure enough . . . . there was the eye-hook on one end. Immediately there was a problem. Lifting one end of the bar wasn't going to work because it would just bind up on the channel. We needed something to lift the other side of the wooded bar at the same time. We went back to the barn and found a piece of scrap 2 by 4. Next we had to rummage around to get a big spike to nail on the end. Good old barn. It always came up with what you needed.

Going back to the dam, the jury-rigged tool we had made worked just as well as the correct tool. Carefully lifting together, we got one bar up and out. That made such a current of water flow out; I took a second wooden piece out. Now, we had a veritable Niagara thundering over the dam. We felt very powerful, almost like Gods. We were changing the whole ecology of the lake. That seemed very satisfactory—for a moment.

Then I had an attack of conscience. I pictured the lake drying up and all the fish flopping around in the mud. That wasn't what I wanted! Jimmy was probably just as sobered about what we had done because he humped to it with me, getting those bars back in place. Thank goodness no one witnessed that misadventure.

Another time Jimmy and I took the canoe into the swamp to get more frogs for the ecology pools we were building below the dam. We ran aground on something in the middle of the soft mucky swamp. This wasn't right. There was never a rock there before.

"Hold still," Jimmy said.

We sat there immobilized, looking at each other, when the canoe shifted.

"Did you do that, Jimmy asked?"

"*I'm* not moving," I said.

Another slight movement.

"What the heck?"

"I think I know," said Jimmy, "Push!"

We stood up and pushed off it, but we couldn't see what it was because the water was all swirly and muddy. Jimmy reached his hand down and muckled onto a huge snapping turtle.

"Gotcha!" It was so big and heavy (typical of a male turtle) he had to use two hands to hang onto the tail

"He's too big. I can't get him in the boat. You paddle."

I dug in as hard as I could, but it seemed like I was paddling through molasses. We finally pulled up to the dock. Its neck seemed as long as a snake and its claws were spread out to shred whatever it could. We carefully lifted it up onto the shore where it was hissing and snapping ferociously. It was the biggest snapping turtle I had ever seen, maybe 28" across the widest part. The turtle created quite a sensation. We would give him sticks to grab onto, but he would snap them in two.

That resulted in the satisfactory screaming of my sisters. But Mother's response was even more negative. Since Dad wasn't there, she called Uncle Bob. The idea was to kill the turtle; since everyone was sure it would come and snap someone's fingers or toes off while they were swimming. Unfortunately, Uncle Bob probably wasn't the best choice to do the dastardly deed, being the laid back pacifist he was, however, somebody found an ax. He took a mighty swing and chopped half the front leg off! The turtle kept moving, though. My sisters' screaming escalated to a higher volume.

A second mighty swing whacked the turtle in the neck, but he kept coming. The third mighty swing did decapitate the turtle, but he still was dragging himself around, like a headless zombie for about five minutes. Finally, all movement ended (thankfully). Later, I asked Jimmy how he dared to reach blindly into the water to grab it. He said he figured the turtle was swimming forward rather than backward.

That hideous experience caused my sisters and me to have nightmares for the rest of the summer.

I took the corpse up to the small field on the west side of the house and put it on an ant hill hoping when they finished with it, there would be a nice turtle shell left. My knowledge of nature was still incomplete, because it wasn't the ants that caused the unpleasant parts of the turtle to disappear. It was probably a bear or coyote, which took the whole thing.

The field was a special place for me. On the edge were some moderate-sized pine trees. I had taken some boards up and put them between two pines to make a tree house. My efforts fell far short of what I wanted to accomplish. I had in mind the Swiss Family Robinson's house with multiple levels and rooms. But it was sufficient for my purpose, which was to get away. I really craved the peace and silence in the trees, because there was so much clamor in the house from all my sisters. The soft whisper of the needles as the wind moved through them soothed my soul. An extra dividend was the sharp acidic scent of the pines that cleared out all the 'people smell'. Sometimes I read up there. Mostly, I just spread out on the boards and imagined the forest was my home.

My sister Elissa was four years younger than I was. She was a roly-poly child with a soft pudgy body. Inwardly, her hardheaded stubborn attitude was in marked contrast to her outward appearance. The thing that bothered me about her was how she would tag after me and whine and tattle so much I could hardly stand to be near her. My opinion of her wasn't completely negative, however. I secretly admired her blonde, tightly curled hair. My hair was straight and would never be 'fashionably fluffy'. Sixty years later I was able to share that thought with her before she died.

My sister Barbara was four years older, and strongly resembled our mother from her cheekbones to her ample bosom. She had a womanly figure and kept her tan hair no longer than the bottom of her ears. She had a fresh open face that only needed a light touch of lipstick to dress it up. Her natural style was accented by a curving smile and outrageously white teeth. She was outgoing and made friends easily. This was a mystery to me, as was her interest in the adults; but since she was the good daughter, maybe it wasn't so surprising. I can't recall having any conflict with her, probably because our worlds hardly ever intersected. She didn't seem to ever get into trouble.

I, on the other hand, seemed to be on the wrong end of the stick most of the time. I was the tallest of my sisters, almost 5'10' by the time I stopped growing (about sixteen). I resembled our father with my completely straight brown hair, lithe body, and dark brooding face. I was serious and introverted. Although I inherited his intellect, I never seemed to measure up to his expectations.

He took me to have an IQ test when I was about eleven. That was great fun, finding patterns in numbers, or remembering long strings of them. Even more fun was the interpretation of common phrases, like 'a bird in the hand is worth two in the bush.' That test was actually counter-productive for me. Now when I came home with lackluster grades, Dad would get after me. He would say, "I know you can do better so why aren't you?" I had no answer to that. I was as completely bewildered as he was. I actually thought those tests were bogus. My concept of myself was that I was completely ordinary.

Dad's solution to the problem was to drill me. He taped numbers on those small children's building blocks. Then he would roll them like dice and whatever numbers came up, I was to multiply quickly, no figuring out allowed. I was not good at that, largely because rapid processing was not a strength I had. What actually happened during those drilling sessions was blackness would envelope my brain. It became empty and void and all functioning ceased. A hot flush would come over me and I felt like I had melted into the floor. My misery was so palpable he would eventually give up. It was completely frustrating for both of us. I still have trouble with multiplication tables. At least now I can take the time to figure them out.

To escape this stress and pressure I would retreat to my tree house and live in the stories I read like Rudyard Kipling's *The Cat that Walked Alone,* Daniel Defoe's *Robinson Crusoe*, Walter Farley's *Black Stallion*, and *Dr. Doolittle*, Being able to talk to animals was an ability I deeply coveted. These were wonderful fantasies and much more interesting than my family. I loved my pathetic tree house. I could look down, enormously pleased with my hideout, while Elissa wandered around calling my name. One of the ways I kept her from following after me so much was to describe the bears and wolves inhabiting the woods with such lurid detail I would almost scare myself.

My other manipulation tool was a pretend secret door in the wall I had next to my bed. This was when all three of us older girls shared a bedroom. I had one wall, Barbara had the other, and Elissa was in the middle. This fake cubby-hole in the wall was where I supposedly left notes to the tooth fairy. If Elissa had been bothering me I would tell her I was going to leave a note to the tooth fairy and next time she lost a tooth she would get nothing. I would make authentic bangs and scrapes, like I was opening up the door and then shutting it. She actually bought it for a few years. Barbara wasn't there because her bedtime was later, but it was late enough to be completely dark.

My manipulation morphed into dominating. Elissa would whine that the only reason I could beat her racing with our bikes was because mine was bigger and had the advantage over her smaller bike. I couldn't let that excuse stand, so I bragged to her I could even beat her with the smaller bike. I almost busted a gut pushing her little bike past mine, but I did it. Then the trick was to conceal how hard I was breathing.

Piece of cake.

(Yeah, sure!)

As we got older, she began to challenge me more. She got in my face once about something I can't even remember. I chased her and gave her a good thump on her back. That ended the conflict but I wasn't happy with getting physical. Fortunately, that was almost the final confrontation. Two more were to come much later down the years.

2   PRIMARY LEAF

My parents began to get a sense of how friendless I was, so they would invite their friends over who had children my age to play with. Years later my daughter Lee taught me the word for this. It's called a 'play date.' Unfortunately, their efforts to socialize me with 'proper' playmates didn't work at all.

The most memorable of these Visits were by two very correct sisters. The girls weren't a bit interested in catching frogs or jumping around from rock to rock in the brook. I'm afraid I showed off terribly, with these great flying leaps that were much more dramatic than I usually accomplished when I was by myself. I actually scared myself on some of them.

I remember the younger sister telling me she had to go to the bathroom. I was having too much fun being Tarzan, so I ignored her pleas. When I finally brought her up to the house, I was mortified to see a brown lump plop out of her shorts as she went up the stairs ahead of me. I realized it was my fault and resolved to be more sensitive next time.

They never came back to visit.

More successful visits were from my cousins. They lived three miles away, so I got to see them often. Jane, Uncle Bob's daughter, was my favorite. We would run around prancing and snorting as if we were horses. I was the black stallion, and she would be my mare; sounds kinky, but it wasn't. We were only eight or nine.

The Barn at Waterlily was a wonderful place. It had stopped being a working barn a number of years before. Mother had turned it into a great library/playroom for rainy days. The main smell was the mustiness of old books, but if the sun slanted in just right, it would light up the dusty air from bits of old hay in the rafters and that would add a visual effect to the olfactory mix.

On the second floor of the barn was a long twenty foot swing that hung from the top rafters. Its height enabled us to push the swinger so hard we could run under the swing itself. The goal was to get the swing arcing so high it would hit the next cross piece, front and back.

There was room up there for a ping pong table, some old beds and a lovely claw-foot round oak table. There was also an old pump organ, and two model trains that actually ran. On the wall was a bow and arrow set from the Amazon that had real animal fur wrapped around it.

One corner was filled with dolls, little beds, and even a dollhouse. Not quite my thing. The best things were the books that covered the walls. One wall was entirely made up of children's books. Mom had subscribed to a Little Golden Book Club, which sent a new book for each of us every month. How I looked forward to those coming in the mail. I still have them now, books with my name in them from when I was seven or eight.

Once I had everything read, I moved on to the older novels and found some real resonance with Seton's *Wild Animals I Have Known*. He was a naturalist who was published in the 1920s. Of course, the chapter I liked best was the "Pacing Mustang". "Lobo, the Wolf" was pretty good, too.

Dad had the other two walls lined with old medical books of his and his father's. I liked going through the incredible pictures of misshapen limbs and horrible tumors or skin conditions. I, also, finally satisfied my curiosity concerning male genitalia. The best find was tucked away in a trunk, in Dad's work shop. That was the "Kinsey Report." I gained a lot of status from my cousins when I showed them that book!

Right off the highest level of the barn was a small balcony. It had a low roof so when the robins or wrens made nests, we could peek and see the eggs and then the fledglings. For some reason, nobody ever used the balcony, until I swung a rope over the edge and climbed down when we were playing Hide and Seek. Nobody could figure out how I could disappear so effectively. Besides the balcony, there were many other odd little places to hide in that big farmhouse. My younger sisters could even fit themselves into the old standup wardrobes that were in the barn. Sometimes we had to give up hiding because it took so long to be found.

I was also hard to find when it came time to do the dishes. The only chores I really liked were outdoors. I liked mowing the lawn, or weeding the pink Phlox that was surrounded by that rampant green and white Bishops Weed. But dishes? Forget it!

The balcony was the scene of yet another time I got into trouble. Elissa wanted to try climbing down the balcony using my rope, but her hand strength wasn't quite up to supporting her weight, so she fell and lay twitching on the ground, squeaking out, "I can't breathe, I can't breathe."

I thought she had broken her back and it was my fault. I ran to get Dad. He came charging out and after a quick look said, "She just had the wind knocked out of her." What a relief that was for me, even though I mostly thought of her as a pest.

Elissa came to regard me as someone that could do her damage, and one time when she was swimming by herself, she went over the dam. Maybe I was supposed to be watching her, but I was in the brook below the dam playing with my frog pond. When I heard her crying, I looked up and there she was, at the bottom on the dam, luckily, not seriously damaged. Her interpretation of what had happened was I had tried to drown her. It's funny how two different memories of the same event can be so dissimilar.

An accident-free place was the downstairs part of the barn. It had two stalls that could have still had horses in them. I was definitely horse crazy, and continually begged for a horse for my birthday. When my father was sent to Japan after WWII, he brought back a collection of ivory horses that he gave to my older sister, Barbara. I was deeply covetous of them. I don't even remember what he brought back for me.

To add further distress, Barbara was invited to ride an English lady's horse called Copper. He was the exact color of burnished copper. I have never seen a coat as beautiful and unique as that on another horse. He was tall (maybe 16 hands) and had a cascading mane and tail. His gaits just floated. Although he was airborne between each foot fall, the vibrations would transfer along the ground through my feet and back into my beating chest. Each time he went by I sucked in deeply that musky horse odor flung up by his hooves. I watched my sister ride him with my heart in my eyes, longing written all over me. It felt as though my eyes were on long stalks hanging out of my head, like a cartoon character.

My parents finally picked up on my feelings and granted part of my wish, which was riding lessons with my cousins and younger sisters. This was the pinnacle of my life up to that point. There was a horse show at the end of one summer. Wouldn't you know, my younger sister Stephie took First Prize? That fact didn't abate my love for horses one bit, though.

Stephie was the fourth daughter in line and nine years younger than I was. She had the slenderness from Father, *and* the fulsomeness that Mom had. Stephie's nose was the opposite of the family nose; hers had a quirky little bulb on the end and she absolutely hated it. What the boys noticed was a little lower than her nose, however, and the boys flocked to her like she was the ice-cream truck.

I got along with Stephie famously, probably because she had looked up to me since she was a baby. I taught her to draw horses when she was still young, and it was as if another dimension opened up for her. She has an amazing capability to transfer what she sees, or is in her head, to paper or wood or wool.

Besides the friends I had in books, one of my best friends came from the shredded wheat cereal box. His name was Straight Arrow. Between the layers of wheat biscuits, was a cardboard with Straight Arrow's Indian lore on it. Things like, tracks of different animals, how to leave signs to other Indians of the trail you had taken, or how to make or find trail food. I collected these and punched holes in them so I could put rings on them to make a book. I spent many hours exploring in the woods, pretending I was an Indian. No one joined me in this fantasy.

One motivation for studying Indian lore was the strong desire to never be lost. I used to get a helpless feeling when my parents became lost on the annual treks driving back up to Waterlily. Having them holler at each other in such a confined space was bad enough. But for me, to lose orientation in space was even worse. I quickly learned the relationship of the sun to the time of day, so I could know where north, south, east, and west were. This reliable connection to the earth, this knowing where I was and where I was going, gave me the security and confidence I needed.

When Cousin Jimmy came to visit from New York, he slept in the lower part of the barn that had a sportsman type bedroom with tongue-n-groove pine paneling on the wall. He even had a toilet in one of the horse stalls, (of all places). We kids thought it was pretty cool. I didn't need fantasy friends when he was there.

Some things we used to do weren't too smart, though. One of them was diving off the ten foot bridge railing into, at the most, four feet of water, with good sized rocks down there. We had to make the dive as shallow and abrupt as possible, sometimes snapping your back in the process, and surely cracking knees on the rocks. I was very much a tomboy, and relished these chances to show off.

My goal was to be as strong and worthy as a boy. One way to establish this was with Indian wrestling. We would start by putting our right feet side-by-side against each other and clasping right hands. The goal was to push or pull with that one hand until the other person lost their balance and fell down. The result was dominance, very satisfying to an 'inferior' girl.

Another side development in my early life was the deliberate effort to be stoic with pain. Do you remember the game "Indian Burn"? That's when you give a person permission to grip your wrist with both their hands. They twist their hands tightly around your wrist in opposite directions, making a friction burn on your skin. You are not supposed to flinch. Then it is your turn to do the same to them. The one that gave in to the pain was the loser. I never lost.

A gentler memory was our life as Water Babies. One of my most persistent dreams was being able to breathe underwater. I thought if I could only squeeze my lips tight enough, and take just tiny sips of water through a crack, I could get some oxygen from the water. That dream seemed very real to me and, I tried it, only once!

Besides the canoe, which we usually stored on the lawn, we had a small flat-bottomed wooden row boat that stayed in the water all summer. This old boat was ideal for fishing because of its flat bottom. We could stand up safely without tipping it over, and tackle boxes or pails of fish had a flat purchase also.

At the end of the summer, we would pull it out of the water which would make the planks dry out and shrink. When it was time to put it in the water each spring, the water would rush into the cracked bottom and it would rapidly fill with water until it almost sank. We would leave it like that for a few days and then we would bail it out. After about a week the boat was fairly water tight. However it rained frequently, so bailing the boat out was usually a necessary first step to going fishing. This was undertaken with great enthusiasm the first time. The younger sisters often got roped into helping with that task, especially if they were coming fishing also.

Dad's favorite activity when he came north for the weekends was fishing. He had found a few spots that wouldn't fail to have perch in them, so our efforts were never disappointed. This was something he always shared with us. I don't remember him ever fishing alone and we loved to go with him.

The first stipulation was that we would bait our own hooks. In the beginning, we would lose the worm after one nibble. Then Dad would demonstrate how to slide the hook the long way down the body of the worm, leaving a tempting loop in the middle and a short piece on the end that would wave attractively at the fish.

The next step was to allow the fish to bump and nudge the worm first. Once a fish had tested the bait, he would be more likely to grab the whole thing. Setting the hook was more successful when the fish had decided it was safe to hang on tightly; otherwise you might yank the bait right out of his mouth.

The next requirement was silence while fishing. Even dropping something in the boat was frowned on. "You'll scare the fish," was the admonition.

These fishing skills usually resulted in a good-sized catch. Now, the final stipulation appeared. We had to help clean the fish and get them salted and in the refrigerator right away. When we were younger, we could only clean three or four to Dads' twelve. As we got older, we got up to speed. A platter of golden, crispy, pan-fried fish was a favorite family meal and much appreciated.

To begin fishing we had to row under the small bridge in front of our house. That bridge was so low we had to crouch to go under, if only to avoid the gigantic cobwebs. Part of the spookiness of it was the metallic echo of the sounds. The other part was the swooping bats that would pile out at dusk. Once we got past the bridge we still had to row out farther to get past the water lilies, otherwise the stems from the water lilies would wind around the propeller and bind it up. Sometimes the early morning fog was so clammy it gave us goose bumps. Of course we wore shorts because when the sun burned the fog off, we would really bake. That sun and the lack of conversation were more than restful—therapeutic would be the right description.

Finally arriving on the main part of the lake we could start up the motor. A large part of the fun of fishing was being able to use that old Johnson outboard motor. It was an antique, even then (probably made in the 1920s). I think Dad used it when he was a boy on the St Lawrence River. It had a clothesline pull-rope we wound around the top of the open flywheel in order to start the engine. I wasn't strong enough to pull it until I was about ten. Putting my foot up on the transom (where the motor was attached) helped me get the leverage I needed to get it running. When I reached that size I was allowed to take the boat out alone. I felt so grown-up and competent.

When relatives came to visit, I wanted to demonstrate how grown up I was, so I asked Dad if I could take them out for a ride on the boat. Showing off again, I had that poor old engine cranked wide open, making tight circles and crashing back over the wake.

Inevitably, the motor came unscrewed off the transom. I hung onto the steering handle with both hands and all my might, but it began bouncing out of the water with the prop going a million miles a second. I couldn't let one hand go to reach the kill switch because it took everything I had to hang onto it with both hands. I envisioned shredded flesh as it thrashed around in bigger and bigger wild jumps. I finally had to drop it.

Down it sank, naturally into one of the deeper parts of the lake.

Again, I had to tell Dad the awful thing I had done.

Surprisingly, I didn't get punished for that one. I'm thinking now, maybe he had done something like that also when he was a boy. The motor was recovered, and we used it for many years after that. As a matter of fact, I still have it down in my cellar carefully wrapped in oilcloth. No one else has any understanding of what that motor means to me; emancipation, disaster, forgiveness.

Mother raised us with all the 'modern' methods of childcare which included bottle feeding, and 'letting us cry' to strengthen our lungs. I think that is part of the reason I did not develop the close bonding that is usual between mother and child. And, as a teenager Mother had become deaf, which probably caused more of the separation we felt from her. Deafness can be very isolating.

She was taking nursing at college when it became apparent that her inability to hear impacted her being able to take an accurate blood pressure measurement, so she didn't complete college. Lack of education was probably another disability (in her mind), therefore she was quite dependent on Dad.

Mom's hearing aid was huge. The receiver was about the size of a cell phone, maybe even larger, with a clip on it to keep it from sliding out of a shirt pocket. Then a wire went from the hearing aid up to the piece that went in her ear. Mom very rarely wore a shirt with a pocket so she usually clipped the hearing aid to her bra. We all knew if she couldn't hear us, we had to speak into her chest.

Mom told us a grand story of when she went to a cocktail party where her problem wasn't as well known. Everyone was well juiced-up by the time Mom received a telephone call. She turned the phone upside down, so the speaking part was by her mouth, and the hearing part was over her breast. Mom said she had to wrestle with them because they kept pulling the phone away and saying, "No-no, Helen, it doesn't go like that." They were sure she had drunk too much, when in reality that was the only way she could use the phone. Mom thought that was as funny as the rest of us did. One of the best things I learned from Mom was her ability to laugh at herself.

Some of Mom's other strengths were her music, both playing and composing tunes; another was solving crossword puzzles. She also was a great list maker—of things other people were to do. She saw herself as the administrator, rather than the worker.

As a child, I very early learned the value and respect that men earned with their careers, and as providers for their families. Mother got her self-respect from being The Doctor's Wife. Since Mom did nothing (in my young eyes) to earn my respect, she didn't get any from me. I regret that deeply now.

Mom did have a powerful influence on my life, however. She was a force to be reckoned with, as were her three sisters. The scalding fury of her anger was monumental especially when she had been drinking. The tragic thing was, she could never admit to herself or others the source of her pain.

Mom used her anger as a weapon. She poured her vitriol out on her daughters *and* her husband. She said I was a slut because I didn't wear underpants under my jeans. Her reason was if I were ever in an accident and an EMT had to cut away my clothes they would know I wasn't a good girl if I had no underpants on. It seemed a pretty poor reason but standing up to her fury was not possible. Another time she dragged me out of bed with the slut accusation ringing in my ears. I never knew what set her off.

Mostly her anger was focused on our father. One time she took a hammer to the bedroom door because Dad was in there trying to sleep. It was the only door that could lock. The rest of us just watched as she methodically hammered until she faded because of lack of strength. Another time we had to pull her off Dad because she was scratching and kicking, aiming for his groin.

He never lifted a finger in retaliation to her. His damage to her was much more insidious. I think she had a certain sense of what he was doing with me at night, and it was driving her to drink. It helped her to cope, I suppose.

The consequences of drinking and driving weren't so serious back in those days. When the police stopped her for erratic driving they would just call up the house and say, "Come get your mother."

Covering up alcoholism was the thing back then. The places that sold Mom her booze would occasionally accept some responsibility and refuse to sell to her. Her response was typical of all of us. She would find a way to get what she wanted. Stephie told me Mom would have her drive the car to an out-of-town liquor store, but when Mom walked in dragging her left foot because of her brain tumor damage, they wouldn't sell to her thinking she was already drunk. It was funny in a sad sort of way.

Life has taught me that covering up anger is no good either because all that does is drive the festering infection deeper. Exposing anger to air and sunshine dries it up, just as they heal physical wounds. What is the sunshine to anger? A compassionate understanding listener—even if that listener is only yourself.

3 SECONDARY LEAF

My connection to my mother paled in comparison to the connection I had to the farm where my mother grew up. Nana and Bompa were our maternal grandparents. They had six strong and vigorous children, four girls and two boys.

Nana's family came down from Canada. She was of small stature and had high cheekbones with little slits for eyes. I saw a picture of a Micmac Indian that looked just like her. I am sure we have Native American in us. All the women in the family have great fire and monumental passion. Our connection to the earth is very strong, also.

Bompa was much taller. He gave his two sons handsome athletic bodies that did well in football. Fortunately they didn't get the prominent and fleshy family nose.

Bompa was a builder and well respected in the community. He built many of the fancy town houses and school buildings. He also built four cottages for city people to rent during the summer, on what was once his farm. Eventually those cottages were bought by his children. The grandchildren were the ones with a care-free life there.

He owned sixty plus acres of land on top of Burpee Hill in New London, New Hampshire. This was hilly farmland with lakes and mountains nearby. Many of the farms had grown up into interesting woodlands so there was a lot of variety in the landscape.

Once we visited Bompa's farm for Christmas. When we went sledding on a winter morning, you couldn't even see the bottom of the hill. Twice down was all anyone wanted to do, because slogging back up in all our winter clothing was dampening, in more ways than one. Besides which, it was lunch time by then.

Other than that one winter visit, our time at the farm was during the summer when we could spread out and experience country life to the fullest.

Bompa's land included a good-sized field by the windmill; also elephant rock field, now planted to Christmas trees. His land continued through the higher cow pastures (now native high-bush blueberry fields) past sofa rock, up to the top of the hill, across some smooth rock ledges covered in soft moss, and down again through the stately cathedral pines (unfortunately gone now). On the way down a dark hidden spring yielded clear earthy water that was redolent of fairies and wood sprites. Taking a ritualistic cool sip as we passed confirmed the connection to our heritage. At the bottom we had to cross the main road, and then walk through some more woods until we arrived at our large peninsula with a narrow long sandy beach. The beach was a natural draw for all of us—aunts, uncles, fourteen cousins, plus the five girls in my family.

I was especially drawn to Bompa's classic barn. It was a large 3-story 'L-shaped' building with lots of rooms, all kinds of interesting tools and assorted junk. It was fun trying to figure out what something was used for. It was there I learned to have a casual disregard for spiders. More fun were the snakes that lived around the warm foundation rocks. I would step on their tails and then grab them by the head: the purpose being to dangle them in front of people just to make them cringe and hopefully scream. Since most of my cousins were girls, it was easy to do.

When I was very young the barn was still a working part of the farm. I could jump into loose hay mounds and be enveloped by a wonderful grassy aroma.

There was a scary place to jump also.

I think it was the room for the ice blocks so there was quite a bit of sawdust for covering the ice (to keep it cold) but there hadn't been any for quite awhile, so it was basically empty. It was tall, narrow, and completely enclosed, like an inside silo. The challenge was to jump from the top of the three-story barn, down to the small amount of hay and sawdust at the bottom.

My boy cousins were more familiar with the barn than I, and jumped down easily. I climbed to the top and looked down into complete and total darkness. Fear grabbed me by the throat. I definitely did not want to jump, but I had a reputation to protect. The palms of my hands got hot but wiping them on my jeans didn't seem to make a difference. I saw my cousins had survived. If they could do it, so could I.

Oh, brother!

One, two, three—

I flung myself out into the darkness. The flight through the air seemed endless. I landed with the great whoosh of a nose-tickling dusty-hay smell as my reward. My heart was leaping out of my chest. What a rush! I must have jumped at least ten times, until I could hardly climb up to the top again.

There was some bad fun to be had at the barn, also. I stole some of the hens' eggs and threw them at the wall. The splatter wasn't satisfying, though. My heart shriveled up as I imagined the murder I was committing.

I wished Bompa still had horses, but they were gone. What he did have was a huge hog. As soon as the pig saw us, he would heave himself up and run around with his enormous flesh quivering, grunting, snorting, and slavering at the mouth. I must admit, he was quite a bit intimidating. Additionally, the smell emitted from the stirred up offal was fetid and foul.

I never visited the pig or the hens again. I did, however, continue to jump in the hay, that is, until Bompa stopped haying.

Bompas' sister Emma lived in the farmhouse attached to the barn. Aunt Emma was a spinster probably because the family nose was a real affliction on her. And although she was very short, her hair was extremely long. Usually she put it up in a loose bun, but when she let it down it touched the floor.

She was an independent and taciturn lady who kept boarders to supplement the pittance she made as a schoolteacher. She didn't have to rely on a man for her living, which was in marked contrast to my mother. Fortunately, her brother (our grandfather) was there to help out with things she couldn't do, so she wasn't alone. Because of her self-sufficiency, I admired her greatly. I even named my youngest daughter after her. Oddly enough, my daughter also has extremely long hair.

When we left the barn to go into Aunt Emma's house, we went through the milk room where she separated the cream from the milk in the separator. It had a long crank that spun a container the milk was poured into. Centrifugal force spun the lighter milk out one spout. The heavier cream came out another spout. Then the cream was hand-churned to make butter. Even after all that processing, the milk still had enough cream in it to rise to the top of the milk jug. Using that cream on cereal or blueberries is one of the epicurean pleasures I deeply miss today. The wooden cheese press was kept in the same room so the air was permeated with the smell of old sour milk, but surprisingly it wasn't that bad. On the other hand, when we walked into Aunt Emma's warm kitchen, we would get the heavenly smell of biscuits or bread or pies, cooked on her old wood cook-stove. Because I was so transported by those smells, I got the idea she was a wonderful cook.

My mother's sisters told me otherwise.

Maybe her fare was plain and simple, while their food was made with nice fancy electric stoves and Julia Child gourmet cookbooks. Having a similar old wood cook-stove myself, I know what an accomplishment it is to cook anything in it.

Aunt Emma also had a blue '32 Plymouth with a rumble-seat in the back. It was a high honor to be allowed to ride in that rumble-seat. She drove like a maniac, but that only increased our respect for her. We couldn't wait to be able to drive it ourselves. Barbara, being the oldest of the cousins, would have been first, but Aunt Emma had piled it up by then.

Barbara learned to drive on our family stick-shift '49 Ford. The first time Dad took her out for The Driving Lesson he thought it would be instructive for Elissa and me to go along; 'kill two birds with one stone,' so to speak.

Well, Elissa and I did die—of laughter.

Every time Barbara would try to engage the gear, the car would lurch and wobble, accompanied by our great whooping laughter; no matter how sternly Dad told us to be quiet, we couldn't contain ourselves.

Needless to say, we weren't allowed to go on another driving lesson.

Aunt Emma's house is the first on the main road. It is the original type of four-square white farmhouses and was built in 1793. Attached to it is the barn which is mostly torn down now, much to my heartache. Peter, one of my cousins, fixed it up to be a rental unit for income to help pay the taxes. In 2010, when the expense of maintaining it became more than the income produced by the rental, Pam (Peter's sister) and her family bought it from the Farm Association, Inc. (which all us cousins are shareholders of now).

Across the street is another sprawling white farmhouse that Nana and Bompa lived in, and it now belongs to my cousin, Persis. (I upgraded the electric service on that building).

Interestingly, Nana had a need similar to mine which was to get away from the hustle and bustle of family. Bompa was able to fulfill this need by converting the carriage house near the big barn into a small cottage retreat for her. When my grandparents sold the farmhouse across the road to their oldest son, Sumner and moved to Florida, they no longer had a place to come to for the summers. Bompa added some amenities to Nana's little cottage and they summered there. After Bompa died, Nana continued to live there for many years. Once she was gone, it was uninhabited, except by raccoons that used the sink as a toilet and knocked Nana's books off the shelves. Their idea of interior decorating was original. They certainly weren't interested in the books and since they are known for cleanliness, sanitary functions were devoted to that one area.

Peter, Sumner's son, completely renovated the little cottage again. He made it his own home for about thirty years. He, also, continued the Christmas tree operation his father started. He mowed the fields; cut down the overgrowth of unwanted trees in the blueberry fields, and trimmed the poison ivy growing on the stone walls around the edge of the fields. He basically became the caretaker for the Farm. More than that, he put his heart and soul into each tree, bush, and rock (figuratively and literally).

It was while he was trimming by the wall that a piece of metal kicked up into his eye. It completely pierced the steel-mesh faceguard he was wearing. If that mask hadn't slowed the metal down it surely would have penetrated his brain. His eye wasn't the only part of his body he lost. He lost a whole hand trying to re-light an unexploded fire works rocket he found, when he was about twelve. Peter's laconic comment after the eye incident was, "I can't afford to lose anymore body parts!"

If you walk onto the driveway of Aunt Emma's farmhouse the next building on the same side of the driveway is Nana/Peter's cottage. On the same left side only a little farther in from the main road is the Lane Cottage. It is named that because the back of the house butts up against the stonewall-lined lane that the cows walked down to get to their pasture. Bompa had the lower fields dedicated to hay production and the cows would have trampled down the winter fodder if the lane hadn't been there. Plus, it is a lot easier to get hay cut on a flat area than on a hill. The cows had to walk almost a half mile to the steeper part of the hill for their summer grazing. That didn't bother them. They knew they were going to be milked and fed grain so they came back to the barn at night on their own.

Since the Great Depression was still vivid in Bompa's mind, and being a typical frugal Yankee, he was very sparing with building materials. Consequently, the Lane cottage arrived on the farm in the winter of 1942. It was actually dragged up the hill on the snow from where it was originally built on another farm. Bompa added a second story, a field-stone fireplace, and also a screen porch. It was used for summer rentals at first but now is occupied by Cousin Tom and his family. His younger siblings, Billy and Mary, don't come back to the farm much.

Across from Peter's cottage and on the other side of the driveway is The Shop. It may have been built around the beginning of the 1800s. It was in use by Bompa's father Benton, and later used as a blacksmith's shop. It was in sad shape, leaning fifteen degrees off plumb, so when Bompa's oldest daughter Gwen expressed an interest in having her own summer place for her family, Bompa was happy to oblige. The huge forge was taken out, the building was pulled away from the stone wall bordering the neighbor's farm, and additional rooms were added. There is a gorgeous field-stone fireplace in there, with lots of Bompa's tools hanging on the walls. (I have a few of his tools on my walls, also.) Then there is the long covered and screened porch, perfect for summer. Cousins Bill, Jane, and Cathy live there now.

Actually, Jane was able to acquire the Wind Mill Cottage and stays there with her children. This was the only cottage Bompa built from scratch. It was the last in the row of three well-spaced cottages on the right side of the driveway. There used to be a windmill there, which pumped the water from the well.

Bompa was very innovative for his time!

The Wee House is in between The Shop and the Wind Mill Cottage. The Wee House was the first to arrive on the farm during the winter (when it was easy to pull across the snow), probably some time in the early thirties. Bompa had built it in 1920 for someone else with very modest aspirations. It was only three rooms on one floor with a porch and was smaller than the other cottages, hence it's name. The fertility of our whole family necessitated the addition of a second story with more bedrooms, so it really shouldn't be called the Wee House. However, there is no possibility of changing the name now. It is currently occupied by Molly, Sally, and Julie, daughters of Aunt Susie (given name Eunice).

All these cottages have porches for the splendid view of Kearsarge Mountain. Another feature they all used to have in common was the weathered siding. In some cases it was grey shingles, a velvety-soft mouse-skin color. The other siding was board and batten which is dark brown with streaks of mellow gold depending on the grain of the wood. Now some of the cottages have had their siding up-dated to new stained shingles. I much preferred the old.

The blueberry fields are still a well-cherished blessing. We had tin pails with hoops on them we would use to pick the berries. The purpose of the hoops was to allow us to hook our belts through them. Then we could pick two-handed and fill our pails up quicker. The only problem was it would bob around as we walked. Sometimes it would even dump its whole contents if we weren't careful. When we heard a "Darn it" float across the field, we wouldn't even bother asking what the problem was. We knew it was a spilled bucket. The answer to that was to use the hoop for carrying only. My method of picking was to put the pail down on the ground so I could pick two-handed. If I used my thumb to loosen each berry with my thumb, being very careful and gentle, I could roll a whole clump into my palm. Since competition was an ever-present companion in our family, there were smaller sizes so the younger and slower pickers wouldn't get discouraged trying to fill them up. However, sometimes I would quietly pour berries into my younger sisters' pails. I would say, "I'm running out of room. Take some of mine."

The first money I ever earned, other than babysitting, was from selling quarts of those blueberries, to the German Lady. She made the flakiest, meltingly sweet, wild blueberry pie that she sold in her little restaurant. I went to work waitressing for her as soon as I was sixteen. Part of my pay was the choice of something to eat. I always picked her pie. She could have won prizes with it!

Through the high-bush blueberry fields is the path to the beach on Little Lake Sunapee. If you didn't bring anything to put berries into, you could still eat handfuls as you trekked by. The path continued past the White Russian family that had fled from the Red Russians during the communist takeover of their country. The Ourusoff's had a tennis court, where we couldn't help peeking at the handsome boys in their tennis whites as we went by. Bompa had sold them some of his property, and then he built them a big summer house with a huge wrap-around porch. It was three times as big as our summer cottages because the whole family congregated in the one building. Inside was another of the field-stone fireplaces Bompa was renowned for building. It was massive, but completely in proportion to the 'great room'. The grand piano didn't diminish the room either.

When we were older teenagers, Barbara and I would pile into their 'woodie' (an old station wagon with actual wooden sides) to go and climb Kearsarge. I was one of the younger ones, and so blown away by their charm and attractiveness, I could hardly speak. They were from the nobility so courtly manners and lineage were important to them. My first marriage was to one of their distant cousins, Michael T. He had their cosmopolitan aura, and then some.

You may have noticed only four of Nana and Bompa's six children have places to live on the Farm. One of the missing is Uncle Bill who showed little interest in the Farm. The other missing family member is our mother. The reason for her not wanting to live there is obvious. Our brother burned to death in the Wee House. That awful experience is why our parents bought a house three miles away. In spite of that distance, our family has remained a close part of the group, although somewhat disenfranchised.

So, between Waterlily and the Farm, our roots were allowed to establish and flourish, even though it was only during the summer.

Most of the Farmland is in a Land Trust now. It can't be further developed, so it will always remain as it is was back in Bompa's day. We all feel this visceral connection to the land. It is a wonderful treasure, for us and our children.

One way we experienced this tie was on the path to the beach. Walking that path was an adventure in itself. Since it was only used a few months in the summer it wasn't beaten down. Following it was a lesson in wood craft. If you didn't have enough time (or inclination) for the long walk from the farm to the beach, you could take the car on the main road and park closer to the Lake. From there it was still a good walk through quiet cool woods. The best way to walk it was barefoot. Your feet could feel the path almost as if they had eyes. This came in handy at night when you had no flashlight and there was no moon. Your bare feet could tell you as soon as you stepped off the path. What were we doing at night with no flashlight? I'll leave that to your imagination.

On the daytime trips to the beach you could leave the path and stop to dig up Indian cucumber if you were feeling hungry. But there weren't that many plants and you had to really look hard to find them. In the spirit of conservation we (mostly) left them alone. Down at the bottom of the hill, the mud squishes up deliciously through your toes. Then you get to Baby Beach on the east side of the peninsula where there are more blueberries. Finally you arrive at the Big Rock on the west side and the path opens out onto—THE BEACH!

To the right is the Point where some of the old white pines still stand. All of us have, at one time or another spent the night camping out on the deep bed of pine needles. The test was to see how many falling stars we could count before we fell asleep. Aunt Gwen, the oldest of the original six children, was married out on that point. She had a canoe carry her across the lake so her wedding dress wouldn't get ruined coming down the path, especially at the sometimes muddy bottom of the hill.

There is a boathouse where a small sailboat is kept beside all the beach chairs, sand toys, etc. There still is a separate changing house, but it may not last many more winters. Usually, we put our clothes on the huge Rock at the edge of the beach. This Rock even had a convenient notch to hold watches and/or glasses.

The beach itself was a seventy-five foot long natural sand deposit that sloped out gradually for quite a distance. There were no rocks, nor even pebbles, disturbing the soft smoothness of the bottom of the lake. There was one exception to that. A lone medium-sized rock was submerged about half way between the beach and the raft. This was the favorite spot for underwater swimming contests and King of the Rock.

There are canoes beside the beach, and you can even swim a hundred yards out to a floating wooden raft. Way out and much deeper is a submerged pile of rocks that supported an older dock. The previous generation used it but it was finally abandoned. It is now a serious hazard to unfamiliar boaters so the Lake association put a white marker on it. Now, bass have adopted it as their home. Once, I took a spear gun to harpoon them underwater. That was really exciting. Then, I was informed by the more correct family members that it was illegal to catch them in that manner. Darn! Other wildlife at the beach are loons with their haunting call, ducks, an occasional Great Blue Heron, and once I even saw a mink swimming across from the Point.

It's hard to describe the effect the beach has on a person. Both body and spirit are touched. I know that when I'm there, a knot in my middle which I'm usually unaware of, unwinds me into loose relaxation, and I am at peace. The water is lovely and clear without the floaty things some lakes have. And when the sun sinks over the distant tree-line across the lake, at a certain moment it turns the water into shimmering molten gold. Then is when you really become aware of the treasure we have.

The privacy of the beach also invites skinny-dipping, which is a very sensual pleasure. The velvety smoothness of the cool water without the encumbrance of clothing allows all the hair on your body to feel the slide through the water. It is a languorous and arousing feeling. Usually skinny-dipping is relegated to the young people, and happens at night. Uncle Sumner, however, continued to skinny-dip in the morning, when no one was at the beach, which was his concession to propriety. As he got older it was not a pretty sight. We all knew of his proclivity, and gave him his mornings at the beach. He did this every summer until he died.

We were not the only ones to indulge in this pleasure. The Russian family would skinny-dip during the day as freely as our uncle. Because they would dive off their boat house it gave our mother the opportunity to use the binoculars, ostensibly to look for wild life. The older of us cousins knew what 'wild life' she was hoping to see. We would giggle and talk in Pig Latin to each other about it. The younger ones were completely mystified. That was part of the fun in having a secret language. We even learned a more secret language called Gaity: That way if someone understood Pig Latin we could switch to a more obscure communication.

Summer was when our coltish abandon had freest expression, but an April Fools joke I played on my mother put a dent in my rowdiness. I got a long nail and put it in Dad's vise so I could hammer and bend it into a shape that would fit around my thumb. I had to get the angle just right to look as though I had hammered a nail through my thumb. Then I made a little cut and managed to squeeze some blood out on a cloth. I used the cloth to cover where the nail went around my thumb. After all my preparations were complete, and with Stephie as an accomplice, I staggered to Mom and showed her the damage I had done to my thumb. Mom totally bought it and lit up with a bloodcurdling scream. She didn't even hear me when I said, "April fool."

She continued screaming for Dad.

"No, Mom. It's okay. It's just a joke—see I'm taking it apart."

It took quite a time for mom to calm down.

No more joking like that to prey on a mother's fears.

A somewhat similar experience happened when I was about ten. My older cousin Tom and I had a great adventure that started at the beach. We paddled across Little Lake Sunapee to the outlet brook. We left the canoe there and my brilliant suggestion was to follow the brook down to my house. I knew it was only four miles in the car so I didn't think it would take long. My expectation of the time it would take to do this was seriously in error. Neither of us had our watches; they were back on the Big Rock. We blithely followed the brook as it meandered through the woods. We finally arrived at a tiny old settlement called Otterville, and the in-between pond, which I had expected. What I didn't realize was it was mostly mud so we couldn't swim it, or walk the shore—there was none. What we did was climb out and walk the old road.

Then we got distracted by the ancient abandoned sawmill that was there. We poked around in that for awhile. When we found a big sawdust pile, we just *had* to jump into it. I remember I buried my legs up to my hips when I landed. Tommy had to hook his arms under my shoulders to lift me out. Good thing he was there.

When we were finished fooling around there, we continued following the brook until it came out onto our own Otter Pond. It was then I realized I had a problem that Tom didn't have. I was completely clothed in jeans and sneakers. He still had his bathing suit on.

I bravely entered the water and tried to swim. I could barely move my legs. I told Tommy to go on ahead, I was going to be slower because of the clothes, but I'd be alright. He struck off down the long part of the pond heading directly for my house. Rather than follow him, I headed straight for the road along the pond. It was not in line with my house, but I knew I needed to shorten the distance I had to travel.

The first thing I did was take my sneakers off and tie them together. There was no way I was going to leave them behind. I had been after my mother to let me have boys' high-top sneakers for a long time, and I had just gotten them. I tried many different ways of swimming with them and settled on a spastic side stroke. My jeans were dragging me back terribly, but I knew if I abandoned them in the water, I would have nothing except my panties to walk the main road. Even I knew that would not have been a good idea. Just about the time I staggered up the bank, Dad, of course, showed up in the car.

Boy, was I in trouble!

The family back on the beach had found the canoe on the other side of the lake, without any sign of us. They were looking for our bodies, convinced we had drowned.

I began to realize what pain our thoughtlessness had produced. Momentarily, I had the curious sensation of being a parent and having a child scare me, as we had just done to our parents. It was eye-opening. Scaring parents isn't fun.

Besides the tie to the land, we had a traditional Sunday evening Hymn Sing. This was quite an event. I dreaded the dressing up, but I loved the singing. Many families from the area attended, but our contingent was the most numerous. It was informal with the younger ones on the floor, and only the adults in the chairs. I remember the clarity of "Fairest Lord Jesus" and the poignancy of the last song, "Now the Day Is Over."

Well, that was what my summers were like. The rest of the years were one place after another.

Dad was stationed in Port Washington, NY, at a Naval Research Center, helping to study the effect of speed on the human body. His specialty in the Navy was Aviation Medicine, although he wasn't a very good pilot. On his first solo flight, he crashed his plane by misjudging where the surface of the water was.

After ten years in the military, he decided to specialize further, so he took a residency in psychiatry, at the hospital in Bethesda, Maryland. It turns out he was a much better psychiatrist than pilot.

Good thing!

His compassion and empathy made him very effective in his practice. On top of that he was attractive and charming; an irresistible combination. His propensity to pun was well received initially, but eventually turned to great groaning.

Dad also had a real gift with his hands. He built a model of "Old Ironsides" completely from scratch. He had a book that detailed the ship inch by inch. It even had templates for the cross-sections of the hull. Basically he started with a two foot block of wood and had a finished product after thirty years. Once in awhile he would take a break from building the United States Frigate, called the "Constitution" and build a less detailed model tugboat or sailboat. They were stunning, too.

I started Junior High in Bethesda. I was tall and athletic but still lacked a womanly figure or grace. I made no attempt to make friends because I knew we would be moving soon, and I didn't have the social skills to make friends anyway. I had discovered science fiction by this time and therefore, had an active, though vicarious, life.

Who needed real people when you had so many interesting friends in books? I remember Dad telling me I read too much. I didn't understand that: Books were my friends.

My tomboy life came in handy when I began to play field hockey. I was quite successful as a right wing. All that running up and down the field kept me strong and thin. I cared nothing about fashion or makeup.

The yearbook picture for that school reflects my disinterest. My hair looked like I hadn't combed it since the night before, which was probably the truth.

I had one abysmal experience in school at that time. While we were passing in the halls between classes, a boy came up behind me, cupped me on my non-existent breast and said, "You really should be wearing falsies." I was stunned into immobility and filled with deep shame. I actually started to stuff Kleenex into my bra.

I began to look at other girls' breasts and discovered how seriously lacking I was. One girl in my class had such massive ones that she could overlap them on the desk when she was writing. I think I admired them as much as the boys did; that is until I saw her in gym class. She could barely run because they flopped up and down so dreadfully. I decided I would rather have a functional body for athletics than a beautiful form for boy attraction. Mine had just started coming in and were so tender and sore I could barely stand the touch of my clothing on them. I shuddered to think of what it would feel like to have what she had. However, it was those gumdrops of breasts that were to become the focus of the most damaging of my childhood experiences.

My problem was I had done so well as a boy, I didn't know how to be a girl. I wasn't even sure I wanted to be one. I wanted to be tough, successful competitive and; not whiney, catty, and manipulative. That was how I viewed women at that time.

I was growing and flourishing, as a young seedling should.

4 STUNTING

While we were living in Bethesda Maryland, Mom developed a large brain tumor that had to be operated on. My two youngest sisters, Stephie and Margo, had been born by this time. That made five of us girls. Aunt Gwen came to help take care of us while Mom was in the hospital. When the operation was over and Aunt Gwen told us that the tumor was benign and Mom was going to be ok, I tore around the outside of the house at full speed about ten times, leaping and caroling with joy.

Then Aunt Gwen left. Since Mom was not yet out of the hospital, Dad was free to get me out of my bedroom with my sisters, and bring me to bed with him. I had no idea what was going on, even though I understood all about the 'Birds and the Bees.' The major focus of his attention was on my 'gumdrop breasts'. The rest of it just seemed to be a lot of wiggling. One good thing was he did not penetrate me, so there was no pain. My effort to understand what had happened made me creep out of bed once he was sound asleep. I got a flashlight and cautiously lifted up his covers. What I saw was something small. It had no resemblance to what I had just experienced, and I was completely bewildered.

Now I *really* knew I was bad, but this time so was he. Strangely, I felt very protective of him and his reputation. I didn't want him to get "in trouble." When Mom came home this didn't happen again—until the following summer.

In our summer home, my bedroom (which I had to myself) was right next to my parents' bedroom. Dad began to visit frequently. I learned to sleep very lightly until I heard the creak of the floor as he crept into my bedroom. In those early days, most of his focus was on those budding breasts. All the fibers of my being became inert. I pretended I was asleep and shut my body down completely. Neither of us spoke about it, or indicated in any way something was happening at night. This activity continued until I left home to get married.

During those years I began to have three different nightmares; vivid, horrible ones. I dreamt that a witch had plunged her sharp icy claws into my back and was about to sink her teeth into my neck. I would flip over to face the danger while crossing my arms tightly across my chest. That dream may have referred to what Dad was doing to me.

The second dream was me as a little thumb-shaped white midget, bobbing along trying to ignore the huge looming menace of a pulsing brain-like mass of wild dark colors. That dream likely had something to do with Budgie's burning death.

The last dream wasn't so dramatic. It even had some lovely moments, but also apprehension. I dreamt that I could dive toward the ground, but at the last second I would swoop up and soar aloft. It was a wonderful dream, but I had to be careful not to lose my connection to earth. If I got too far out, I would have to fly really hard to get back, not sure if I would be able to make it. It was easy to fly away and much harder to get back. This dream probably was about my separating from people and escaping into fantasies.

Because of these dreams my ability to fall asleep was deeply compromised. I would read until morning. If I didn't have a book to bury myself in, I would get quite agitated. I lost my rowdy humor and became serious and brooding. My default expression was a scowl.

I started my high school years when we moved to Pennsylvania. There, I carried the dark secret of my father's visits within me like a malignant tumor. I actually had trouble standing up straight, because I needed to curl around it. Adults would say, "Don't slouch." That was impossible. I was ashamed of my breasts, not proud. Here I was given the third floor bedroom which, again, allowed Dad access to me.

My cousin Molly went to the same high school as I did. She was a bit of a tomboy also, so I got along famously with her. I especially remember our gym class where we would race each other up climbing ropes. Since she was a violin player, she had well-developed upper arms. I was still chinning myself on every door frame I went through, so I was strong, too. I can't remember who reached the top first; maybe we did so together.

Another buoyantly happy time in gym class was dancing the polka. Molly and I were again paired, and we would gallop around the floor in time to the music. It was quite uplifting.

For Molly's sake, I tried to rouse myself into being a normal teenager, and made my one and only friend, Amy. It was a bit of a strain being "girly" and going to sleepovers, but I managed it.

Since, we were living in Pennsylvania during the school year the treks back to our summer home were marathon events. There really wasn't room enough for all of us to fit comfortably in the car. Barbara being the oldest, was given the preferred front seat between Mom and Dad, that is, until Elissa began to have spells of carsickness. None of us wanted this, because after she had thrown up it was almost impossible for the rest of us to keep our own stomachs from following suit. To prevent this, Elissa got the front seat where it was easier to keep her stomach steady. Focusing on something far away through the front window, supposedly, helped eliminate the queasiness. As soon as Elissa realized the power she had to get the best seat, she continued to wield it for many years.

Rather than have four of us wedge in tightly in the back seat, I would take Stephie on my lap. She was a cute, bubbly child with long, curly blond hair. I would tell stories from my vast repertoire of fairy tales and could keep her distracted for long hours.

She was my little "punkin" even in spite of being responsible for the demise of several of my pet parakeets. With one, she tried to see if it could swim like a duck and she drowned it in the sink. Another bird disappeared when she opened up the cage door to play with it and, of course, it flew away.

Margo, the youngest, was another cutie pie in a sturdy sort of way. She also was fearless. On one occasion, when I was dropped off at the farm to paint a watercolor of Nana's cottage, I was startled to see five-year-old Margo arrive barefoot and dressed only in a lightweight cotton two-piece bathing suit. She had walked the entire four miles by herself, and Mother hadn't even missed her. Margo had unfortunately overheard Mom say that she was an "accident", and felt down in the mouth and unwanted. I let her know she was my "munchkin", and definitely wanted. I loved my younger sisters enormously and made sure they knew it.

That next summer when I was almost 15, I took a Red Cross lifesaving swimming course. The instructor's name was Gordon. He was almost six and a half feet tall with a lean-muscled swimmer's body, handsome in a craggy sort of way, with dark skin and penetrating eyes that could see into your soul. I could barely make eye contact with him: it was like looking into the sun.

Gordon was an artist in wood and leather and actually good enough to make a living at it. He was also an alpine skier and bird hunter. His long-legged stride was perfect for woods walking, and he had a striking gun-metal grey Weimeranner for his hunting dog. The dog was thigh-high and sleek but muscular. He had floppy velvet ears, and a smooth satin coat. More notable; his eyes were always on Gordon's face.

I fell Hopelessly in Love with Gordon—and his dog. Fortunately, Gordon was a bachelor. Unfortunately, he was 35 and I had not yet reached 15.

The lifesaving class involved escaping from the drowning swimmer's panicked clutches. This needed to be practiced on land before we tried it in water, and Gordon paired up the group for this. We also had to swim all four different strokes for fifteen minutes each. You really had to be a strong swimmer, which I was.

At the end of the class, I had to miss the final exam because of my monthly. When that was over, I took the final with Gordon alone. Playing the role of a panicking swimmer, he had to grab me in the water. It was my job to escape his clutches and then swim with him in the life-saving hold. Being grabbed by a drowning Gordon only added fuel to the fire in my breast. Although he was always perfectly correct with me, I still knew that he found me attractive, also.

During my sophomore year, I managed to attract the attention of a junior, and he invited to his prom. I was not one speck interested in him, because of my crush on Gordon, I went anyway. I got my First Kiss which I found to be a disgusting, slobbery, tongue-thrusting debacle. I didn't go out with him anymore.

That same year when I was 16, I wanted to see what all the sex fuss was about. I decided to get rid of my technical virginity and, again, it was not a heart-stopping experience. My partner in crime was thoughtful enough to take the necessary precaution, but I was totally ignorant of what the interruption was all about. When He got back from the mystery interruption, and we got going again, it seemed to take forever. I asked how long it was going to take him, he replied, "Just a few more minutes."

That's all it did take, and neither my heart nor my body felt a thing. I was completely numb. What on earth was everybody getting so hot and bothered about? I realize now that my coping with what Dad was doing to me, had shut down my ability to respond to any sexual advance at all.

In my junior year the family moved to the Naval Hospital in Chelsea, just across the river from Boston, Massachusetts. Here I shared a bedroom with my older sister so the pressure from my father ceased during the school year.

Dad was a high-falutin Captain, and director of the Psychiatric ward. Mom was very impressed with her social standing, which required her to put on white gloves and "call" on the other officers' wives. If they weren't home, she would leave her (engraved and not printed) Calling Card on the vestibule table provided for this purpose. These activities kept her busy for a long time.

I got my license that year. Dad happily remembered not to have anyone else in the car while I mastered the intricacies of the stick shift.

One time when I was doing some practice driving with Mom for the hours required on my learners permit, two handsome sailors crossed the road in front of me. I turned my head to watch them, hit the curb, and blew both front and rear tires on the right side. Imagine my chagrin, explaining to Dad that I was ogling sailors instead of watching the road?

When I got my license, I discovered that I was a natural for Boston traffic. Basically, it is a diluted game of Chicken. All you need are the old nerves of steel. To get into traffic, I'd jump into the tiniest break with no hesitation once I'd committed. Eyes in back of the head were a necessity, as was knowing where you were going. There was no time to slow down in order to read signs; if you did, you'd lose your place in the flow, and getting back in was difficult. Route 128 at rush hour was a feeding frenzy.

One time Mom and I went into Old Boston to buy Christmas presents. We were inching along in stop-and-go traffic, when I sneezed. During that millisecond when my eyes involuntarily closed, traffic stopped—while I was still rolling. With a loud bang, I broke the tail light of the car in front of me.

Yet again, I was in front of Dad, trying to explain my stupidity.

The one really serious accident happened during the summer in New Hampshire. I was driving along Route 11, when a car in the other lane crossed the center line and clipped the rear end of the car in front of me. I had been going about 50mph, but I immediately stomped on the brakes and swerved to the right—to no avail. I still got hit. Dad's big expensive

Buick gave such a wallop to the beat up junk that was the other car, it disintegrated. I mean, it literally fell apart.

Two drunken men lurched out of the mess cussing me. The other person that got sideswiped stopped and got the drunks away from me. All I could think was, *I've ruined Dad's beautiful car*. I wasn't hurt, just a little bruised—thanks to the size of that Buick. By the time the police showed up, the drunks had disappeared into the woods. The police traced the address from their license plates and staked out their barn. When the men came back to feed their horses, the police nabbed them. Don't you just love country living?

Dad didn't discipline me in any way since it was obviously not my fault. I have to admit that he was usually fair, in spite of his other downfall.

During the school year we lived in the opposite of country; pure city, actually, on the property of the Chelsea Naval Hospital. Since Chelsea was a poor section of the Boston area and the school there was substandard, the Navy kids were bussed over the Mystic River to a much better school in Brookline. There I met my only friend at that school. His name was Bill Wasserman. He was in the same art class as I was, and we were the top students.

We both were in the running for a scholarship to a summer program at Massachusetts School of Art. I ended up getting it, but when I entered the program, I was blown out of the water by the huge talent of these students. Since I only had a modest talent, I thought, *I'm never going to be able to make a living at this. My best bet is to educate my mind. That part of me has more potential for success.*

Ironically, Bill was the one who had the guts to stay with art. He made a nice living as a photographer for 30+ years. He should have won that scholarship, not me.

I brought Bill home to meet the family and they all liked him. He took the family pictures that we did each year for Christmas cards, and had the gift of seeing who we were on the inside. This was reflected in his photos and was eye-opening.

When we were living at the Naval Hospital, I dreamt that Dad was dying. I could see his face, purple and contorted, and even noticed what pajamas he was wearing, light blue with darker blue triangles on it. I told my sister Barbara about the dream, but all I said was, "I had another nightmare. I dreamt Dad died".

The following week, when I got off the school bus, my sisters came pouring out of the house, and said, "Dad is in the hospital!"

"What pajamas was he wearing?" I asked

"The blue ones" they responded.

With a sinking feeling I said, "Oh no, my dream is coming true." But fortunately, I misinterpreted the dream. Dad was not dying, but simply choking on coffee that Mom was forcing down his throat. Apparently, they had been fighting (as usual), and after several days of staying up all night arguing, Dad was desperate to get some sleep so he took some sleeping pills, not to die, but just to get some sleep. Mom, furious that he would try to escape her that way, tried to wake him, only to have him aspirate some of the coffee.

I have no explanation of how my dream happened, except that it must have had something to do with the suspension of our linear time dimension.

At this period of my life, I began seeking answers to the universal questions people ask about the purpose of life. I got unsatisfactory answers from every source. I especially distrusted those from my father.

One person whose answers I did listen to was my Godfather, Morton Bartlett, whom we called Bart. He was tall and broad shouldered, with heavy brows and gentle, deep-set eyes. His melancholy air wasn't a bit off-putting because the warmth of his baritone voice enveloped you in his presence. Bart volunteered his time to make 'talking books' for the blind. I wish I could get some of his books now so I could hear his voice again.

He was one of Dad's oldest friends. They had been roommates at both Philips Exeter Academy and Harvard. Although they really didn't do much together, they sure could they talk. They were both storytellers and when they got to punning, there was no holding them back.

Bart had lived his whole life in Boston, so his citified long trench coat and silk scarf were natural for him. He was a long time bachelor because he had lost the great Love of his Life. You can imagine how romantic that was to a teenage girl like me.

He made his living as a self-employed commercial artist, and although he was good at it, the artistic life must have been a struggle. You could see his clothes were dirty and threadbare. After we moved to the Boston area, we saw a lot of him and were probably the closest thing to a family he had. Plus, he did our Christmas card pictures until Bill took over.

The best thing about Bart was the undivided attention he gave me when I was talking with him. He saw me as a seeker of truth, with ideas worthy of consideration. This was a novelty in my young life, so instead of being in my usual turtle shell, I expanded when I came into contact with him. Bart was a scientologist though, so his ideas about the universe were strange and didn't seem to me to have truth in them.

The ideas he had about people were more useful. He said you could categorize them into six groups according to the questions they wanted answered.

1. "How" people want to know how something is made, or operates. They would be the engineers, scientists, mechanics, builders, plumbers, electricians, etc.

2. "Why" people are the psychiatrists, doctors, diagnosticians, troubleshooters, sociologists, etc.

3. "Where" people are mapmakers, explorers, travelers, guides, etc.

4. "When" people are historians, archeologists, etc.

5. "Who" people are journalists, reporters, gossipers, etc.

6. "What/Now" people are musicians, dancers, artists whose creations are ephemeral rather than concrete.

These groups are usually a combination of two or three. "How and why" go naturally together. Also, "Who and when" go together, with "where" sometimes added.

Like to take a guess as to my combination?

Yep. That's me . . . . "How and Why".

I always seemed to learn something while I was around Bart, but my high school years were drawing to a close.

My graduation present was a family trip to visit Dad's mother on Florida's Sanibel Island, a place well-known for the many different varieties of sea shells you could collect. My grandmother, Gonny, lived right next to the water on the leeward side of the island. Since she was too old to enjoy being out on the water and had sold her boat, Dad asked the neighbor to take us out for a ride on the Gulf of Mexico.

The neighbor warned, "Small craft advisories are up."

But Dad responded, "Look how calm it is," not remembering we were on the leeward side. Dad's powers of persuasion prevailed over the neighbor's caution, so we piled into the boat and took off. Once we swung around the end of the island, we got into really choppy water, and the wind began to increase the farther we went. Because we were broad-side to the waves the boat began rolling fearfully.

The neighbor said, "There should be a passageway through the island along here somewhere."

Elissa started bellowing hymns, thinking that would save her, I guess. I was thinking about Moby Dick and Captain Ahab, and what was happening to our little boat seemed very minor compared to that.

Finally we reached the calm of the inlet, only to run aground on a sand bar. We saw the fins of sand sharks in the water, but somebody had to do something, so I jumped into the water and pushed. You never saw anyone get out of and back into a boat so fast. The rest of the trip faded into insignificance after that.

Two other experiences that were exact opposites. One should have gotten me into trouble, and didn't: The other should *not* have gotten me into trouble, but almost did.

I'll begin with the first one. A guy on a Harley Davidson stopped by our picket fence and began flirting with me. He was in his 30s and handsome in a long-haired sort of way. He wore a black leather vest and a short-brimmed leather cabbie hat. When he asked me if I wanted to take a ride on the back of his bike, I was thrilled. I can't remember why this was so easy. Mother must have been away for some reason. I took him down to the lake where we sat by the water in total privacy, and he never laid a finger on me. I rather expected he would, but he was just tender and respectful.

The next situation wasn't as pleasant. Ernie was a local man, out of work, and Mom wanted me to have nothing to do with him. He wasn't even handsome. Although he was in his middle thirties, he was toothless and he smoked up a storm. He asked, "Have you ever been hornpout fishing?"

"No, but I'd like to go."

"You have the best luck at night. I'll take you there tomorrow night. Better make it around 1:00."

"Okay." So I snuck out of the house late the next night. We paddled over to the swamp—and then passed it. He said he wanted to stop at the beach for a minute. We both got out of the canoe. He started kissing me and took my clothes off. Next thing I knew he was pumping away. When he finished he completely floored me with the question, "Are you grateful?"

I guess he was getting gratitude from his forty-something girlfriend, but he didn't get it from me! I was disappointed that I didn't get to go hornpout fishing. That was what I really wanted. Going fishing should not have gotten me into trouble, but it almost did. I was extremely lucky I didn't get pregnant (that time). Luck was not involved in sneaking back into the house. It was a piece of cake, Mother being deaf and Dad being gone.

After I graduated from Brookline High School in 1958, I went to Colby Junior College in my mother's home town of New London, NH. This was a relatively small school for women that Barbara, Mother, and aunts had attended, also. I was nestled in at a place where I was not anonymous and consequently, I felt right at home. The professors were distinct characters and quite challenging. Not surprisingly, I got my best grades in biology which was right down my alley.

I think my physical side might have been stronger than my academic one, because the thing I liked best at school was the ski hill that I could connect with right from the campus. I spent every winter afternoon after class time on the slopes, partly because Gordon (my former life saving instructor) skied there, too. Rampant hormones may have played a part, also. I was only a beginning skier, but he gave me some hints, and I was soon more accomplished. The method I used was to go down the steepest most difficult run first, wound up tighter than a spring. Then I would go to the intermediate slope, where I truly belonged, relaxed into grateful relief.

That next fall I talked my family into letting me bring my bicycle to school, ostensibly just for exercise. But what I did was ride four miles over to Gordon's house to see if he would act on the impulse lurking behind his eyes. He told me that he had been attracted to me when I was only fourteen, but knew better than to do anything about it then. Now was a different story, however. He asked what I knew was a very pivotal question. He asked if I were a virgin. I didn't want to tell him of the sad truth of my deflowering. In my heart I was still a virgin, (although technically I wasn't).

So, I lied to him.

Dear reader, don't ever lie.

Nothing good can come from a lie—and nothing good came from that one. Gordon's response was he didn't want to be the one to take that from me.

See how that backfired on me?

I was very unhappy and stopped eating. I dropped from 145 lbs to 118 lbs. When Dad came up from Marblehead to his consulting practice at the college he would take me out to eat. He was concerned about my dropping weight but I lied about what I weighed. Somehow I would choke down the food and that satisfied my father. Those weekly meals were the only good nutrition I had, which was probably what kept me from getting really sick.

One more time, I went over to Gordon's house, using as an excuse that I wanted to buy some of his handmade leather belts for my sisters. We soon got to the real topic which was whether our relationship would move to a more intimate level or not. Gordon said it was not just the virgin thing. He told me he was seeing Dad for counseling about his problems. That was a surprise. But the next statement was even worse. He said Dad had given him an ultimatum. Gordon was going to have to choose whether he was going to date me and discontinue with Dad, or stop seeing me and continue with Dad. He added that Dad had said he couldn't properly counsel him if it involved his own daughter. The final blow was Gordon's decision that counseling was more imperative than dating me.

What could I say to that?

My sadness deepened.

I began to see Gordon at concerts. He always had a woman with him. Once, it was a young single teacher from the college, but she wasn't much to write home about. Another time it was the local doctor's German Nanny. She was stunningly beautiful, taller than I was, and with a *Playboy* figure. Plus she had that sexy German accent. There was no way I could compete with my father *and* these beautiful women. I surrendered my hopes.

My second year at college, I decided to go to one of the 'mixers' at Dartmouth, a school for men not far away. A group of us, none of whom even knew anyone there, got on a bus that would take us to the dance. When we got off, we walked through the line of men and were selected according to some mysterious attribute that appealed to college men (probably how quickly they thought we could be bedded). We were just cattle going through a chute.

I got picked (finally) and we danced maybe two dances before the offer came to go to his room. I didn't care much one way or the other, so we went. Again I was in the position of receiving slobbery kisses, with no response on my part. I asked to go back to the bus, where I waited long hours until everyone came straggling back. Good thing I brought a book to read.

I did go on a real date that year, though. Nick Ourusoff, from our summer farm friends, came up to visit me from Harvard. He had brains coming out of his ears, and possessed that cosmopolitan charm all those Russians had. Plus, he was the handsomest of the lot. I was quite in awe of him. We got into some very intense conversations about life, but our relationship stayed completely platonic, which was just fine with me.

During my second year of college, Dad retired from the Navy after 25 years of service. His actual rank at retirement was Captain, but part of the retirement package was bumping him up to Admiral benefits. Although this gave him a hefty allotment, he set up a private consulting practice to bring in extra money. Mother, of course, was very impressed with her Position and wanted to live in the manner that befitted it, so she continued to spend every penny and then some. Her desire was to move to the upper crust of Greystone Beach in Marblehead, just north of Boston, so that is what we did. We even were able to have a cleaning lady come in on a biweekly basis. I'm sorry to say, my response to this was to live in squalor in my own room. My room was again, interestingly enough, on the third floor. Elissa's room was up there also.

Many years later, Elissa told me that she could hear when Dad came to my room late at night. She said it made her feel wanted when Dad came to her room. I had no idea that Elissa was experiencing the same thing. I thought I was the only one.

I graduated from college in June of 1960. I was twenty years old and still a child; stunted, in fact.

What did I learn in college?

First of all, academic pursuits were extremely enjoyable because of the answers they could provide about the "how" and "why" of the natural world; human, animal, and inanimate. I wasn't as intensely drawn to the "who, where, and when" of history but it was still useful information to have. Somehow, history gave me an orientation in time, as reassuring as my personal sense of place.

I also began to realize that whatever I set out to do could be accomplished, and this concept was vastly different from the inadequacies I'd experienced as a child.

Unfortunately, I had no inkling what I was going to do for a career. I agreed with my parents' suggestion and took a year off from school to figure that one out. I got a job at Filenes working in the Lingerie Department—of all places. I was totally, a duck out of water.

My cousin Jane was at Endicott College in Beverly, Mass., studying to be a teacher. She had a plan for her life (unlike me). She would visit occasionally and we had great rapport. Her brother Bill was studying geology, and cousin Molly really went to town. She got *two* masters in Asian Musicology. I, on the other hand, was seriously adrift.

I decided to take advantage of the location on the ocean and bought a rubber diving suit and weight belt with the money I was earning amidst all the lace and perfume. I began snorkeling and was amazed at the large number of lobster. I tried to catch them, but they scooted backwards so fast, it was impossible. I tried pinning them down with a stick, but the buoyancy of the wood made it difficult. The next try was a solid iron rod, which worked well. I started catching lots of lobster, but needed something to contain them. I rigged up a fishing net I hung from my belt to stuff the lobster into. Now I had the method perfected and was providing lobster for the family.

I never ate lobster, because it made me seriously nauseous, as did coffee. Even then I knew where my aversion came from. Dad always smelled of coffee when he came to my room, and lobster was his favorite food. How's that for moronic? Providing something I hated. Beats me.

My marine interests also included setting up a saltwater aquarium with the plant and animal life I found in the ocean. I had small crabs, sea anemones, barnacles, seaweed, starfish etc. I tried to make it a balanced life cycle, but I had to add brine shrimp eggs periodically. When they hatched out, the aquarium came to life as the various animals waged death on the baby shrimp. To keep the temperature cold I ran the aerator hose outside my window. It worked fine in the winter but when summer came, things started dying so that ended the marine phase.

Since I was living at home, instead of college, I was expected to help more around the house. Barbara got the meals (under Mom's direction), so I was able to successfully avoid the kitchen. My main job was to take the cleaning lady home. What a pain that was—NOT.

I also dug up a little plot off the kitchen to plant some things. Other than that, I was really at loose ends.

I decided I would go back to school and finish my education. I applied to Boston University and was accepted as an off campus student.

Once there, I felt like a pebble in the ocean. My civics class had about 700 people in it. We sat in a huge auditorium and the professor was so far away, he looked about 3" high. I felt disconnected to everything and lacked the sense of belonging. My answer to this was to visit Peter Ourusoff who was going to school there. He was a friend from years ago in New London, New Hampshire and I felt quite comfortable with him. He had an apartment across the street from the campus that he shared with his tall, good-looking cousin Michael Tatistcheff.

Michael was interested in me and the inevitable happened. This country girl fell for the aristocrat. When he said he hadn't "gone all the way" yet, I decided to help him out. Next thing I knew, I was pregnant! The shame of this was added to what I was already bearing with the incest and all.

I resolved to run away to New York and raise this baby as a single mom, but the prospect was extremely daunting. I knew I didn't want to lose touch with my family completely, so I went to my Godfather, Bart. I asked him if he would send me news of them from time to time. His input was really eye-opening. He said that the baby was only half mine and that it would be unfair of me to eliminate Michael from his part in the conception. I saw the truth of that and I went to Michael to tell him the sad news.

But he didn't think it was sad at all and immediately asked me to marry him. By this time, I was very intimidated by the struggle I knew I would have, trying to raise and provide for a baby all by myself. I knew there would be no more education for me, and suddenly college looked much more appealing than it used to.

My Father realized the emptiness of my heart and volunteered a solution. He offered me an abortion, even though it was illegal at the time. I was completely appalled. All I had learned about family and love shouted at me.

WRONG! WRONG! WRONG!

Next, I was surprised. Where did that certainty come from: My love for my baby sisters or grief for my lost brother? There was no doubting its presence, and it was the first solid rock I could stand on.

When I look back on my life now, I shudder to think that my wonderful, Lee might have been terminated. I am so grateful to that inner voice that spoke up.

Since I was about to leave my childhood behind, I decided to take action to protect my three younger sisters. I found some time with Dad alone and dug deep. Confronting him was harder than I thought. I seemed to be afflicted with lockjaw. My voice could hardly get past the stiffness in my jaws. My stomach was (strangely) both clenched and flipping. I forced it out: "Dad, you know that my having to marry Michael is your fault. Because of what you did to me, I was used to having my body handled. Please don't do it to my sisters or they'll end up having to get married also."

Dad was crying by now, and I was exhausted with the effort it took to unlock my jaw, so I left it at that. Eight years later, I found out my herculean effort to overcome the silence was pointless. He continued his abuse with all three of my younger sisters.

So what had I figured out during my childhood? The first concept had never changed and that was that I was bad, as was my father. Because he hadn't hurt me physically, it didn't seem like abuse; just screwed up love. My love for him never abated. Although I knew he was morally wrong, there was no way I was going to blow the whistle on him.

What I couldn't figure out was the contradiction between his behavior and the fact that he went to church. The hypocrisy of that made me distrust religion.

As far as his going into psychiatry is concerned, I see that as a very logical step in his trying to understand the dark places within himself. You've heard the expression, "the shoemaker's children go without shoes?" That's close to applying. More accurately would be, "the shoemaker goes without shoes."

Twenty years later, I learned from a reliable source that a bad sexual thing had happened between Dad and the nanny when he was a boy. Realizing that my father had been on the receiving end of harmful behavior helped me to understand; have forgiveness and compassion for him.

The next principle I learned was that I could trust no one. Growing out of that idea was to question authority. That way I wouldn't get stuck believing in something false.

I learned to make my own judgments, rather than rely on someone else's.

I learned that anger was destructive and it should never be used to wound.

I learned that safety lay in having control.

And, I learned that sex was, at best, uninteresting,

Amongst all this negativity, I learned three positive things: the natural world was fascinating, family was valuable, and a sense of belonging to a place was precious.

5 NEW GROWTH (MICHAEL)

I took the easy way out and married Michael in 1962. Further college was not going to happen for me, but Dad reassured me that when I was ready to finish my education, he would cover it; because of this promise, I expected that the money would be available later. But for now, Michael would continue with school, and I would not.

Our marriage ceremony was a continuation of the bleakness. Mom bought me an ugly brown dress (because I wasn't a virgin). I forced my feet into heels and tottered through the ceremony, so shaky that I almost keeled over in front of the minister.

When Bill Wasserman took our Christmas pictures that year, not many people realized my true feelings, but even though I put on as good a face as I could, the darkness in my life is still visible in the photo.

In the middle of the following summer's heat, when I was very pregnant, I went apartment hunting for a more family-sized place. Walking along Commonwealth Avenue, I checked signs in windows advertising places to rent, and when I stopped to wait for a bus, I heard, "She just toppled over!"

I opened my eyes to find a crowd of people around me. I was on the ground. A policeman came over and helped me sit up but I could go no further.

"What happened?" I asked.

Boy, that's original! I guess people really do say that. I leaned against the building behind me, totally washed out.

"What's your name?" the policeman asked.

I had to take a breath between each word I spoke. "My . . . . name . . . . is . . . . Pat." *Forget my last name,* I thought. *It's too long.* When I realized that the only thing that hurt, and that only a little bit, was my thumb. I thought, *imagine that! After crashing down on cement, all that hurts is your thumb?*

After about 15 minutes I felt well enough to board the bus and get home, nothing serious, just heat and pregnancy.

I wasn't able to find a place to rent until I went to the other side of Fenway Park, where I found an apartment on Peterborough Street, near where the Boston Strangler would later do his thing. Since the Fenway was so far from the campus, I bought Mike a 10-speed bike to ride to class. I bought it with money I had been saving to get myself some scuba diving tanks. I figured I wouldn't be going diving in my new life as wife and mother. The irony of this is that the bike got stolen three months later (somewhat like my life).

I never really connected with this pregnancy. It seemed more like a trap that had caught me and I just had to endure it. My mother's voice reverberated in my head: "You made your bed and now you're going to have to lie in it."

My labor crept up on me. Since Mike and I couldn't afford a taxi, we had to walk about a mile, through the Park to Boston Lying-in Hospital. They had a clinic there for poor women, (and I was definitely feeling very poorly). Fortunately the park benches under the trees were spaced just right for each contraction. My progress getting to the hospital was slow due to having to stop every five minutes, but it turned out that didn't matter as I was in labor for 36 hours.

The labor room was quite an experience! Other women there were screaming and cursing. I couldn't believe the ruckus they were making. Whenever my pain became too intense, I thought about my brother experiencing the pain of his whole body burning. That would make the pain of my labor seem insignificant. His pain was constant, but mine came and went, giving me a break from the worst of it. Doctors finally got impatient with my progress and gave me a spinal so they could drag the baby out with high forceps. The rigid steel of that instrument tore and scarred me far more than the baby would have. My daughter, Elizabeth Michael Tatistcheff, was finally born, January 4, 1963. We called her Lizinka for short, but then that was shortened to Lee when she was in elementary school.

After her birth I was in a lot of pain and gobbling aspirin like candy, so desperate for relief that I would take them eight at a time. My ears started ringing to the point where I couldn't hear the phone when it rang. I thought the aspirin might have something to do with this, so I stopped taking them. After three days, my ears were still ringing so badly that I thought I had gone deaf, the way my mother had. When I finally called the doctor, he just laughed at me. He said it would take at least a week to clear that amount of aspirin out of my system. He was right.

There is an old expression, "it was so bad that my toes curled." Well, I don't know if it was the overdosing on aspirin, or the pain of first childbirth, but my dead-straight hair became curly! The body certainly can do mystifying things.

I think my daughter sensed my unhappiness even in the womb, but even more so after her birth, while I was still in so much pain. And, I seriously doubted that my small breasts would have sufficient milk in them for her. I was so anxious about this that I would weigh her before and after a feeding. I was only giving her one or two ounces, and felt that couldn't possibly be enough, so I conceded quickly, and turned to bottle feeding. Michael was really good about giving her the bottle, and she probably picked up on his joy. I was definitely *not* joyous. After a few weeks, I was able to care for her, but it always seemed to be at arms length. To this day, I haven't been able to bridge that distance between us. Contributing factors to our lack of closeness are probably due to the emotional turmoil during my pregnancy and the inability to breast feed.

The disconnection between my daughter and me, however, did not compare to the increasing distance already beginning to grow between Mike and me. One example of this was when I taught him to drive. What a rotten experience that was. When I first met Michael he didn't have a driver's license. His family lived in New York City, used the public transit system, and had no need for a car. Now, for his first job he needed one. I volunteered to teach him how to drive, but he was too proud to take instruction from me. When I offered a suggestion, he would flip out; full-blown shouting is extremely uncomfortable inside a compact car. As a result, I vowed to avoid letting the teaching experience ever enter our marriage again.

Michael graduated with his degree in journalism and landed a job as the editor for a small weekly newspaper in Methuen, just outside of Boston. His relationship with the owner was tumultuous, which resulted in his getting fired and rehired about five times in four months.

The insecurity of this job resulted in Michael's accepting an offer to teach at Hampshire Country School, in Ringe, NH. Dad got him this job because he was doing some counseling there. Both Mike and I were considered staff, because we were house parents to five boys who lived with us. The school was for emotionally disturbed children of high IQ. Michael taught math, which was easy for him. I was a surrogate mom, which was easy for me having mothered my younger sisters.

One of the basic tenets of the school was: "Disturbed children come from disturbed parents." All we had to do was be normal and that was a refreshing change to these children.

One boy was still a bed-wetter at the age of eleven. Since nobody gave me a strategy to deal with this problem, I just did what seemed normal to me. I woke him up to go to the bathroom before I went to bed at 11:00. If there were wet sheets in the morning, he helped me put those in the laundry, and fresh ones on the bed. No big deal. After a few months the boy was no longer a bed wetter.

Another interesting boy was a full-blown paranoid. If he was a boy, he was living on Uranus. If he was here on Earth, he was a Trachodon (duck-billed dinosaur). His father was a Tyrannosaurus Rex; his mother, a Brontosaurus. I thought these things said a lot about what his parents were like. Mike said this boy was a genius, but the only way he could teach him was to become a Pterydactle (flying reptile) himself.

Eight months later, I became pregnant again and chose to go to my family's home town for my care. It wasn't that far away, and it would be nice to see the family again.

This pregnancy was a completely different story. All I wanted to read about was babies. I stopped reading the science fiction that had been ever present with me. The most riveting book pictured the embryo as it grew. Every week I visualized the changes as my baby became more and more recognizable. I'm embarrassed to say how much I pored over that book. It might have even been close to an obsession. What a relief it was to feel the baby's first movements! Of course, I hoped this one would be the boy I didn't get the first time.

Nicholas Michael Tatistcheff was born September 8, 1964. The doctor induced labor three weeks early because he feared the baby would be too big for me to deliver. As it was, he had to be dragged out, again with high forceps. His birth weight was nine pounds, thirteen ounces, and had he been full term, he would have been over ten pounds. Nicholas had dark brown hair and dark eyes with long eyelashes that would be the envy of a little girl. I connected with him immediately. The way we sucked in to each other was like opposite poles on a magnet.

While I was in the hospital, I met a woman there with even smaller breasts than I had, and she had plenty of milk for her baby. I realized breast size had nothing to do with milk production. If she could do it, maybe I could. Sure enough, I was able to relax enough to nurse my second baby successfully. I couldn't get enough of the way his neck smelled and the softness of his skin on my lips. I probably nuzzled on him as much as he nursed on me. Every little thing he did was an occasion of wonder and/or hilarity. I was completely wrapped up in this baby.

Nicholas, whom we quickly began calling Nicky, was a robust eater. Nothing fussy about his eating preferences. His inquisitive mind even attempted to find additional ways to ingest food. He tried putting peas in his ears and up his nose. That one was a little scary, once I got over laughing.

I was so focused on my son that I almost forgot I had a daughter. I'm sorry to admit that if it had not been for Michael, Lee might have gotten lost by the wayside. She was definitely Daddy's little girl.

The strain of the disturbed children at the school began to get to Michael, so he applied to other schools to teach math. Bridgton Academy in Maine accepted him, and, once again, we became dormitory parents. We lived in a small apartment on the bottom floor of a large three-story building. Bridgton had a strong sports agenda, and Michael took over the tennis program and also became the soccer coach. He continued to teach math and started summer school courses to get his masters in this subject. Fortunately, I had no role to play here, so I concentrated on child-rearing.

We were not much older than the boys going to the school, so it felt unnatural taking a parental role with them, however, some experiences made us grow up quickly. Michael's job as dorm parent was to check everyone in at night. He would cover each floor saying good night and making sure everyone was accounted for. When he walked by one bathroom he noticed something on the floor of the stall. He found the body of a boy who had fallen off the toilet, his pants around his legs. Apparently, the boy had blown an aneurism in his brain that ruptured as he was straining. That was the first dead person Michael had ever seen and it weighed heavily on him.

My personal experience was not a serious matter at all; compared to Michael's, quite the opposite. But it was definitely a wake-up call for me. I was sunbathing behind the dorm and since those were the days of sun worship, I had taken off the top to my bathing suit as I laid face down on the towel. Nothing out of the ordinary here. When someone dumped water on me from the dormitory window, I had the presence of mind not to jump up, but I was definitely mad. I gathered my belongings and went to find Michael, expecting him to ream out the students for their disrespect. But Michael had a very different response. He said I was teasing the boys by what I was doing, and they were probably trying to get me to jump up so they could get a good eyeful. I saw his point and it was a learning experience for me. After that, I did my sunbathing at the beach.

Another self-discovery moment happened when our cat learned she could catch mice—although she hadn't got the part about killing them yet. On one hot summer night, I was sound asleep in my shortest lightweight nightgown when I felt the cat jump up on the bed. Then something light ran across my upper thigh. I shrieked, jumped up to turn on the light, and discovered a mouse just disappearing over the side of the bed. I felt like a fool to make such a fuss about a little mouse, but my excuse was the surprise of it. What I realized was my veneer of bravery was only an outer layer; deep down, I was just as afraid as anyone else. I just didn't like to show it. (Weakness, you know).

Because Michael received a salary only the months he taught school, he needed to get work for the summer. He found a job as a photographer at a girls' camp, tutored math privately, and set up a program to teach tennis on the school courts. I was involved in this, by distributing posters for his program in laundromats, summer campgrounds, variety stores, etc.

Michael had been playing tennis since he was a child and was very good at it. He had a crushing serve and a wicked drop shot. It looked like such fantastic fun, I broke my resolve and asked him to teach me to play. At that time, I discovered Michael's teaching style. It was sarcasm and ridicule. I asked him if this was the way he taught math. He responded, "Yes," then added, "It's very effective." It was not effective with me, however, because I didn't stay a pupil for long. Instead, I moved into playing with anyone else available. Many times a single player would come to the courts without anyone to play with, so I would get my chance, and because of the long hours I was able to play, my game improved, thankfully.

I started playing doubles but my net game was nonexistent, so I asked Mike to give me some net practice (not a lesson). This entailed his shooting a bucket of balls at me while I was at the net. I was supposed to hit them before they bounced. Half the balls I hit were going into the net and rolling around by my feet. Mike had me going from side to side at full speed. The only way to connect with the ball was to keep your eyes on it, so I wasn't watching my feet. Sure enough, I ran onto a ball and tore my ankle. Down I went, curled around my foot. The pain was excruciating. Again, my brother, Budgie, came to mind, as I panted, "It's only my foot. It's only my foot."

I went to the hospital and they said I hadn't broken anything, just torn all the ligaments. They put a cast on my leg and said they'd change it to a walking cast after six weeks and I'd have that for *another* six weeks.

I went home with crutches. After a few days, the swelling went down, which made the cast too big. When I stood up the cast would slip down and rest on the injury. Because this was extremely painful, I'd swing my foot up behind me to keep the cast horizontal. I wanted to have my hands free for work, so I would hop around with the cast up behind me. Because of the weight of the cast, I could only do this for fifteen minutes before my muscles started to cramp.

We were all still in our summer location and needed to move back to the Academy for the winter. Being the Navy brat and accustomed to moving, I had always taken care of the packing, but now was a different story. The crutches made it extremely difficult to carry anything so I hopped around until my leg cramped before deciding that my packing was out of the question. I needed help. Michael volunteered to do the job, but his idea of packing was to dump everything into plastic bags.

When we arrived back at the Academy, I collapsed in the kitchen surrounded by all these bags. I began to pull the clothes out and discovered everything was wrinkled. Nothing was suitable for the children to wear to school the following day. I became so frustrated that I actually cried. Nobody could see me since everyone had gone to bed, so I didn't feel badly about expressing my weakness.

It didn't take long, however, for the story of the Spartan boy to come to mind. Do you remember that story? The one where he hid a wild fox cub in his clothes? He allowed that animal to gnaw his vitals rather than let on he was concealing a forbidden pet. My troubles seemed laughable compared to that, so I dashed my tears away and thought, *what's the obstacle that needs overcoming here?* The answer was obvious; the cast. So I stuck my foot into a kitchen wastebasket full of water and soaked it off. My thinking was I would be able to hop much longer without the weight of the cast on my leg. Now, I could work!

I'd just read Linius Pauling's book, *Vitamin C and the Common Cold*, so I also began taking massive doses of vitamin C (about 10,000 mg/day). Three days later I was bearing a little weight on my ankle; seven days later, full weight. Apparently, Vitamin C helps as much in the healing of soft tissue as it does with the common cold. This was the beginning of my life-long interest in naturopathy/alternative medicine.

This interest in ailments and healing got me into an embarrassing situation once. Do you remember Uncle Sumner, my mother's brother who liked to skinny dip at the beach? One summer I had brought the children to Mom's house for a visit, and he stopped by also. Of course both Mom and he had been drinking. I didn't have that excuse.

He casually asked, "How would you like to see my vasectomy incision?

In my naïveté I thought I would see something like an appendectomy scar on his abdomen.

"Sure."

"Why not"

He dropped his shorts. There we are, looking at a wrinkled testicle with a band-aide across it. He started to remove the band-aid, but both Mom and I protested,

"No, no."

"We've seen enough." *I guess!*

Stunned and appalled at my ignorance, I struggled to show neither on my face, but probably was not successful. A few words of wisdom: Never agree to look at someone's scar—I guarantee it will be ugly.

A phase of my life that I deeply regret began when Michael came to me with both a statement and a proposition. He said, since I was the only woman he had ever known intimately, would I mind if he tried someone else? I was stunned into immobility. He saw my reaction and started gibbering about this cute, little tennis student he had, and his fantasies regarding her. "Little" was the word that unfroze me. I have never been described as "little," and my self-esteem took a big hit—but no way was I going to reveal that. So I said, "If that's what you want to do, go ahead and do it."

I began to cast my eyes around looking for someone to do likewise with. If he was going to have extra-marital affairs, then I was going to darn well have them, too. After all, this was the day of equality for women.

I chose several different men to be with and it was exhilarating to receive such a positive responses from them. I didn't really believe I was attractive. Although my flat chest had improved somewhat, inside I still felt ungainly. I began to revel in my sexuality.

I can't believe I'm writing this . . .

You might be asking, "What is the difference between what happened to you as a child and what you are doing now?" The answer is simple. Back then, I had very little choice about what was happening to me. Now, I was actively choosing. The really sad thing is it didn't seem wrong to me then. Remember, this was the '60's. Woodstock had happened and free love was the mantra. I even got a book titled, *Open Marriage*. Today, I realize that what you learn from books is not always good.

At the time, all that hanky-panky seemed very modern. I thought, whatever happened between consenting adults, as long as it didn't cause anyone pain, was all right. I now know, because of the damaging effect of that behavior, the kind of bonding that should happen in a marriage never happened between Mike and me. That was the first terrible thing that happened in our marriage

Now, another terrible thing happened. At two and a half years old, Nicky was still taking afternoon naps. One day, when he raised his arms up for me to take his shirt off, I noticed a golf ball-size lump under his arm. We took him to the doctor who asked if we had a cat. We said that we did, he continued, "It's probably Cat Scratch Fever and it will go down in about a month."

After a month, it had not gone down; in fact, it was even a little bigger. I called Dad, who said, "Any suspicious lump should be biopsied immediately."

We had to move fast. We prepared to leave Nicky in the hospital. He had been in training pants during the day for a few weeks, but I still put diapers on him for nighttime. Our babysitter put him to bed one night still in his daytime training pants. They were dry the next morning. This was one week before the biopsy. I fully expected he would revert to needing a diaper in the hospital, especially when I saw the high-sided crib they locked him in at night.

I had to leave my baby boy in the hospital and go home. The next day, bright and early, I returned and asked the nurses how he had done. They answered, "He didn't ring for us, but he crawled up over the sides of the crib himself, to get to the bathroom." I was really surprised and proud of him.

When the biopsy came back, it was MALIGNANT, so I called Dad again, who advised, "Take him down to see Dana Farber for a second opinion."

Dr. Farber had been one of Dad's teachers at Harvard Medical School. He taught Histology and Pathology, which is the study of microscopic/diseased tissue. Dad had flunked Dr Farber's course, so he took a summer job in his lab to become more familiar with the material. Dad did pass the course the next time around. Because of all that, he was sure Farber would remember him.

We made the appointment to go down to Dr Farber's office, which turned out to be the Jimmy Fund Building. We brought the test results of the biopsy with us, but they still wanted Nicky to go through the clinic for an exam. When it came time to talk to Dr Farber, we went all the way to the top floor, which was definitely the Executive Suite.

Dr. Farber said, "Certainly, I remember your Dad." Then he gave us the bad news. "Yes, Nicky does have a late-stage lymphosarcoma, and he has maybe an 8% chance of survival."

I was devastated. My son was as good as dead. My next question was weird. Don't ask me what my mind was thinking.

"What do you think of my getting pregnant again?"

Dr. Farber answered, "Not a good idea. When your son gets terminal you're going to have to choose between staying with your dying child or your living child. No matter which one you choose, you'll always regret your choice."

I saw the wisdom in that.

Now began my treks to the Jimmy Fund Building every three weeks for chemotherapy. His treatment was the simple procedure of injecting poison (a derivative of cyanide) into his blood, which would be collected by the lymph glands, thereby killing the cancerous cells. Little Nicky fought so hard when they injected the Cytoxin, it took four nurses to hold him down. As soon as the poison entered his blood, he would get the bitter almond taste and throw up. He would continue dry-heaving for the next two days. We would try to keep fluids in his stomach so he wouldn't rupture a blood vessel and start throwing up blood.

I will never forget the look a visitor gave us when Nicky was quietly retching while we watched TV and nobody was doing anything about it. There was simply nothing we *could* do, except shrink inside—and die a little.

My reaction to Nicky's sickness was to take up smoking. I usually have no trouble passing time in waiting rooms because I always bring reading material with me. Now, I was too nerved up to be able to read. There was a cigarette vending machine in the waiting room. That looked like a possible way to pass the time so I bought a pack and struggled through it. By the second pack I was hooked.

Really Brilliant!

Although Nicky's cancer didn't get any better, it didn't get any worse, either. Michael's mother Agrippina (but usually called Grousha by her friends) organized a prayer chain for Nicky, and had Masses said for him. I was very grateful because I knew I was truly bad, and no way would God listen to *my* prayers.

Michael's mother was a statuesque Russian Lady with an erect bearing. Her warmth towards me was very different from her husband's aloof detachment. Additionally, she was very spiritual. I went to an Easter service with her and watched her on her knees through most of it, crying the whole time. What were the tragic circumstances that brought her to such a state or was it just the intensity of her worship experience? I never gathered enough nerve to ask her.

My mother-in-law made several other huge contributions to my life. Besides the prayers on Nicky's behalf, she was an accomplished mycologist (student of mushrooms) and taught me to recognize the edible mushrooms, Boletus and Chanterelle. The whole family went together on many foraging trips in happier days. More central to this story, she volunteered to babysit, so that Michael and I could get away for a camping trip in Baxter State Park. We wanted to climb Mount Katahdin.

Can you guess what important thing I forgot to bring on that trip?

We went camping only that one time. Our excursions into the woods were mostly for hunting. We shared the love of venison, which is gamey like lamb, but much less fatty. However, I wasn't all that keen on killing, still respecting the sanctity of life. What I did enjoy was the Hide and Seek aspect of trying to find deer in all those great woodlands. It was so wonderfully incongruous to see such a large animal creeping around in the woods, when all you were accustomed to seeing was small game and birds. The beauty and grace of their form precluded my destroying them. Still, I didn't want to be thought of as not tough enough to do it, so I went along for my own reasons. But when I saw a deer, I deliberately shot wide. I don't think Michael ever caught on to my duplicity. These hunting experiences were a grown-up version of my Straight Arrow days in childhood, and I felt no hypocrisy in them. Actually, I found hunting for mushrooms just as much fun.

Once, while hunting on top of a mountain, something bad happened to my knee. I couldn't straighten it out without dreadful pain, so I had to walk with it bent. That brought up the unusual choice of how to walk. Should I bend both knees and walk evenly, or bob up and down on one short leg and one long one?

My bad knee needed fixing fast, so I decided to gather a little data of my own. Dad had scorned chiropractors and osteopaths as quacks, but there was an osteopath nearby, and now was the opportunity to decide for myself. I walked in with crutches.

The doctor said, "This will be an easy fix. It will hurt for just a second, and then you will be fine."

"I can stand anything for a second," I responded.

He yanked really hard on my leg, and was as good as his word. It only hurt for a moment. I walked out of his office without crutches, and with my own opinion about osteopaths, based on personal experience. I would go to another one in a heartbeat, that is, if I needed one. Being as sturdy as I was, the opportunity didn't present itself all that frequently.

The next medical incident began when my sister Barbara bought an expensive, wooden jungle-gym for her children. I wanted one for my children also, but was unable to afford it on a teacher's salary, so I copied my sister's, very carefully measuring and drawing everything out. My few tools included an old fashioned screw-auger bit and brace (crank type). Michael gave me a hand drilling the holes for the dowels (cross pieces), and soon it was together.

All that was left to do was make the slanting rope ladder (easier to climb than a straight up and down version). I should have whipped the ends with a smaller gauge string to keep the cut ends from fraying. This would have been the nautically correct way, but because it was nylon rope, I put a lit match to the cut ends and flattened them out.

Lee couldn't wait for the project to be finished, so she started climbing around, passed under where I was working, turned her head up to speak to me, and a piece of melted rope fell on her cheek. I snatched it, sizzling and bubbling, off her cheek. It almost landed in her eye.

I think it is a miracle that any children survive their childhood.

That's not to say there weren't many happy times. I spent as much money on children's books as I did on science fiction (and cigarettes) because reading to them was so enjoyable, for me *and* for them. We had an overstuffed chair which was also a rocker and it was big enough for all three of us when it came time to read.

Another good time was taking them to the beach close to us. Constructing sand castles and floating on the air mattress were favorite activities. Both children learned how to swim early and easily.

Unfortunately, brother and sister fought more frequently than played well together. That discord was to be a permanent fixture of their childhood.

Michael's mother had a very different relationship with her three sisters that reminded me of the way I related to my own sisters. These Russian women were extremely well endowed with enormous breasts, especially the one who was an opera singer. Competition between them expressed itself by controversy over who had the biggest boobs. To resolve this disagreement they flopped their breasts onto scales. (Naturally, the opera singer won.)

I got double enjoyment over this last story. Let me tell you how that happened. One summer at the family farm, I had the unusual opportunity to hang around after the meeting because I was spending the night instead of rushing back home. Four cousins and I (Molly, Sally, Julie, and Jane) were winding down on the porch. The conversation turned to Molly's daughter, Lura who wanted to take her mother shopping for a bra. Lura's objection concerned the shape of the bra her mother was wearing, and she said, "Women don't have breasts shaped like pointy cones. What you are wearing is an orthodic bra and it's not natural looking." We all chuckled over the image and tried to come up with other instances we had seen cone-shaped breasts: The Valkyries were one, and Madonna was another. I then, offered my story of the Russian sisters, their breasts, and the scales. Knowing the chic New York style of Michael's family, we whooped with laughter.

Not so funny was Michael's father. He was a stern patrician. One time he criticized me so strongly about my children's lack of table manners he brought me to tears. We were all at the table when this happened, and I had to leave because I did not want my children to see me cry. His criticism centered on the fact that they should wipe their mouths with napkins before they took a drink so there would be no greasy marks on the glasses. I had not taught them that because I had never heard of it before. Michael's mother, Grousha, told me not to get upset because her husband brought her to tears, too. I dearly loved her for her compassion and I felt better.

Another quality my mother-in law had was the spirit of play. She enjoyed playing Tag, and Hide and Go Seek with her grandchildren, but going to Storyland with them was the absolute best. Michael and I had already taken them there on someone's birthday, but her ability to get down with them was unique.

So, the first part of my marriage to Michael was full of possibilities, but it also contained the seeds of destruction.

6 LIGHTNING STRIKE

Michael got tired of working at the rather ordinary academy he was teaching at and his aspirations were to lead him to one of the highest ranked private schools in Maine, Hebron Academy. He became chairman of the mathematics department and because of his high status we were given a house to live in. No more dormitory living. Three cheers!

I became house proud. Although the dining room contained floor to ceiling bookcases, it wasn't enough for my science fiction collection, so I decided to build more. My handiness with tools was quite a surprise to Michael. Next, I painted the dining room burnt orange and had a rust colored carpet under the table. Warm earth tones were where my comfort lay.

The house was built in the 1800's and it had an intriguing dimension between the first and second floor. I noticed it when I stood on the stairs. I could see the distance between the downstairs ceiling and the carpet of the second floor was at least fifteen inches, much more than the eight inches you would expect it to be. In my mind's eye I could see some splendid hand-hewn beams hiding in there, and could not resist pulling down some of the ceiling tiles.

Score! When I eagerly showed Michael the timbers, his horrified reaction was an eye-opener.

"What have you done?" His voice escalated.

"You know this isn't our house. It belongs to the academy."

I saw his point, recognized that I had clearly overstepping my boundaries, and thought, so *what else is new*.

"You better tell the headmaster what you've done."

That sounded like a good idea so I went right over to the headmaster's house, even though it was a Sunday afternoon. His wife came to the door and when I explained what I had discovered and that I wanted to expose those beams, she said her husband was napping but she would check to see if he was awake. I heard the murmur of her voice followed by his bellow, "I don't give a god-damn what she does with the house!"

I reported back to Michael an edited version of the headmaster's words, and the project was good to go. I even got Michael to help me expose the hand-hewn beams in all their glory.

Then I wanted to set-off the beams with contrasting white sheet rock, but Michael's salary couldn't swing it. I came up with another brilliant idea of spraying that expanding foam insulation between the beams. All I'd have to do would be to tape plastic over the beams. I priced the job and it was inexpensive enough, so now I was on a roll.

After the insulation applicators left, I couldn't believe how awful it looked. Even after I took down the plastic to allow the beams to show, it was just as bad. The ceiling looked as if something alien had landed on it, as in some weird kind of fungus.

I tried cutting off all the lumps and bumps off with a knife, but that didn't make it look any better. Then, I got out my trusty flat sander. It didn't make any improvement either. Finally, I put a coarse disk in my drill and that removed the alien growths. Now the problem was feathering the finish lightly enough that the surface would be even.

The entire process was quite an ordeal. I had to wear a mask for protection against all the particles, and working over my head was extremely tiring on the arms. Michael quickly got bored so I lost him as a helper. Although I struggled for months until the project was finished, the end result was stunning and well worth the trouble.

Next, I turned to the fireplace and chimney. Because they were covered with sheetrock, all I could see was the fireplace opening. I thought exposing the red bricks of the whole chimney would go well with the hand-hewn beams of the ceiling. Imagine my dismay when I uncovered the hidden part of the chimney only to discover that the mortar between the bricks had never been pointed. (Pointed means the point of the trowel is used to smooth the lumpy, drippy mortar.)

This was nearly as bad as the ceiling. How was I going to solve this problem? Much as I hated to, I covered the whole thing with unifying paint, so the weeping grey mortar was not so obvious. The asymmetrical chimney, now a lovely ivory, made an impression that was both unexpected and unusual—somewhat like me I thought.

When I couldn't think of anything else to do in the house, I turned to the outside and discovered the former resident had left a patch of rust-colored chrysanthemums—just my color. My interest was sparked and I started gardening like crazy. I continued the flower garden all around the perimeter of the lawn. I admired my left side neighbor's pink mallow, an old fashioned plant sometimes called a friendship plant. Fanny, my ancient neighbor down the road, said it was called that because the only way to get it was as a gift from one woman's garden to another's. Greenhouses rarely, if ever carry it, seeming more interested in selling fancy expensive hybrids.

I discovered that my natural soil was almost pure sand. It smelled completely sterile, and although importing good loam for the flowers was possible, not so for a decent-sized vegetable garden. I turned to my right-side neighbor and asked if I could use the area behind her barn for a vegetable patch. She agreed, and I found a deep layer of dark rich soil that had been deposited as organic waste from the animals that had been in her barn many years ago. Basically it was the manure pile that had broken down into the perfect growing medium. It had a heavy peaty fragrance redolent with something like musk, and I had a blast growing fresh organic vegetables in that medium. Michael was not one speck interested in helping with vegetables, but he enjoyed the results.

One thing he did help with was tapping the huge sugar maple out front. I had read about how to do that and got the formula for the dimension of the tree and how many spouts you could put in it—one for every twelve inches of diameter. The maple was so big that we could put three spouts in it. The 30 gallons of sap we collected boiled down to one gallon of syrup.

Usually sap is boiled down in a separate sap house so the steam doesn't affect anything and cheap wood is used as the fuel. I felt badly about doing this on the electric stove because the school paid our utility bill. I half expected to hear about our high bill, but never did. The result was liquid gold it was so good. But I ran out of ways to use it so gave a lot of it away.

Stephie entered my married domesticity at this point by asking us to help her get married to Robert, a summer neighbor from New Hampshire. She was desperate to get away from Mom's drunken tirades. Mother was very much against the marriage, but I said I would help, and the minister at our local church agreed to do the service. I became convinced that Mother needed to be at the wedding or we would never hear the end of it, so we invited her—and warned the minister. Stephie must have painted a vivid picture of Mom because the pastor was the one shaking the most at the wedding.

Unfortunately, I still incurred Mother's wrath, and she began calling us late at night, drunk and loaded for bear. Michael couldn't deal with it, and left the phone off the hook, which only increased her fury. So she called the headmaster at 3 a.m., barely able to talk, told him there was an emergency, she couldn't get us on the phone, and something must be terribly wrong. The next thing we know, the headmaster calls to see if we were alright. Michael apologetically told him that he had a drunken mother-in-law, but otherwise everything was fine on our end. The next day he called Mom and told her never, *ever,* do that again. She almost didn't remember what she had done, and I think was a bit ashamed that she had gone to those lengths; thus, she respected his proscription.

My dysfunctional family was making me retreat into the quiet and healing balm of my garden. Besides growing and harvesting, I was drawn to making things of beauty. I got a spinning wheel and spun my own wool. I even dyed some of it with natural products like onion skins and flowers. I wasn't interested in knitting but I made a loom and started weaving. I also learned how to dye cloth using the East Indian method of batik.

Let me tell you how domestic I was becoming. I even started making bread and pies, getting the children to help me roll out crusts and make little tarts with the leftover dough. Once they were old enough (six and eight) I also taught them how to fry an egg or meat for themselves. I thought it important for them to be self-sufficient.

I read cookbooks almost as much as my science fiction, developed a reputation as a good cook, and even experimented with making wine. The very best one was dandelion wine, another arduous task. I picked a paper bag full of blossoms before reading the recipe thoroughly, and then I discovered I had to get every speck of the green underside off the yellow blossom; otherwise the wine would be a nasty green color. I spent long hours doing that. Another part of the recipe was bananas, skins and all, (probably where the yeast came from) and lots of sugar to feed the yeast. The by-product of this combination is alcohol and fumes. All I had to do was put a balloon over the mouth of the jar and its contents fermented away, filling the balloon. When the balloon went limp the wine was ready to bottle and put on the shelf. When we opened it six months later it was smooth, liquid sunshine.

I began to get itchy feet and would take the kids with me when I went exploring country roads. I loved going down a road I hadn't been on before and seeing where it came out. Their interest would flag toward the end, however, so I'd get them singing. When we neared home, we'd start singing Dvorjak's "Going Home" theme from his New World Symphony. I had a marvelous time but I don't know if they remember these jaunts with as much pleasure as I did.

All of this didn't seem to satisfy the yearning I had for something but I didn't know what it was. I began to get restive in my role as wife and mother, not seeing it as worthy of respect.

As a child, I'd seen my mother not earning a living, while my father did. So work became how I measured myself; it was what gave me self-respect. I'd gotten off to an early start by picking blueberries, baby sitting, and waitressing, but I was certainly was not setting the world afire.

So, I decided to see if I could make money with my art, specifically with macrame belts and necklaces. I made up a sample board and took it to Carol Reed in North Conway, NH. This was an upscale women's dress shop, and they ordered three of one thing, five of another etc. I got so sick of doing the same thing over and over that I filled that one order and never took a second order.

The art teacher at the academy left, so I saw an opportunity and volunteered to fill in with a crafts class. I taught what I knew, which was macramé, batik, weaving, spinning, and pottery. It was great fun, but soon expanded into a full teaching load.

The second year, I went to the Headmaster, and said I wanted to be paid. He responded that Michael was the only one they'd pay. I got pretty miffed about that, and decided to teach in public school where I'd be fairly paid. Michael didn't need a teaching certificate to work in a private school, but I needed one to teach in public school. To remedy this lack, I'd need to return to college to finish my degree.

My next step was to call Dad to tell him I was ready to go back to school, and I needed the money for the tuition (which he had promised me before I got married). His answer astonished me with its flatness; "Sorry dear, you are your husband's responsibility now."

At that moment, I realized that I was no one's responsibility except my own. This was my Emancipation Moment. I enrolled in the

University of Maine in Gorham taking the night school degree program in elementary education.

Life did not improve. To top off the load of: full-time job, night school, wife, mother, housekeeper, *and* Nicky's sickness, I got pregnant, again! The unimportant item I forgot to take on our camping trip to Baxter State Park was contraceptives.

I was ambivalent about getting pregnant, but my mother-in-law was delighted. She later told us, that this had been the ulterior motive in offering to stay with the children when we went on that trip.

Other than craving Fritos, my third pregnancy was uneventful. I found a local doctor, and because of my history of large babies, he induced labor early, as had been done with my second child. I chatted with the doctor after the IV started, and because what he was saying was so interesting, I made no indication that things were moving along rapidly until I told him, "The baby's head is crowning."

He said, "That can't be."

I replied, "I've got to p-u-u-u-u-u-sh!"

That got him moving. He quickly lifted the sheet and said, "By Jove, you're right," then hollered for the nurses.

I'm telling you, transferring from a bed to a stretcher while in second stage labor, is no picnic. Once I got in the delivery room, I think the baby was out in about ten pushes. The pain was so intense that I left my body and floated around in the corner of the ceiling. I looked down when the nurses said it's a boy, and my body down there said, "I'm so glad, I'm so glad, I'm glad." My ceiling body thought *Stop babbling, you idiot.* Then, snap; I was back in my own body.

Timothy Michael Tatistcheff was born, May 21, 1968. I called Dad to tell him my wonderful news, that I had another son. Dad was in the hospital struggling with the final stages of emphysema. He didn't seem to understand what I said, and began talking about planting trees. In alarm, I called back and asked to speak to Barbara, who was right there. She said, "Dad is taking a lot of morphine right now. That's why he's so out of it."

Thinking back on it, I think Dad was talking about a generational thing, and I was the one who didn't understand. He died a few days later. I missed his death, but I did get to go to his funeral.

Timmy seemed to be a twin to his older brother, as far as looks are concerned. From what Dr. Farber had said, I was sure my first son was going to die, so I viewed this second boy as my (possibly) replacement son. The baby's physical resemblance to his brother made me think that my mind had influenced the genetic combinations.

If it wasn't my mind, then maybe it was God granting me my heart's hope.

By this time, Michael and I had a king-sized bed, so Timmy just moved into it with us. No more late night bottles for Michael to feed. I don't believe those who say sleeping in bed with a baby is a dangerous thing to do. There is no way you lose awareness of the baby, even in deep sleep. But it *is* a good idea to put a rubber sheet under the baby. Lee and Nicky often crawled into bed with us in the morning, so no one felt left out. Those family moments are the ones I cherish the most.

Because I was nursing the baby, Mike took over the trips to the Jimmy Fund with Nicky. The monotony of that was interrupted by some good news. After three years of chemotherapy, the doctors thought there was a possibility that the cancer might be more specific, possibly Hodgkin's Disease. They needed to remove Nicky's spleen to determine that, which they did. They found what they were looking for, so a different therapy began; cobalt radiation, no more awful chemotherapy. The doctors were hopeful that this would cure Nicky's cancer, and said if he got past puberty he was home free. As of this writing, Nicky is now 47 yrs old—and what a blessing he has been to me.

My richness and joy come from the fact that all my children lived.

I had given up smoking while I was pregnant with Timmy, but went right back to it now. Because I still played a strong game of tennis, I didn't think smoking impacted my performance. I had, in fact, just won a women's doubles tennis tournament at the country club, which was an interesting experience. Halfway through the second match, I knew we were going to win. We still had four more matches to go, so that certainty was premature. I think it had something to do with what they now call "visualizing success," but it's more than that. It's *knowing* that something will happen, no matter what it takes to accomplish it. So, win we did, and I had a nice little trophy to show off. Everyone should have some area they are really good at and can be a winner at. Having a trophy helps build a feeling of confidence.

That certainty/confidence was REALLY put to the test when I decided to give up smoking once and for all. I wound myself up so tight to keep from reaching for a cigarette that my neck locked up and I couldn't turn it. I went back to the osteopath, and he tried something called the 'Indian Clamp'. Remember the Indian Burn of my childhood? This was similar. The doctor muckled onto my trapezius (neck muscle) and squeezed with all his might. I yanked right out of his grip and asked, "What did you do that for?"

"Sometimes it works, he said, "but I guess it won't this time."

He gave me some Flexeril, which did work—but made me seriously nauseous, unless I went to bed.

Now the osteopath was diminished in my eyes. He was no longer a miracle worker, but just like regular medical doctors; they are right sometimes, and they are wrong sometimes, not gods, just humans, like the rest of us.

I had another mixed doubles tennis match coming up with Michael as my partner. Because I was in a neck brace I couldn't play. He got another woman as his partner, and there I sat on the sidelines, missing my opportunity.

The hell with this, I thought, and went back to smoking.

The stress of the load I was carrying resulted in my getting really sick. My night-school professor told us that in order to discourage people from missing the final and requiring a makeup exam, his makeup was twice as hard as the regular test. Even though I knew I had a good fever, I didn't want to take that makeup, so I struggled through the exam, but driving the hour back from Gorham was even more difficult. I was shaking so hard, that I could hardly steer straight. I crept into bed at 11:00pm, but by then, could only take little sips of air. The pain felt like a hot knife pinning me to the bed. I woke Michael at midnight and said, "You better get me to the hospital." When the nurse told me I was going to have to stand up for the chest x-ray, I was so sick I had lost my civility and said, "You've got to be kidding."

Sure enough, I had pneumonia. The hospital was such a relief! It felt like sinking into a feather bed, and I slept for three blissful days.

Because of this experience, I decided to really and truly give up smoking. I knew my self-esteem was riding on the success or failure of this attempt. I spent the next six months totally convincing myself that I was not getting a reward with a cigarette, but actually a punishment. This talking to myself was almost a form of self-hypnosis. Timmy got pneumonia during this period also, further reinforcement for me.

Finally I felt ready. I got through the first week. Reaching that goal was a mistake, because then I relaxed a little bit, took one of Michael's cigarettes, and had three puffs. It tasted terrible—and wonderful. The only thing that saved me was the thought of the last week of pain that would amount to nothing if I gave in.

Although this was the last cigarette I ever had, I had to practice constant vigilance for 10 years, still craved them for 20 years, and had bad dreams about going back to smoking for 30. Frankly, giving up smoking was the hardest thing I ever did, including childbirth.

The reward in achieving my goal, however, was stupendous. I felt 10 years younger, as though I was 18 again. And it was not just an illusion. I started jogging in the evening when it was cooler, and was up to five miles a day when I discovered the euphoria that happens with that kind of exercise. It felt like I was effortlessly floating above legs that were disconnected from me.

I was so enthusiastic about this new body that I entered the yearly 27-mile bike race around Long Lake, without any preparation other than jogging. I was surprised to discover that in a bike race everyone pedals just as hard going downhill as uphill. The only other memorable thing that happened was I said to a woman, who was racing beside me, "I'm so dry I can't even spit." She passed me the water bottle she had clamped to the cross-bar of her bike, and I was really impressed with her sportsmanship.

I finished fourth in my class: Women Over 16 Years, (even though I was 30-plus). This was a big race with over 200 participants and I was so pumped that I set myself the goal of finishing first the following year. I'd used Michael's heavy touring bike the first time, but I got a brand new racing bike for this next race. I started training on my new bike that next summer. I would ride the seven-mile loop from North Bridgton, to Waterford, to Harrison, and then back—three times every evening (if it didn't rain).

I wanted to ride in a group the way I had seen bike clubs do. They'd draft off the leader and then shift the leader back into the pack to rest. I talked Mike into partnering with me on the training loops, but he only lasted one loop before quitting because his legs cramped up. Somebody I played tennis with volunteered to be my racing partner, and because he had been in other races he gave me some good tips. One was to get foot clamps which enabled upward pressure on the pedals as well as downward.

The day of the race there were 250 participants. The bike clubbers wore fancy helmets, tight spandex shorts in matching colors, special shoes for foot clamps, and racing gloves. I was hoping all those do-dads weren't going to give them a distinct advantage. I did have my own water bottle this time, and my tennis sweatbands for forehead and wrists.

The race began by the Sportshaus in Bridgton and then went east through town taking a left onto 117. As we turned to leave town, everyone stood up to sprint up the hill. I hadn't thought to train for sprinting and discovered that I started honking on each inhale. I sounded just like a goose.

Yep, smoke some more, why don't you.
Oh, well there's more to the race than this sprint.

Once we got past that hill my racing partner and I worked as a team, trading off the lead position. It worked just as I had hoped. If I could keep my front wheel as close as six inches from his rear wheel, I could lighten up my pedaling. We alternated about every five minutes. Unfortunately, he hadn't trained for the race at all, and his endurance only lasted to the halfway point. I pressed on without him. Michael was in the crowd at the halfway point, spotting for any women that might have gotten ahead of me. He held up one finger. I caught up with her, and we traded the lead back and forth. No helpful drafting now.

When we got into town again, I started the sprint for the finish. There was a real knot of racers at the left turn, where a policeman was holding back the traffic. I cut across the gas station to avoid them and heard the other woman biker holler, "F . . . You," at me. I kept looking back to see where she was, but that was the last I saw of her.

When I got to the finish line I almost fell off my bike. I had forgotten how to walk, but when I got my feet under me again, I went to the officials to discover I had the winning time. But there had been a protest lodged against my time because I had left the roadway. I didn't know any of those rules, but ignorance is no excuse.

I said, "That's why she hollered "F . . . you," at me.

The official responded, "She did?"

"The policeman there can verify it," I said.

The official said, "There's a rule against unsportsmanlike conduct so you can protest her time, and since they cancel each other out, your time stands."

I was not the first woman to finish the race, however, because Michael had missed a 15-year-old girl that had short hair and was in with a bunch of men. Her time was 90 seconds ahead of my time, so I probably would have been able to catch up with her, had I known she was ahead of me. She wasn't in my group of Women Over Sixteen' though. Still, I won my class and got a pair of nice cross-country skis for my prize. I was satisfied.

I was not too happy at the next event, though. Six-year old Timmy was so excited to have his mom a racer that he wanted to go bike riding with me. We set off down the hill, only to have him show off by turning his handlebars back and forth. Next thing I knew, he was flying over those bars, then crashing helmetless to the pavement.

I tried to sit him up, but his neck just flopped. I laid him back down and went racing back home to get the car.

By the time I got back, Timmy was sitting up and talking. We took him to the emergency room and they sent us home with instructions to wake him up during the night to check his pupils for uneven dilation. If nothing had happened by morning, he would be OK.

Timmy was fine the next day, but I'm telling you, it's a bloody miracle that children survive childhood. If we don't permanently scar them physically, we do a number on them emotionally.

Let me give you an example. Michael's mother Grousha, whom the children called Babushka (which means grandmother in Russian), came to Maine for another visit. We decided to take the chairlift up Pleasant Mountain and have a nice picnic with a view. Going up was no problem. I rode with Timmy, Nicky rode with Babushka, and Michael went with Lee. Coming down was a different story. Nicky absolutely refused to get back in the chairlift because it was too high and scary. I offered to ride with him, but his refusal was as hard as the boulders under the chairlift. No adult was going to convince him it was safe, certainly not me, and not even his father or his grandmother. I finally threw up my hands and said, "We're going down in the chairlift, and if you aren't in the parking lot when we get there, we're going to leave without you."

This ended the stalemate. Nicky took off on the path at a dead run and we all piled into the chairlift. I kept my eyes on Nicky, and when the path took a turn away from the lift, I saw him leave it to stay under the chairlift. This was where all those giant boulders were! I saw my six year old, leaping from rock to rock at breakneck speed, trying to keep up with us. The embarrassment I had felt for my fearful son, evaporated when I saw the jeopardy he was in. Now all I felt was fear. Happily, he survived that episode of parental stupidity.

That experience began to wake me up. I worked harder to accept my children as they were, without the overlay of my own fears, hopes and disappointments.

When I look back on my life then it seems that I remember only the difficult things, but they are what stand out from the ordinary.

My relationship with Michael came to be in that difficult category. He was critical of my house keeping, which didn't get any better because of his attitude. Actually, my housekeeping *wasn't* anything to write home about, but he could have helped instead of criticizing. He also didn't like the way I dressed in jeans all the time. Well, I spent most of my time outside gardening etc, so I *didn't* look too sharp. Then one time I dressed up to go to a faculty party, I had on a black lace top with a black chemise under it, and although I had no breast showing, he accused me of "advertising." I was totally crushed. I thought I looked pretty good. I tried to figure out where I had gone wrong. It couldn't have been from showing too much leg because I had long black pants on with black boots. I did have bare arms, but what was wrong with that? Michael never did explain it to me.

Another criticism was my uncouthness, as opposed to his aristocratic refinement. An example of this is when I used to do something he called "hawking," and I called it, "clearing my nasal passages." If I blew my nose I'd pop my eardrums, so generally I would sniff and swallow. This drove him nuts, I tried to do it when no one was around, but he would notice even if he was in the other room. And, it would sometimes happen without my even being aware of it.

Another example was how we ate chicken. I would pick it up and eat wings and thighs with my fingers. He would tidily use knife and fork and never touch it. Of course, I didn't eat that way when we had company or went out to eat, but I still was naturally "too common."

When I had been attracted to his ways, I didn't realize the arrogance that went along with it. He thought I didn't give him the respect he thought he deserved. The problem was I actually *didn't* respect him. When it came time to change the storm windows to screens, there was no way he was going to climb up there. SoI did it.

I could also beat him at arm wrestling.

And then, he was afraid of dogs.

You can imagine how well that went over with me. I managed to talk him into getting a dog, with the argument that the children needed to grow up with one, otherwise they would be afraid of dogs, too.

One day when I was exploring on a back country road I passed a dilapidated shack swarming with children and puppies. The parents' main source of income was selling worms at twenty-five cents a dozen. There was also a sign, "free puppies." I couldn't help myself—I stopped. I was drawn to the one that looked like a little round fluffy ball. All the others had short black coats with skinny bodies. He looked like a little bear cub. His attitude was not a bit forward. He actually was the shyest one, the one that ran under the porch to hide. I went against all the good advice I knew about picking out the liveliest and most alert puppy. After all, I didn't want him jumping up on my children and frightening them, so I asked the adults to get him out. I flinched when they got a hard rake to drag him out. When I got him in my arms he tucked his nose under my elbow. That did it. I was hooked. I gave the family twenty-five dollars for the dog, which made me feel good (and probably did them, too).

I kept the puppy tucked in my shirt until I got home, slept on the couch with him that night so he wouldn't cry and annoy Michael, and did this for two weeks before he stopped whimpering.

I wanted to name him Isaac for Isaac Asimov, my favorite science fiction author. Michael agreed with me, but said that it should be for Sir Isaac Newton, the famous mathematician. That was so typical. Even when we agreed, we disagreed.

The dog wasn't as big a hit with the children as I had hoped. He actually was more my dog than theirs (probably that nighttime couch bonding).

Cats seemed to fit in the family more comfortably. Lee loved cats as strongly as I did. One of the first cats we had was a male Siamese named Coffee and he slept wound around her neck at night. When he decided to leave our summer location in North Bridgton, and return to our winter home in Hebron where his little black paramour was, Lee was devastated. I made up lost cat posters and we put them all around anyplace people would let us put them up. He was actually found a week later in Harrison by people who had seen that poster. Coffee had already made a good start on that journey back. Lee continues to have cats in her life even as an adult.

Michael did not especially care for cats or dogs. However, we did share some common interests. Besides hunting, Michael and I both enjoyed science fiction. I had introduced him to this genre by sharing the collection I had since I was fourteen-years old. I added to this collection about three times over, during the marriage. We had so many books we needed a place to put them. I showed Michael how to make a bookcase sized just right for them, and I think this may have been the start of his lifelong interest in woodworking. He made many classic pieces of Shaker style furniture. I did respect and admire him for that. Too bad I never got a chance to tell him.

Another recreational activity was cross country skiing. We got skis for the whole family. Having the kids with us was an added bonus. One time we decided to make a real ski trip up to the Wild River National Forest in Gilead, New Hampshire. The road there was closed in the winter which made it perfect for skiing; wide and smooth. Going up using the herringbone method was easily accomplished. Coming back down was a different matter. One of the boys buried the tip of his ski in the snow and fell forward. Hearing your child howling with pain is galvanizing to a parent. Both Michael and I were at his side, but later had no memory of how we got there. Happily, as soon as we got him out of the boot he was fine. He didn't want to go skiing after that, so instead of forcing him, we let it slide. That put a damper on all of us going together. However, I liked skiing enough to go skiing by myself (which isn't a safe way to go about it.)

One of our family projects was to find a tree for Christmas. If there wasn't snow so we could ski, we would still go out hiking, scouting around until we found something half-way decent. The kids were just as likely to spot the best tree as Michael or I were. Sometimes I had to discretely add a branch here and there to get enough room for all the ornaments.

Christmas was always a big event for the family. Stockings were not hung by the chimney with care but laid on the bed of each child. We used my stretchy nylons so more could be stuffed in them. The goal was to give the kids enough to keep them busy and quiet just a little longer in the morning. They were not to go to the tree until both of us adults were up and had our tea in hand.

Christmas also involved taking Christmas card pictures which was great fun while the children were young. It soon became a chore I dreaded, so it was a big relief to be able to phase out that tradition.

I started taking the children to church but there weren't enough children to make Sunday school classes interesting so church didn't click with them. Michael didn't support this effort, being the dedicated atheist he was, so this might have influenced their lack of response.

I did not have that problem with another project, however. Somewhere I picked up a mini-bike which the boys got a bang out of, but it was too small for us grownups to use. That was probably part of the appeal. Later I got Nicky a larger dirt bike which he really enjoyed crash banging through the woods.

Something Nicky did *not* enjoy nearly as much was music lessons. He took piano, and Lee took piano and oboe. Timmy took piano also, but he was more impressed with a musical we went to see, called *The Fantastiks*. There was a haunting song in it called September, which he can sing to you today. He has continued with his love for music and sings a wonderful tenor in adult choirs.

Lee also sang in a female choral group as an adult. She sang bass and could hit notes quite a bit lower than I could. Singing seemed to be a way of connecting to my children. When Timmy woke up in the middle of the night screaming about spiders on the wall, I would go and lie on his bed and sing to him until he fell asleep.

Because I was a very busy person with all that I was working on, I didn't have much time to be a playmate for my children, but I think/hope they realized that I loved them very deeply.

I buckled down really hard with my studies, and graduated with a summa cum laude, higher than Michael's magna cum laude. I needed that affirmation to counteract his low opinion of my intelligence.

Next, I went merrily out into the school system, only to discover that children in public school are savages to each other. I wanted no part of that and decided teaching was not for me. As my career plans disintegrated, so did my marriage.

Michael's idea of an improvement in our marriage was to get me out of the academy where all the wives wore tweed skirts and hide dirty jeans me out in the boondocks. This suited me just fine, and we found a lovely old classic house to buy. We really didn't have enough money to swing it, so Michael talked his parents into sinking their life savings into it. This way they could have the vacation house in the country they had always dreamed of, a place to escape the city. Although I was uncomfortable using his parents like this, Michael prevailed.

The complete and utter destruction of the marriage happened about our tenth year, (although it took another four years for it to be completely over). I discovered him with my younger sister—in our bed! The specter of our father disinterred itself, and pole-axed me right between the eyes. I later learned that this had been happening since the first part of our marriage, and as if this were not enough, another sister had been involved with him, also.

Something shriveled up and died inside me. I began drinking, just as my mother had done. I understood her feelings a lot better now.

Michael realized the impact this had on me, and retreated to our friends the Hendersons, where he got very drunk. After about thirty-six hours I called to forgive him, as I had done already with my sister. But when something dies, it can not be brought back to life. My relationship with Michael was as good as dead.

Like a tree that has been cleaved by lighting, it still stands even though it is half dead. It just takes a few more years for the dead part to land on the ground.

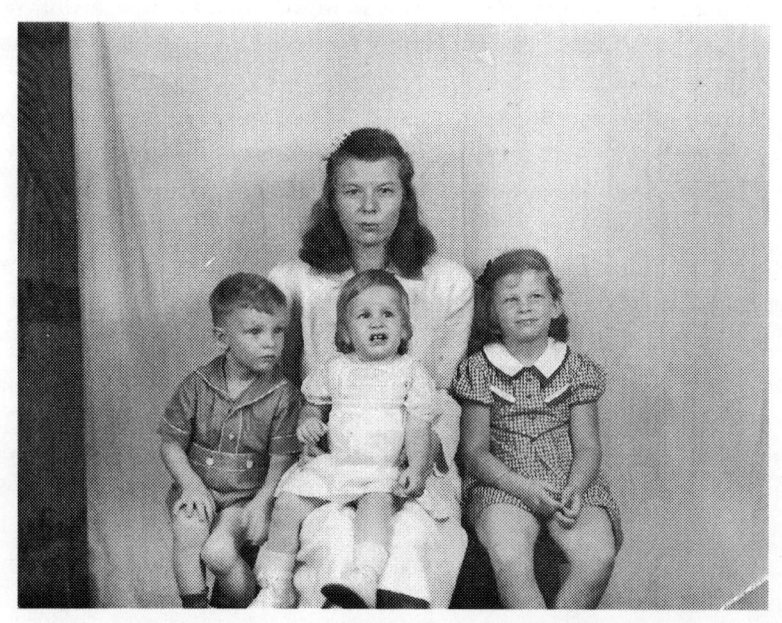

Budgie, Pat (in Mom's lap) and Barb @1942

Nana and Bompa, and Aunt Emma when she was young

Barb, Pat, Elissa with Mom 1946

All 5 Beal girls—Bottom row Steph and Margo 1951

Dad, early in Navy career

Stanley cousins 1952

Waterlily Cottage

1962 Christmas card (I am pregnant with Lee)

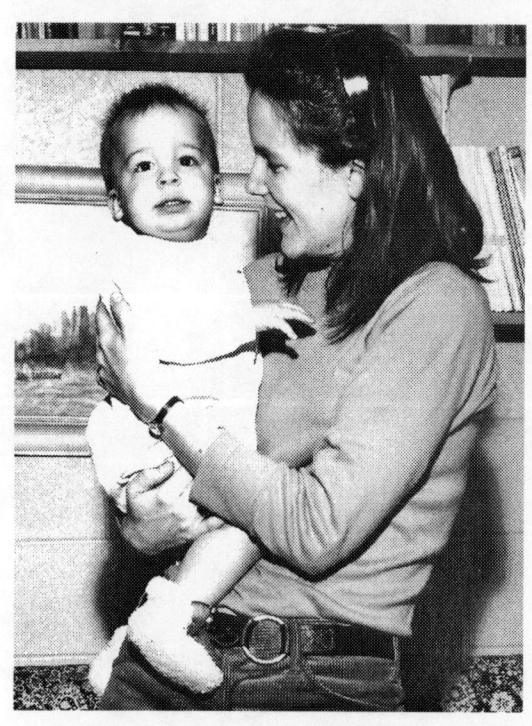

Babies are great! 1969

Nick, Tim, and Lee in the dreaded lederhosen 1970

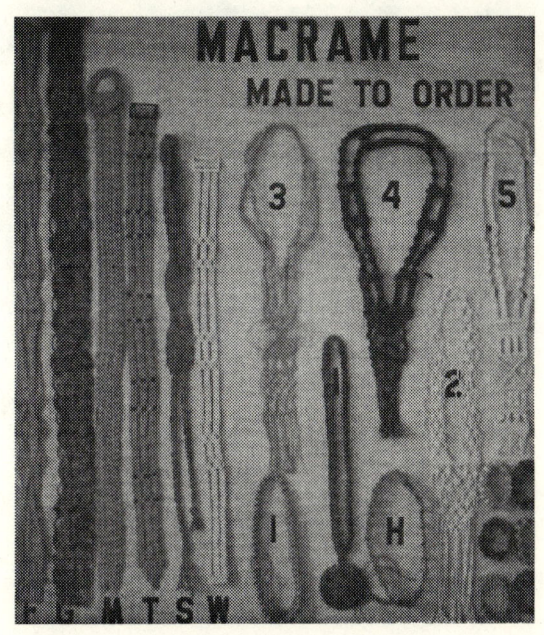

Craftwork for sale 1972

Tatistcheff family 1974 Pat and Mike, bottom-Lee, Nick, Tim

Bike Race 1975 First in class (second woman finisher)
27 mile bike race-250 entrants

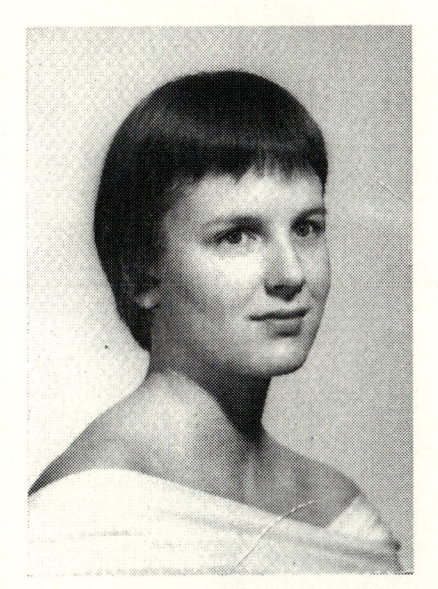

Nurses Aide picture (15 years after graduation picture) 1976

Harry on motorcycle

Pat and Emma with Goats 1981

Pat, Harry, and Emma at Turnbulls 1989

Emma on Arizona in Parade 1992

Chantrel 1998

Work Truck

7 BRANCHING

My life took a new direction at this point. I had gotten a CNA certificate (certified nurse's aide) and was working the night shift in a nursing home, which additionally accomplished my desired distance from Michael.

I was considering becoming a physician as my father, grandfather, and great-grandfather had been. With my grades, I figured I could do anything, but just to be sure, I took a year of post-graduate work in sciences. After all, doing well in the humanities (right brain) is a far cry from doing well in the sciences (left brain).

My grades were uneven. I almost flunked physics and chemistry, but did much better in anatomy and zoology. This really shook my confidence in how well I would do in medical school; and even more than that, what kind of doctor I would become.

Working in the nursing home I saw people die from medical mismanagement and decided I didn't want to be responsible for people's lives. If someone died as a result of my possibly inferior training because I had achieved only mediocre grades in medical school, what a horror that would be! Thus, I closed the door on becoming a doctor.

At that point I decided to investigate another half-shut door. I wanted to see if the first love in my life still had the power over me he had when I was younger. I went back to visit Gordon, my swimming instructor when I was a teenager.

He was as magnetic now as he had been fifteen years earlier. Gallantly rising to the occasion, he invited me to accompany with him on one of his exhibitions. When I thought about how I would be just another number in his long line of conquests, and would never have the importance to him that he had to me, I decided that I valued myself more than that. So, I declined. I think it surprised me as much as it did him.

When, I went back to the nursing home, I met Harry, who was head of maintenance there. One night he had to pass me in the corridor so he put his hands on my shoulders to let me know he was there. His touch was like an electric current that almost made my knees buckle, which is only natural I suppose, since he was an electrician.

Harry had strawberry hair and a rusty moustache over a wide smile. His bulky shoulders and arms combined with lean hips and legs gave him a muscular presence that was commanding. Fortunately, his glasses moderated this effect. I could tell he was no shrinking violet, so it came as no surprise that he was a scrapper. He showed me a slit in the back of his hunting jacket that he said he got in a bar-room brawl with a Frenchman.

He told me, "Don't ever trust a Frenchman." I should have listened to him. (I'll tell you more about not trusting Frenchmen later.)

Harry, told me was a bachelor with no children, so he seemed available. I got together with him and finally discovered what everyone else thought was so wonderful about sex. My bones actually melted. This affair was different from the others I had. No one else had been able to make my body sing as Harry could.

My husband Michael liked to talk about his exploits and expected me to do the same. It was a kind of foreplay for him. My relationship with Harry was something different and powerful. I did not want Michael to take voyeuristic pleasure in it, so I told him I didn't want to talk about it. Michael grudgingly accepted that, and I was able to hug my relationship with Harry in close.

Even though I still lived with Michael and the kids, sadly, my relationship with the children began to disintegrate. I found myself snapping at them with very little provocation. I did not want to turn into Mother, but it looked like that was happening. My drinking was getting scary, too.

Life went along like this for about six months. We began talking about a trial separation. Michael insisted that I talk with a psychiatrist he knew through tennis. I was appalled that he would be talking about our personal difficulties with someone that wasn't even a friend. But I reluctantly agreed to meet the man for lunch. His assessment was that I was "driven by penis envy," and this was why I was so competitive and desirous of freeing myself from Michael and my duties as wife and mother.

I was deeply insulted. I told him he was totally unprofessional if he could make an evaluation without having even met me. I also said he was completely wrong. Because I had no more interest in what he had to say, I got up and left.

My goal was to be the best I could be—as a woman. The idea that I wanted to be a man was laughable. I was completely happy to be a female, and still have my so-called male accomplishments.

However, I was still on the horns of my dilemma; torn between my children on one hand, and Harry on the other.

I thought I'd found the perfect solution by moving across the street and taking a room in my neighbor's house. That way the children could visit me easily, and Harry could also.

I thought I could have my cake and eat it too.

WRONG!

But I didn't fully realize it then.

I'm stalling because I don't want to get into the next section of the story. It's so unbelievable that even I have a hard time accepting it as truth. The important thing is I believed it at the time. Here goes.

Harry said that he learned to be an electrician from his father but his real job was as a pilot for the Mafia. He said he didn't do anything bad, he just flew the plane; He said he was considered an expert at landing in the local airports because of the dangerous crosswinds caused by the New England Mountains. He wanted me to come and go up in the plane with him. I refused. I wanted absolutely nothing to do with that part of his life.

Then I discovered there was a woman living with him called Clara. She was a petite, perky, Polish woman. He said he used to be with her, but now he was with me. He added that she was higher up in the "Family" because she was the bookkeeper and he was only the pilot. He also said that he couldn't leave her because she would put a contract out on me. In the beginning I accepted everything he said as the complete truth. I had no reason to believe otherwise, no matter how outlandish it was. So I went along with it.

After about six months of agonizing, I finally made my choice and told Michael that I wanted a divorce.

Here is where I made a terrible blunder. We got one lawyer for the two of us. In an effort to save money, I lost an advocate in my corner. Our first meeting with the lawyer established that we would seek a no-fault divorce, and we would share custody of the children. I was served a summons to appear before the judge to see if divorce was necessary.

All he asked was, "Do you love Michael?"

This was an easy answer, "No."

"I never really did," went through my mind, but I didn't voice it.

That fall, I took a leave of absence from my job to join my sisters as we stayed with Mom. She was dying of cancer. We did a round-the-clock watch with her as she died—although my older sister Barbara had been with her since the beginning of her hospitalization that summer.

I called Michael at Christmas time to talk with the children and find out when the divorce was going to happen. He said not until next year.

When I returned on New Year's Day, I asked Michael what the date was for our divorce and he said it already happened on the twenty-eighth of December.

I couldn't believe it!

"Liar," I threw into his face.

"You knew when the divorce was going to happen when I called on the twenty-fifth, didn't you?"

He just ignored me and said, "Because you weren't here, the judge awarded me sole custody of the children. You, apparently weren't interested enough to show up."

"What? How could I show up if you had given me the wrong date for the divorce?"

"You could have called the courthouse if you were really interested."

"Of course I'm interested. What makes you think I'm not? And why didn't I get a summons, like I did for the hearing?"

"I don't know. Maybe they didn't know how to get in touch with you."

"You could have told them."

I was beginning to wind down because I was starting to get the picture. However, there was more in store for me. Michael, at least had the grace to look sheepish as he said, "The judge awarded me alimony of one dollar a year."

I was dumbfounded.

"Why on earth would you want to do that?"

He replied, "If, or when, you become a doctor and start earning a lot of money, I can get support money from you then. And if you decide to fight me on this, I'm going to bring up the incest."

This last salvo took the knees right out from under me.

I said, "That's past history. It doesn't have anything to do with now."

Michael responded, "Everyone knows that incest re-occurs from generation to generation. I'm going to have you declared an unfit mother."

This last blow completely knocked the stuffing out of me, and although I said, "That's bullshit, and you know it," I was defeated.

Early in our relationship, I had told my horrible secret to Michael, the first person I had ever mentioned it to, and now he was using it against me. Because I was not a fighter, I retreated and tried to focus on the positives:

1. Michael could send the children tuition-free to the academy.

2. Their housing and meals would be provided by the school. What could I offer them? I had no house. I was going to school. It looked like Michael could do much better for them than I could.

Even though Michael's accusation that I would inflict incest on my children because I had been a victim myself was a horrible lie, my surrender was total.

My father was weak. He could not control his impulses even though he had made his life-work the study of the mind. An example of his weakness was his inability to give up smoking in spite of the harm it was doing to him. He died of emphysema. His death wasn't from ignorance: it was from lack of will power. Not much discipline or control there.

In contrast, I *had* been able to stop smoking. My will power was stronger. I could also halt the cycle of incest. No way would I allow that kind of harm to my children.

I returned to the hospital where cancer was consuming my mother's body. She looked so frail that I could not imagine her as the powerhouse she used to be. But she still had enough spunk to ban Margo from her room. Even though all Margo wanted to do was pray with her, Mom would have none of it. It broke Margo's heart. Mom was too busy dying to want to get into theological discussions. I can see it from Margo's point of view as well. What better time to pray than now, before it's too late?

Once Mom died, I was all set to go back home. The funeral was for the living, and the important part was done. Barbara said we've got to start dividing up Mother's things so we can sell the house. I wasn't ready to do that so I found some cross country skis and boots, strapped them on, and tromped out my sadness with sweat. Four hours later, I was in a better frame of mind and plunged in to the dreadful task of Who Gets What. Basically, we decided to take turns in our birth order for our number one pick. After we all got our first pick then we would go to our number two pick and so on.

It quickly became apparent that Elissa had been carting things away in her car before we all arrived for the death watch. This didn't bother me, because anything that had disappeared was just less to handle. What I didn't like was the ugliness of the fight between Elissa and Margo for the TV. Stephie and I showed little desire for most of it, just a few mementoes.

Very late that night Elissa and I had a typical confrontation. She asked me, "Have you seen the bag of can openers?"

"No, I haven't." Curious, I asked, "How many can openers are there in the bag?"

"About seven," she said

"What would I want with seven more can openers? I already have two at home."

"I saw you with it in your hand."

"I never touched it."

"You took them."

I felt myself flare. My eyes dilated and the hair on my neck stood up. I roared, "You're calling me a liar and a thief!"

When Elissa saw me get larger, she shrank, and this had the immediate effect of diminishing my anger. I didn't want to hit her, but she thought I was going to. Not going to happen. What *was* going to happen was my exit. "I'm outa here," I said.

I marched over to my gloves, hat, and coat, jamming them on.

Barbara begged, "Please, Patsy, I can't do it myself."

"You'll do just fine without me. I don't want any of this stuff anyway. The important part is done. The rest of this is just for the living." I headed out the door empty-handed.

Barbara said, "I'll burn the house down, I don't want it either!"

My last sight of Barbara was as she lit up some paper towel in the waste basket.

I didn't have a quiver of care.

Go ahead. Do it!

About ten miles down the road I realized I had left so empty-handed I didn't even have my purse. I wearily turned around and headed back. There wasn't a light on, but I was glad to see the house still standing.

I quietly went into Margo's bedroom. "How bad was the fire?"

"What fire?"

"Sorry I woke you. Go back to sleep."

I crept into Elissa's room. "What happened to the fire Barbara was lighting?"

"Oh, she put it right out. She only burnt a couple of paper towels."

I went into mother's bedroom. It was empty. No one was going to sleep in the dead woman's bed.

I guess it's up to me. I was so tired I fell into the bed, almost sleeping the sleep of the dead myself.

Sorry, Mom. I guess I really do care about your house.

I learned a Big Lesson that night. Monumental anger can over-ride other honest emotions. Once the camouflage of anger is gone, you're back to how you really feel.

Anger is a no-good, dirty-rotten thing!

After Mom died, I wanted to lighten the load my children were experiencing with the divorce and all, so that February vacation I decided to take the kids to Disney World. Lee was not interested in going, but Nick and Tim were. I wanted to bring Isaac (the dog) with us for security. I'm afraid his presence almost made the entire trip unbearable for the boys. My trusty Volkswagen Bug was not really big enough for all of us, our gear, *and* a dog. One boy could sit in the preferred front. The other would have to sit in the back with the dog dripping saliva all over him. That was such a dreaded position in their eyes, it had to be alternated.

Three really unexplained things happened on this trip. I hope I don't alienate you by describing them as miracles, but suspension of natural law, is a good definition of a miracle. By the way, my faith at this point in my life was nonexistent, even though I was going through the motion of taking the children to church occasionally.

It began like this. We stopped somewhere down south to do laundry (all that saliva, you know). I noticed a young couple bent intently over a book they were reading together. Being a reader myself, I wondered what the title of the book was that was so intriguing, so I asked them. They said it was the Bible. You could have knocked me over with a feather. The Bible was *that* interesting?

One thing led to another, culminating with an invitation to go to their church barbeque. I agreed, much to my sons' dismay. They spoke up, "You don't know these people, they could be ax murderers:" They had a point, but I was going. I think in hindsight, the boys would have agreed with me that it was a nice break from the trip.

The barbeque was out in a field somewhere. The people were just regular folks, and I felt perfectly comfortable with them. The food was great. There were some campfires with the youngsters making S'mores; you know, those toasted marshmallow, chocolate, graham cracker things.

That night, the whole church group gathered around to pray over me. Their prayer was that I would 'experience God'. While they were praying, I had the strangest vision. I saw the inverted cup that had been over me my whole life, keeping me in darkness and from God. Then the cup started to lift and a bright light came streaming in under the edge of the cup. I felt a wave of happiness flow into me. But when the cup got up to about my knees, it came slamming down and I was in darkness again. Regret replaced the joy. I don't know if I slammed the cup down, or if Satan did. All I know was the light was gone: and I had not eaten any funny brownies or anything. That was the first miracle

The second miracle happened while we were in Disney World. I lost my wallet with all the money for the trip in it, such as it was. I was really sunk. I started praying like crazy while I hung around the Lost and Found. An hour and a half later it showed up, completely intact. Nobody had touched a penny. If that isn't suspension of natural law, I don't know what is.

The last one happened on the way home. I carelessly let the car get low on fuel. We were traveling at night on a turnpike without stations on it, in the middle of nowhere. You had to get off the turnpike to find fuel. By the time I realized my predicament, I was almost on empty. The next fuel station was 30 miles away. I coasted into the station on empty at 11 at night. It was closed. My only recourse was to get back on the turnpike and continue. I went another 45 miles on empty before I was able to pull into a station that was open.

Guess what! Miracles *do* happen, and answered prayer made a big impression on my doubt. God's watch care over me was getting to be something I could count on.

My youngest sister, Margo, began an adventure of her own when she borrowed my German backpack and hitchhiked across the country.

By the time she reached California she was a mess. She had gotten into drugs and had been passed from one trucker to another. Eventually, some people tried to help her and they asked if she knew anyone in California. Fortunately she remembered our cousin Bill, so she landed on his doorstep, dirty, spaced out, and quite a sight to behold. Bill's roommate was not impressed and started spraying everything with Lysol.

Bill and his roommate had plans to go to a folk dance that evening, so Margo went along with them. Bill's account of this evening is very different from Margo's. He said she was tripping out of her mind. Margo said she hadn't taken any drugs for weeks and what she had was a Pentecostal experience. Margo then joined a hippie commune.

Our oldest sister Barbara and her husband went to visit Margo, basically to see if she wanted to come home. They were stunned by the commune's casual nudity and lack of cleanliness. As for Margo, she was amused by their reaction and had absolutely no interest in their offer.

Her next step was to go to a Bible School and, with her gifted mind, she learned a great deal. Further schooling was a good idea, but we didn't quite know what to make of her tendency to burst into prayer at the most unexpected moments. All of the family dismissed her as a "Jesus Freak", and we insulated ourselves from her experience. But I wondered if the spiritual encounter I had experienced on the Disney trip was in the same realm as what Margo was studying. I began listening to her with a more open mind.

When I got home from the Disney World trip, the immediate necessity was to go to the Laundromat. As I was taking my basket out of the car I heard this high-pitched screaming. I went over to where a crowd was gathered around two men. One grey-haired heavy-set man was on the ground scrabbling to get under the cab of a pickup. He was the one making all the noise. The aggressor was a lot younger and all muscle. He was hanging onto the open cab door and kicking the older man hard enough to lift him off the ground.

I felt the hair on the back of my neck stand up as I sprang into action: I jammed my basket down, charged up to the younger man, and yanked him off the door. I hollered at him, "What the Hell do you think you're doing?" He swung around and looked like he was going to deck me. I could tell he had already decided I was the next one to be on the receiving end of his rage. I thought, *Oh brother, now you're in for it!* I didn't back down, though. I just locked eyes with him in the full flare of my anger. His eyes shifted from mine and he looked over my shoulder: Then he shrank, turned, and ran away.

Since he had looked over my shoulder, I turned and looked also. There was nothing there that I could see. The other people were to my left and right. I was amazed. What could have intimidated him? Certainly not me. I think it was my guardian angel he saw.

Now a branching occurred in my life path. I realized that besides visions, and answered prayer, God's watch care over me would protect my life and limb. This was an extraordinary change in my approach to life.

Another fork was in the area of work. I was earning my own living and was no longer dependent upon a husband to provide for me. This was a great source of satisfaction for me. Being independent was where I wanted to be.

The final area of splitting was the exchange of my first husband for the man who would later become my second husband.

After Mom died in 1976, I could not go back to the nursing home; too much death and dying there. On a personal level, Dad had died in 1968. Plus, Nicky's nearness to death for three excruciating years had completely used up my ability to handle sickness and dying. I needed to find something else to do for work.

When I looked at my life I saw that my previous choices for employment had been stereotypical female positions. Women had been nursing and teaching since time began. You could almost say it was in our DNA. But now was the age for new opportunities for women. Feminism was in big swing at this time, so I looked around to see what else I could do.

I hadn't realized how unique and precious my background was as "Dad's 'little helper." Since he had no surviving son, I filled in that place and followed after him as he did little repair jobs around the house. I was exposed to—and acquired—the spatial awareness that males traditionally have. I, not only learned the names of tools, but also how to use them, such as righty-tighty, lefty-loosey. Because of this background I determined to go into the construction trade, the choice being between carpentry and the electrical trade. Since I wasn't too keen on heights, and carpenters have to go up on roofs, I was leaning towards electrical.

When I got back from Florida, Harry took me on one of his weekend jobs to wire up a cellar. He walked down the hallway and said, "Put a junction box here, a switch here, and a light here."

Then he walked to the next room and said the same thing. I said, "Huh?" So he drew it out and it made perfect sense to me, being as visual as I was. When he had me drilling the rafters overhead with the big 3/4" drill and 18" long bit, I realized I was plenty strong enough to handle the equipment. At the end of the day, I was really pumped about how we had installed a fully functional electrical system. I asked Harry if this was what an electrician's helper did and he said, "Yes."

I said, "Anyone can do this."

He said, "Oh yeah?"

The way he said it challenged me so, I composed a letter of recommendation, which was only a 'slight' exaggeration. I had Harry sign it and armed with that, went down to the local employment agency. The first place they sent me to, Pineland Electric, hired me basically on the strength of that letter. So you see, I was right to present myself strongly. Now remember, this was the start of women in the trades, before they had the umbrella of protection they have now.

The employment agency asked me to get back to them, to see whether I was accepted as an electrician's helper. If I was, they would send more women into this type of job. That was in August of 1977. In September I signed up at the local Tech school to take as many of the night school electrical courses I could squeeze in. I managed to take three that semester.

One of the differences between a trade school and a liberal arts school was in the number of times a fact was stated. At the university I was exposed to information once or twice, and expected to learn from that. At the trade school, a fact was presented six times before we could move on to the next item. I found the pace to be laborious.

Out of the total of the eight courses I took, only two were of much practical use in the field. The one course I couldn't have done without was the National Electrical Code course. It was taught by Ray Pellitier and he had a way of slicing through the convoluted wording of the code, making it understandable. He also had lots of show and tell items he had come across in his work, as the city of Auburn's electrical inspector. These items were suitably crisped, scorched, and melted reinforcing the seriousness of the job we were undertaking.

At Pineland Electric I was quite a hit with the guys. Everyone wanted to ride with me to the job. We had to jam four across in the front of the pickup, so it was quite body to body.

I had Harry pick me up at work a few times, so he was a distinct presence and the guys could get the idea that I was Unavailable. The few other women in the trades were either VERY available, or tried to be men themselves.

I chose a different path and kept my manners. I wanted to show that a woman could do the same job as a man without having to become coarse to do so. The men didn't understand that at first. They would try to get a rise out of me by telling dirty jokes in my presence. I completely ignored them, but at times it was quite a struggle. Some of those jokes were sidesplitting, and an occasional snort would escape me. I've always had a hard time remembering jokes, but I tried my best, so I could share them with Harry later.

I had to keep my guard up though, not getting too familiar with my co-workers. When they stopped for a beer after work, I would only get a soda—not that I wasn't drinking, I just didn't want things to get out of hand. I developed an attitude with them which was the typical WASP stiff arm; come in only so far and no closer. This was very different from my Velcro relationship with Harry.

I'd been at Pineland about a month, when an interesting thing happened, quite naturally. Because I didn't usually swear—my worst expletive was "rats"—the guys stopped swearing and telling dirty jokes around me. Perhaps they were responding to the concept I had of myself.

Three months into the job, I had my "rite of passage." I'd been working roughing-in a retirement home complex and I was pretty much the only one on the job, even though all I had was a helper's license. This was highly illegal: a helper is not allowed to be working alone without a master on the site.

The office pulled me off that job to help on the rough-in at a completely different place. The sheet rockers were coming in and they were going to close the walls. The electricians on the job assigned me the light circuit. in the living room and stairway. No one showed me the wiring plan so I just wired it up the way that seemed logical to me. The next day the electricians said, "You wired it up wrong." The plan called for a three-wire from the switch to the light. All I had put in was a two-wire.

They sent me back there to argue with the owner of the company who had the master's electrical license. I had to convince him that it would work the way I wired it. He finally agreed with me, but I was shaking in my boots. Here I was, a lowly helper arguing with a master.

I thought that was the end of it, but it wasn't. A month later they brought me back to the same room and said, "You wired it, you finish it." When it came time to energize it, the whole crew showed up to see what would happen. I wouldn't be surprised if there had been bets placed on it. When it lit up without going 'POP,' I got a round of applause. I was an electrician!

Later I had an experience that was a lot more than a POP. Our assignment was to rip out old conduit and wire at a nunnery that was being converted to low-cost housing. The copper and metal were worth quite a bit at the junk yard, and my job was to remove the copper wire in a 400-amp panel that was supposedly dead. This wire was as big around as my wrist. I took out the neutral wire first and as I yanked it across the main breaker lugs a huge ball of fire leapt out at me, with a BOOM! I jumped a mile and kept stumbling backward, as my supervisor came roaring around the corner. His face was so white that I gave him a shaky smile.

"Are you all right?"

"I guess so," I croaked.

"I thought you were dead. Are you sure you're not hurt?"

"I had my hands on the insulation so I didn't get any of it."

"Thank God! Do you know you shut the whole building down?"

"I'm sorry."

"Well I'm to blame," he said, "Not you. I should have made sure that panel was dead before I put you in it. Good thing you didn't try to take out the hot wire first. You were really lucky."

I was touched by his obvious concern.

That night after work I got my own tester, and I'm never without it. First big lesson learned. Don't ever take anyone's word in electrical. *Always* double check for yourself.

The owner of the company was what Mainers call "a real piece of work," and the exact opposite of my supervisor. He was a big man about 6' 4" and tipped the scales in the neighborhood of 290 pounds. Because of his imposing presence he could intimidate easily. He actually enjoyed bullying. Every morning before we went to work, he had to humiliate someone, while the rest of us were required to stand around and uncomfortably watch. Every other word he spoke was filthy, and he'd actually froth at the mouth!

No one spoke back to him, not even the other masters, and no one came to anyone's defense, either. It was amazing. I resolved I would not allow myself to be on the receiving end of his wrath.

Well, after about three months I got invited to his office to discuss whether I was going on the out-of-state job. I had heard of these as big party events. The guys had a per diem amount which they spent on having fun. I knew this would be a difficult scene for me, so I'd told everyone I would quit before I went.

I was mightily relieved that the Boss wasn't hollering at me. He told me that the guys were betting on whether I would go or not. He also said he would lose face if I didn't go, and the next thing that would happen, was others would refuse to go, using my refusal as support for their not going. Because he was reasoning with me instead of bellowing, I agreed to go.

The trip didn't turn out as badly as I thought it would. The Boss, amazingly, flew out in a private plane to pick me up, so I wouldn't have to spend the night in a motel with the guys. I think he was trying to make points with me, but it didn't take much to discourage any possible advances. Actually, looking back on it now, I can appreciate his gesture for what it was, sparing me the hassle of coping with the guys and their out-of-town behavior.

Unfortunately, that was not the only time I spent in his office. My turn to be on the receiving end of his wrath had come! Fortunately it was not a public spectacle. As soon as I sat down, he was screaming about what an awful mistake I had made, and how it had cost the company so much money. I was dumbfounded! I went over in my head what I might have done that could be this bad. He finally got to my dreadful mistake: I had put the panel covers on upside-down!

I breathed an audible sigh of relief because no one had gotten hurt, and it didn't look like property damage had happened. This just increased The Boss's fury. He was waving his arms, pacing back and forth, his face an apoplectic purple, and spittle was collecting at the corner of his mouth.

I sat there pondering what he had said and arrived at the conclusion that there was no way I could have put the panel covers back upside-down.

Not possible!

I knew when I had taken off the covers; I had put them down under the panel exactly as they had come off. When I picked them up to put them back on, they were in the same position they started in. I wouldn't have spun them around.

So where was the real problem?

The whole reason I was working in those panels was to install isolated equipment grounding bars. This involved removing the bare grounds out of the neutral bar and putting them into the new bar. I had to do this for twenty circuits in ten panels, so it took me almost a whole day. The person who had originally installed the panels had forgotten to install those grounding bars; therefore, it was not my mistake. So, I spoke up. I didn't raise my voice, but I wasn't going to take this abuse if I didn't deserve it.

What a mistake that was! The Boss wasn't accustomed to anyone talking back. Now he *really* went ballistic. He bellowed, "You're too big for your britches. You think you'll make master some day but it'll never happen;" and, of course, F . . . ing this and F . . . ing that the whole time.

When he finally wound down about a half an hour later, I left to join up with the others, but they had already gone to the job site. I got in my car, supposedly to go to work, but instead I drove around to the other electrical contractors in the area.

Nobody was hiring!

The next day I went to Portland and got hired at the first place I applied, Curran Electric. Now that I had a job, I called Pineland up to tell the Boss I quit.

He said, "I figured as much but I'm glad you at least let me know." He added, "I was going to give you a bad recommendation because you quit without notice, but now I won't."

Imagine how pleased I was to tell him I didn't need his recommendation because I already had a job. Even better than this, I ran into him at the supply store about ten years later. I said, super casually, "Oh, by the way, I wanted to show you this," and pulled out my master's license.

He said, "I knew you could do it." That was a surprise; quite a bit different from his parting words when I left his company.

8 ROOTING: (HARRY)

The period of having both Michael and Harry in my life was drawing to a close. Michael couldn't stand me living across the street, and was so furious at me for walking out on him that he needed to leave the state. He applied to teach in Massachusetts and was accepted.

That summer he took off—with our children. I was devastated. My neat little plan to have both Harry and my children in my life had failed. The emptiness of life without my children was unbearable. So, I asked Harry if he would father a child for me without my naming him as the father. I wanted a child that no one could take away from me.

Two months later, in autumn, I was pregnant. This didn't stop me one bit. It didn't even slow me down.

Curran Electric was a much smaller company than Pineland. It mostly sold appliances but it also had a master electrician and a journeyman, plus me with only my helper's license.

I partnered with the journeyman for two weeks, traveling with him in his truck. I had my first exposure to a service upgrade then (60 amps to 100 amps). Actually, it was only half a service since he did the outside, while I did the inside.

After those two weeks they gave *me* a truck and had me go out on my own. This was scary. First of all, I didn't know Portland all that well and, secondly, I was still pretty green. More importantly, with only a helper's license, I shouldn't have been on my own. But here I was so it was sink or swim.

Most of my first jobs were on Monjoy Hill, the slummy area of the city. I met some pretty rough people and the electrical was from another century! The work up there was mostly trouble-shooting circuits that were malfunctioning. Being analytical helped—and so did being stubborn. "Never give up" definitely was my modus operandi.

Harry meantime, had left the nursing home, and was working for another electrical company in Portland, and our carpooling made commuting easier. About my second month at Curran's I put up my first 100 amp service. I was so nervous about getting it right that I had Harry look at the job before I called the inspector. Everything was good to go, in spite of my worrying.

Another area I learned was pipe-bending, which drew on the spatial awareness I had acquired in my childhood. Nobody really taught me. I just did it.

The building where the pipe had to be put in was some sort of theater which would have the capacity of seating more than 100 people. In such a building, code specified that the plastic covered conductors had to be in metal pipe because burning plastic is incredibly toxic in a fire; enclosing the conductors in metal diminishes the fire hazard.

Unfortunately, I had to work in the ceiling while the insulation guys blew in the insulation. Because it was summertime and a million degrees up there, sweat just rolled off me; wearing a mask was hopeless because it just clogged up.

My face swelled up like a football. Some fire retardant in the insulation set me off. I got the job done though, and without taking a medical.

Being a woman in a man's job, I felt I couldn't/shouldn't complain. How does the saying go? "If you can't run with the dogs, better stay on the porch."

A few weeks after the theater job, I got hit with 220 volts when I was hooking up some electric heat (with the power off, of course). Someone else was on the other end of the circuit, putting it in the panel. They just thoughtlessly turned it on. Boy, I got it GOOD! I ached for about two hours in my wrists and chest. Getting bit is part of the job, but I was six weeks pregnant! I was frantic with worry about whether the baby was hurt or not, but the doctor said she would be alright.

I didn't make out a claim for this as an injury since it was gender-related, and the theme of my work there was, "I can do the same job a man can do."

Can you see a man claiming pregnancy as a work-related accident? Nevertheless, if it had harmed the baby, it would have been a totally different story. I would have kicked up a storm in a heartbeat!

The next thing that happened was the master quit. That left me the only one running the show, with my puny helper's license. I went to the management, asking who was taking out the permits for the work. They said that the company had a blanket masters license, but this did not make sense to me. Who was the person backing up that company license? It had better not be me.

Curran Electric finally hired on a master electrician. He was older than I was, but something about him didn't seem right. He wouldn't make eye contact. I, of course, took it personally, thinking it was my misshapen pregnant body, but I just let it roll off me.

I learned a few months later it wasn't me that was the problem. He had lied about having his master's license! All he had was a journeyman's license.

I continued to work, even to the point of being three days overdue. I remember the look of great dismay on the home owner's face when I showed up for work in my advanced condition. I thought *he* was the one that was going to need medical attention. Perhaps he anticipated my water breaking on his living room floor. Actually, I couldn't blame him but I was there to install a dryer outlet, *not* deliver a baby. The job necessitated crawling under his trailer. Even though I was up on my hands and knees, my belly was still dragging on the ground! That trailer job was the last I worked at Curran Electric.

I was ready for the baby to be OUT, but the baby didn't agree with me. She had a mind of her own, even then. Ten days later I went to the doctor's office and he pricked the amniotic sac, which he said would get labor going. Nothing much happened, though, until later that night when contractions finally started. I waited until morning and then drove myself to the hospital. Harry didn't live with me then, because he was still living with Clara (more about that later.)

The hospital put a fetal monitor on my belly, which was reassuring. I panted away for 17 hrs without dilating to more than 4 centimeters. I needed to be at least 10 centimeters before the pushing could start. Because of all the ripping and high forceps of the other deliveries, I was too scarred to dilate sufficiently. They decided to go caesarian because the baby was in distress now (as if I wasn't!).

This is the point in my life that I learned that DOCTORS LIE! They gave me a spinal which they said wouldn't hurt, but it did. That wasn't so bad. The worst part was when they started cutting into my abdomen. I told the anesthesiologist that it I could feel it and it hurt like crazy.

He said, "We can't stop now"

I groaned, "The pain's so bad I've got to throw up."

He replied, "Turn your head."

Apparently I almost died. My blood pressure dropped to 40 because I was losing blood so fast. Harry had arrived at the hospital by now and he said nurses were running out of the delivery room to get more blood. I don't remember the rest of it because finally they put me out with gas. Good thing!

The baby was born August 23, 1978 and she was beautiful, not mashed up like the others were with the fierce forceps of my other deliveries. I wanted to call her Emma to be strong and self-reliant like my Great Aunt Emma. Harry wanted to call her Rose for his grandmother. I said Rose is too wimpy a name, but because of the baby's beauty, we named her Emma-Rose.

Harry wasn't available to get me home. I thought I could manage it myself, but the hospital wouldn't release me unless I had a driver. They said having a caesarian precluded my being able to lift my foot to brake quickly enough in case of an emergency. I felt really bad having to ask someone to help me when I knew I was fully capable of doing it, but I relented and asked my minister to drive me home. This was the beginning of my lessons in humility.

Another lesson was learned when it came time for Emma's birth certificate to be recorded. Having to put down "unknown father" made me feel like something that should be wiped off a shoe. Filing for welfare was hard too, but I wanted to stay at home while I was nursing the baby. This part was wonderful. I had an old rocking chair from Water Lily that I used when nursing. Its arms were at just the right height to support the baby in the crook of my arm. Once I stopped nursing her, I still used the rocker to soothe and sing to her. It was as much a comfort to me as it was to her. For sleeping, she was nestled in bed with me, for many years actually.

Until Emma was a toddler, we lived in the apartment across the road from where Michael and I used to live in Hebron. Then Emma and I moved to our very own home, the Little Red House in South Paris.

Emma was the spitting image of Harry; long bodied, strong, strawberry blond hair and a proud German nose. All she had from me was my lips and attitude. That was enough, I guess.

Harry loved Emma deeply. And he also knew how to woo me; with tools. He gave me a Makita skill saw, brand new in the case, which I still have. When it finally wore out (cutting metal roofing which it was never designed to do) I took it to be rebuilt. The bill was only a bit less than a new one, but they are mostly plastic nowadays and not built to last (of course, the sentimental value was priceless).

"You are only as good as your tools," Harry used to say. Another favorite was, "The right tool for the right job." I say that frequently to my helpers. You wouldn't believe the number of tools helpers return to me, bent or broken because of misuse.

Harry came up with the idea that I should go for my masters; then we could start our own company. He couldn't work in Maine except under another master since his Florida master wasn't reciprocated in Maine. He had what was called a 'grandfathered' license in Florida. That meant when Florida began licensing electricians, they gave all then-working electricians a grandfathered license, even though those older electricians had no electrical courses to support it. So, Maine wouldn't accept his out-of-state grandfathered master's license. Consequently, he wanted *me* to get the masters license. I told him I didn't feel solid enough to be a master, but he said, "Don't worry about it honey, I'll back you up." So, I took the exam and passed it, smooth as silk. I was flying; I was now a licensed journeyman electrician. *Whoo-hoo!*

I thought it would be a good idea if Harry got a Maine license also, but *he* was sure he wouldn't be able to pass it. I knew he was a far better electrician than I was (at that point), but I was a far better test-taker than he was. I sat down immediately after the test, writing down as many of the questions as I could remember. I managed to remember forty-eight out of the fifty. With the extra coaching on the specific questions, Harry got his Maine journeyman's license, also.

Harry was pumped up and proud of himself. He was like a little kid in his happiness. He couldn't wait to call his brother, also an electrician, to tell him the good news. I guess not having his journeyman's really rankled him, so his pleasure now was irrepressible.

The next hurdle was the master's test. Usually people had to take it numerous times before passing it. So, I decided to take it the next time it was scheduled: That way I would know what I needed to study. Four months later I was at the test site again. This time I was so eager I asked them to grade it while I was there. I passed again! Yet, this time I wasn't so euphoric. I didn't feel like a master. But together with Harry, we could do anything. Turns out, I was the first woman in the state of Maine to get a masters license (my only claim to fame).

Excelsior—(onward and upward).

After Emma was born it became much more difficult for me, especially when Harry and I started our own electric company. Harry kept all the electrical stock at his house and calls for work came in there also. It was actually my master's license that was making the business legal, but I was supposed to be married to a man called Don. This mythical Don that also supposedly did the work, was really me. He was also the father of my child, another fabrication of course. This whole thing was almost as bad as the "unknown father" bit. It is such a relief now being a straight talker. Deviousness like that will not enter my life again.

Unfortunately Harry always seemed to have lies floating around him; about stupid inconsequential things, like his going to college. I knew he wasn't college material but he seemed to need that validation. He also claimed to have hand-carved a small wooden duck that was decoration in his house. I guess my disbelief was obvious enough for Emma to remember. We were just talking about it the other day. Another lie was that he had built the gun cabinet. He had no affinity for wood. It scared him. I knew all this sprang from his feelings of inferiority so I couldn't destroy him with my unbelief. I let it all go.

All these negatives were minor compared to the positives in our relationship. Harry and I had an electro-chemical attraction that just melted me when I came in close to him. He was much bigger and stronger, so I could relax when he was near. There is a level of defensive alertness that is necessary when you are single parent. With Harry near, I could pass that role over to him and relax.

Another way I experienced Harry was through the olfactory sense. His smell was similar to that horse smell I discovered as a child. Harry had a moustache so when I kissed him I could suck in that horsey Harry smell. My kissing was always more of an inhale than throat probing, anyway. All of this is because I just might have the family nose. I *have* heard my nose described by others as 'long' (thankfully not bulbous). Who cares what it's called, when it gives me such pleasure.

Harry was fifteen years older than I and called me 'kid'. But it was a love word rather than a 'dis' word. Nobody else has ever called me that sweet word.

I loved and respected him completely, as he did me. However, our life together was not a bed of roses. He was unreasonably jealous. This was the basis of all our fights, some of them pretty massive. He thought I was capable of flopping down in the woods to lie with a real estate broker I had met for the first time. He also accused me of the same thing with a man that was cutting pulp wood down the hill from me. I had heard that the woods were being clear-cut where I used to cross-country ski, so I did go to look, but never approached the man. This kind of assessment of me was so far off the mark that I would become infuriated. Granted, I had gone with Harry while I was still married to Michael, but there had been no concurrent intimacy with Michael after I had been with Harry.

When Harry made these accusations, I would get so close to the fury mom had, I was afraid of losing control. I saw the damage her rage had done to her loved ones, and I resolved to never hurt people with my hostility as she had. That attitude crippled me emotionally and physically for many years. As an adult whenever I would get furious, I would run away. One time when Harry accused me of unfaithfulness I was so angry I had to get out of the car. Since he wouldn't stop to let me out, I leapt out anyway. I almost *really* crippled myself because the car was moving at about 30mph. The scars on my knees as a result of my landing are still visible today. Unfortunately, I also scarred my seven year old daughter, Emma, who was in the car with us. She jumped out of the car (after it stopped), and ran after me, crying my name. I had disappeared into the woods, and could not bring myself to respond, even to her. This had quite a negative impact on her. To this day, whenever she gets angry, she cries.

Another time when I got so angry I had to run was when Harry and I were fishing for white perch from the shore of Range Pond in Poland. It was about eight o'clock on a spring evening. Harry made the same old accusation and I simply couldn't bear it. I took off into the woods to get away and back home. I didn't go too deep into the woods, only about 50 yards from the road: then I turned and paralleled the path of the road. I could see Harry driving back and forth, but he couldn't see me. About midnight he gave up, so I got back on the main road to make better time. Because it was twenty miles home, I didn't get back until six the next morning.

All that wonderful exercise completely dissipated my anger, so I was able to talk calmly with Harry about why I so mad. He still didn't get the picture. He didn't even believe I had spent the night walking. He thought

I had hitched a ride with someone. Unfortunately, that jealousy reared its ugly head probably five times a year.

I even tried communicating to him in other nonverbal ways I thought might reach him. One time, I threw a birthday cake at his feet. On another, I snatched a necklace I had given him off his neck. We ended up wrestling around on the ground, but we both took care not to hurt each other.

I'm ashamed to say, that wasn't the only time I got physical, but it was with Clara, the woman who was living with him. Emma was about six, and by this time word must have gotten back to her about how much Emma looked like Harry. Her response to this was to make trouble for me.

One day, my babysitter asked, "Who's Clara?"

When I asked, "Why?" she responded, "She came over and said you better watch out for Pat. She has such low morals she doesn't even know who the father of her child is."

I could feel the hair stand up on my skin. Not only did my eyes dilate, but my whole body swelled up. I roared over to their house.

Harry wasn't there, but Clara was.

I raised my voice, "What were you trying to accomplish at my babysitter's, and where did you get that information?"

She said, "I looked up Emma's birth certificate."

I said, "That's none of your god-damn business, and I'm going to tell Harry what you've done."

(When I start swearing it means I've totally lost it).

She didn't want me to tell Harry, so she blocked the door. That was a laugh. Puny little Clara wasn't going to stop big ole me.

I wanted to hit her but I didn't close my fist to her, so I wasn't *completely* out of control. All I did was grab her by the left wrist and throw her into the wall. Then I piled into the car and she jumped onto the windshield to obstruct my vision. I was so mad I accelerated, bumping over the ruts in the driveway, while Emma screamed from the backseat, "Mommy, Stop!" I swerved and braked to dislodge Clara, who was screaming, too. I wondered *who's going to be the one to give up*. As I slowed down to enter the main road, fortunately for all of us, Clara decided to slide off.

This kind of rage is incredibly corrosive. One year later, Clara's left arm (the one I grabbed) swelled up with cancer. The way I see it, my hate and her hate met in her arm and screwed it up completely.

The mind has enormous power over the body. Being a psychiatrist's daughter didn't teach me that: personal experience did. Let me give you two examples from my own life. When I was sixteen an incredible itching started on my arm. Obviously, the more I scratched it, the worse it got. Dad took me to a dermatologist who took scrapings, did some other things, and then gave me the diagnosis, neurodermatitis. I knew enough to realize it was my nerves. I willed myself to stop scratching and it cleared up shortly thereafter.

A similar thing happened about ten years later when I saw a Walter Cronkite program called *Here's to Your Health*. He described the seven signs of cancer, one of which was a change in bowel habits. Well, I had been having diarrhea for about a month. I became convinced I had colon cancer. Eventually I went to a doctor and he gave me that awful barium enema, then took me into his office and said, "You seem like a level-headed girl, but there is nothing wrong with you". I was so embarrassed. Three days later I no longer had the problem. That's the power of your mind. It can make you sick—and it can keep you well.

In the thirty years I worked for myself, I never took out health insurance. I couldn't afford it. There was only one time I ended up in the hospital with a high fever. The doctors couldn't figure out what the problem was, but they put me on antibiotics and I got better. I think it was food poisoning, eating from the 'pig run' I had. (I'll talk about the pig run later on.) I had in mind that I couldn't afford to get sick, so I didn't. I also could decide to stop hiccupping, once I realized I was doing it. I couldn't seem to make it work for coughing, though.

Clara's cancer got worse so Harry took her back to Florida where her family lived. He had to stay with her because she wanted him with her as she was dying.

I had no problem with that, but expected that he would come back north when it was over. I didn't realize that Harry thought he was too old for me, and this would give me the opportunity to find someone else. Not bloody likely!

Before he left in 1986, he officially transferred the business over to me. I focused on work and got a really good 'bread and butter' job, installing a new computer system for Casco Bank in all of their thirty branches, from Kittery to Augusta. This involved hard-wiring the teller line for each station. We couldn't start until the bank had shut everything down at 5pm, Because I needed enough people to get the job done by opening time the next morning, I had to hire two helpers for this job.

These were marathon night events, and driving back home, I'd often hang my head out the truck's open window to freeze my face in an effort to stay awake. After we got the first phase done, we returned to all thirty branches to install computers for the administrative officers. When that was completed, we went back *again*, to install PC's for the presidents. What was really good about the job was we could charge them for travel time. You can see why I called it my bread and butter job.

One time when we were at the bank in Fryeburg, I moved the desk to drill down through the floor for the computer wire. This was around 2 at night. Even though we were making a lot of noise drilling, I heard some banging outside. I looked at the front door and saw a bunch of people were trying to get my attention. Apparently, I had set off a silent alarm in the sheriff's office and he had called the bank president to get the keys to open up. The president was so discombobulated at that hour, he brought the wrong keys! So, there they were, trying to stop a 'robbery in progress' by banging on the front door!

Small towns in Maine. Can't beat 'em.

I got my helpers from this category (small town people.) The first was Freeman, a really good soul who lived down the road from me, but he wasn't the sharpest knife in the drawer. His best quality was he never had a bad word to say about anyone, plus he didn't swear (in front of me, anyway). He was so eager to be a good helper, he'd run to the truck and back, panting like a dog on a hot summer day, and sweating buckets. I didn't dare have him do much other than be a gopher. (You know, go fer this and go fer that). I did ask him one time, to cut a piece of half-inch metal conduit, about 6" long. He wanted to be so careful to get it right; he lay down beside the pipe to mark his cut, his face right on top of it with his tongue sideways in his cheek. How could I possibly fault him?

Another helper Ray, was another story. He was the most accident-prone person you ever saw. If he wasn't breaking something, he was getting hurt. His most spectacular event occurred when we were working in Portland. We off-loaded the material from the truck at the front door, but the only place we could park was in the underground garage. I told Ray to do that.

After about an hour I asked my other helper, "Where is Ray?" He went to find out and came back with his face several shades lighter.

"What's wrong?"

"Ray is afraid to come in."

"Why on earth is he afraid?"

"He ripped the top of the truck off, in the garage."

"Good grief! How did that happen?"

"You know that low spot in the garage? Well he didn't even think about the cap being that high and he smashed into it."

I thought about that for a minute. *Whose fault was it? Mine for not anticipating this—or his for not noticing?*

"OK. Tell him to drive to the junkyard and get rid of it, and also tell him not to be afraid, because I'm not going to fire him."

(I had been meaning to get rid of that old wooden cap anyway).

However, the very next week, when we were installing lights in the drop-ceiling Ray lost his balance on the ladder and grabbed the track supporting the ceiling tiles. Of course, he pulled the whole thing down on top of himself. Fortunately, he didn't get hurt, but I had to let him go. Enough is enough!

I still needed two helpers for the bank work, so I hired on Bob. He lived just across the street and was out of work with a bad back. This was light work so I thought it would be fine. It didn't turn out that way though.

A few months later Harry called to tell me Clara had died. I was frozen. I really didn't know what to say, ambivalent as I was. I must have mumbled something. A few weeks later I got a birthday card from him.

>It said: Happy Birthday.
>
>I'm here and you're there.

Something's wrong with this picture.

This galvanized me into action. I called him and announced, "I'm coming down with the truck and bringing you back up north with me."

Harry said that although he liked the idea, he didn't know how that would be possible because he had a boat and motorcycle he didn't want to leave behind. I sold Emma on the trip with the inducement of visiting Disney World, which we flew through at a dead run. Fortunately, it was a stormy day so there were hardly any lines. I'm quite sure we set some kind of a speed record.

What we found at Harry's was a shock. Nothing was packed and it looked like he had been drinking. His voice was slurred and he could hardly stand up. But I couldn't smell any booze on him. He had been taking Clara's pain medication and he was in a drugged haze. Two minutes after I got there he was nodding off. I went into the medicine cabinet and flushed all the drugs down the toilet. He had a fit when I told him what I had done.

I just started packing and ignored him when he tried to pick a fight. The motorcycle went in the back of my truck. He hooked the boat and its trailer to his van and everything else got packed in and around all the vehicles. Because Harry was more familiar with the route back, he led off. Emma sat with Harry to keep an eye on him even though she was only eight. This probably marked the beginning of her being the parent and him the child.

The trip back was horrendously long. Harry was going through withdrawal and was really weak, so we only drove a few hours a day. I was grateful when we finally got to Portsmouth, New Hampshire at five in the afternoon. Although we were nearly home, Harry pulled into a motel! He didn't have it in him to go another 90 minutes. So close to home. I think that was when I finally got irritated with him. But—there was no getting around it. He was doing the best he could.

When we finally arrived home, I unloaded Harry and all his stuff at his house and went back to mine. I had by this time bought my first home, a little red fixer-upper. I had work scheduled and couldn't stay home so Harry watched Emma, or maybe it was the other way around.

I took Harry on a job soon after, but it was totally embarrassing. He leaned against a door jamb (probably to keep from falling down), and with a silly grin on his face, gave a wide wave and said "Hi-i-i-i-i-i," obviously cooked. I had to dump all his pills again, but now I had the pharmacist alerted.

Once Harry was no longer into the pills, he reconnected with his jealousy. He was especially suspicious of the new helper, Bob. He accused me of immoral behavior with him, which got my temper up wicked awful—and Bob was even madder than I was.

Things went from bad to worse. First there was the original shouting match between them. Then someone (?) took a gun and shot pellets into

Harry's van; and also spray-painted obscenities on the road in front of the red house.

One day, when Bob went past the house on his bike, Harry went after him with a baseball bat. Bob called the police but mistakenly accused Harry of assaulting him. When the police showed up, Harry bristled and said, "If I had assaulted him he'd be covered with bruises".

Nothing came of that incident but then one of my pigs turned up shot. Harry was convinced Bob had done it. So, the next time we saw Bob at a small variety store, Harry was all ready to go for him. Actually Bob started it by pointing his finger and shouting at Harry. The owner of the store then joined the screaming match with, "Not in my store. Not in my store!" So, Harry and Bob took it outside.

Harry was big and strong, but he was also 55 years old. Bob was smaller, wiry, and 20 years younger. Harry began throwing haymakers but couldn't land anything. Bob was kickboxing, and Harry couldn't get inside the barrage. Harry had his glasses knocked off and a bloody lip before he managed to land a good one. Bob didn't like this and yelled, "Get this old man off me. Call the police." He's going for his gun." Well, Harry did have a gun, but he had a permit for it—and he wasn't going for it anyway.

When the policeman showed up, he got out of his car with his hand on his holster and his eyes all wide. He asked Harry, "Are you packin?"

Harry answered, "No, but I've got one in the back of the motorcycle."

Nothing came of this episode either, since both of them had agreed to the fight by going outdoors. Bob decided to move away, thankfully. And I decided I could do without helpers, if Harry would give me a hand. Peace reigned, but only temporarily.

Having Harry go to work with me was definitely an improvement, now that he was off the drugs. He would run interference for me with the home owner while I did the work. That was really a big help because otherwise they'd be hanging around, asking me questions about how I got into the electrical trade, etc. Although I didn't mind talking about it, I was on the clock. Also, when it came time to fish for a wire in walls, having a helper is crucial. Harry's presence also gave me a legitimacy that was helpful back then when women weren't in the electrical trade at all. (As of this writing, it is pretty much the same now.)

Some of the work we did was for the main branch of Casco Bank in Portland. One job was to install a wiring system for cameras inside the vault. To do this, we had to stand on tables with stacks of money we had to shove aside with our feet to get better footing. I was nervous as a colt, especially when the guard left. My thinking was, if he wanted to steal money, he could blame it on us since we were unsupervised, and there were no cameras to say differently. Was I glad when that guard returned! No problems developed later, so that was good.

Another time, the bank wasn't so casual. The bank building was five stories high, and the electrical panels weren't always on the same floor as where the problem was. We wasted a lot of time going up and down the floors before we could get the right circuit turned off. Harry had some old handheld walkie-talkies he got for hunting, but for some reason, they didn't work well in the bank. So, he bought new headset walkie-talkies. When we came around the corner on the main floor, with those on our heads, the guards drew on us. That got everyone's adrenaline going, Big Time!

The solution to this problem was to get some nice light blue shirts with "Anytime Electric" embroidered on them in big letters. Now the guards could immediately identify us and not get spooked.

We did another job for a different bank, this one twelve stories high. (So much for not being a carpenter due to fear of heights!) We were supposed to hang a great big refrigeration unit on the outside brick wall. It would have been easier to work on the roof, but who said being an electrician was going to be easy? It was only on the ninth floor, but same result if we lost it.

We had to hammer-drill a large hole through the brick for the pipes to bring the cool air inside, and the hot air outside. I spent a day and a half rigging the ropes from the fire escape before I was satisfied it would be safe enough to hold us. The hammer-drill itself was about sixteen inches long and the drill bit was the same length (total thirty two inches long)! When it was time to begin the job, I looked down and almost came to a dead stop. "Nothing ventured, nothing gained," carried me over the railing and into the rope sling.

The first of the drilling was difficult because I had to bend way back, holding the drill over my shoulder as far as I could. When the drill bit became buried in the brick, then I had the problem of the bit catching on the side and twisting me up. It took a lot of strength and it was very tiring. The job required both of us because we needed to spell each other to keep it going. There was none of Harry's lollygagging around with the owners, thankfully. I really appreciated his strength. He could hammer twice as long as I could, but I contributed a good amount, also.

Teamwork like that is what makes light work of a heavy job. As a team, we did pretty well. An example of how we complemented each other on the job was when we had to install a new outlet in a finished wall. The first thing we had to do was cut a hole in the wall for the box that we would put the receptacle into. Harry would go down one floor and drill up to get through the floor. Then he would push the wire up through the wall. The wire could be anywhere in between the wall studs, but I could get my smaller hand into the cut opening, almost up to the elbow. Since his hands were much larger than mine, he would need a metal snake to grab the wire. This made it a lot easier for me to find a wire in a sheet-rocked wall. Thus, I cut holes and grabbed the wire. He did the drilling and feeding the wire; teamwork at its best.

We also got some work in Portland at different print shops. That was really challenging. They had four-color Heidleburg Presses that were HUGE. The control panel with all the interlocked magnetic starters was seven-feet high and four-feet wide. When something wasn't working we had to open that up and start trouble-shooting. I would get the schematic diagram out, and try to follow it. Harry would take a live wire and start energizing a control here, and another there. He was what is called a 'seat of the pants' electrician. I was the locked-in logical one. Between the two of us, we always got it going.

One big job involved the move of Seavey Print from one building, to another about three blocks away. We had to disconnect about 30 machines at the old location and then reconnect them again at the new. Although other people moved the actual machines with fork-lifts, it was just Harry and I doing the electrical part. We started early on the morning of the move. After midnight, around two in the morning, Harry saw me fading. He took me in his arms and swung me around the floor in a high-clumping polka, which got me laughing and my blood flowing again. We worked around the clock, getting them up and running after only 36 hours. It was important to the owner that they be out of operation for as short a time as possible. Harry and I managed that to their satisfaction. Our wiring job wasn't pretty, but we went back and got them wired up according to code later. That probably took us another three weeks. Good bread and butter job.

Harry's belief in me, allowed me to start believing in myself. One time that got me in trouble, though. Emma and I had a kitten that the dog chased up a tree, a white ash that had to have been at least 150 years old. The first branch was about 30 feet off the ground. Harry said the kitten would eventually come down, but after two days it still hadn't come down. I was getting worried about it not having any water for 24hrs, so I left a message on his answering machine asking him if he would call the fire department to see if they would get it down.

Apparently they don't do that anymore. When I got home our 30 foot ladder was on the lawn near the tree. I thought, *Harry must think it will reach.* I didn't think so, but Harry apparently did, so I set the ladder up. I saw that if I extended the ladder all the way, and stood on the third-from-the-top rung I could reach the branch the kitten was on. As I set the ladder up, I was thinking more about the top of the ladder than the bottom. I got most of the way up the ladder when the ladder decided to leave the tree. I had the choice of going with the ladder or sticking with the tree. I chose the tree. As luck would have it, the tree was so big I couldn't even reach halfway around it. I squeezed with all my might; arms, knees, legs—and ended up in a heap at the foot of the tree. The ladder landed on top of a pile of debris. Ominously, there was a pipe sticking up through the ladder, about where I had been. Thank goodness I made the right choice.

But, I was still pretty skun up and madder than a hornet. I called Harry and told him what happened. I said, "Will you get over here and foot this ladder for me so I can get that kitten down?" He came over and squared the ladder up: I guess I hadn't put it on level ground. That was why it had tipped away from the tree. I was still mad enough to get up that ladder without even thinking about it. Or, maybe it was the security of having Harry holding the bottom of it. The kitten was rescued, none the worse for the wear (unlike me!)

My oldest son, Nick, once told me that the highest accolade you can give a person is: they are a "hold-your-roper." To do that job well, you need to have secure footing, or grounding. Harry was that for me. Plus, he taught *me* how to do it. I sank my roots deep and wide, securely grounded.

9 SHAPING (Wear and Tear)

I was beginning to feel the wear and tear of electrical work. It took 90% of my strength to accomplish what took a man 30%. When I got home from work, I'd be so wound up it was difficult to relax into sleep. If I had work the next day, that involved heights, or heavy drilling, I would worry about that. The reason for the tension was because I broke something in my wrist while drilling attic rafters. The drill bit had hung-up on a nail, and when it catches like that, it makes the motor whip around. Because it was overhead, I couldn't brace with my body, and my wrist snapped. Now I have a weak wrist and drilling really tires it. To solve this deficiency I learned to sharpen the bits with a flat file so they were super sharp, which made drilling easier and safer for me.

Another problem that kept me from a good rest was recurring nightmares. The witch dream with her claws sunk into my back didn't happen anymore, perhaps because I had gotten past what Dad had done to me. I also no longer had the flying dream because I was no longer tempted to escape into fantasy. My new worst dream was forgetting I had a child and having it starve to death. The crushing sorrow and shame for that neglect was shriveling. The symbolism here was obvious. It was the result of the loss of my first three children.

My second nightmare was the classic one of being nude in a group of people. That probably had to do with my fear of exposing myself and my vulnerabilities. This dream is a universal one. We are all in the same boat, afraid of our weaknesses. Speaking of weaknesses, in reality as a woman I did not have the physical strength of a man—but I learned ways to compensate for this lack.

The first tool I bought when I started my own company was a $1500 hammer-drill for driving ground-rods. Maine soil is consistently rocky. Rather than bust a gut pounding on an eight-foot ground-rod with a sledge hammer and brute strength, I bring out my trusty ground-rod driver. Someone from the utility company that hooks our service up to the power line told me that my driver was the envy of other contractors. I can just see the linesman watching an electrician struggle with getting a rod into the ground, and saying, "You should have Pat's ground-rod driver." (Not half bad.)

Not all my compensators are expensive, though. It requires great hand strength to bend two-hundred amp wires, which I lack, so I'd screw a plastic bushing on the end of a threaded 12" piece of a larger diameter rigid pipe. I put the end of the wire in the pipe. This increased length gave me the leverage advantage that makes shaping the wire much easier. It turns out the best tool I have is my brain. It makes up for deficiency in strength.

But, tools that help you out—don't always help you out. Remember the huge white ash tree the kitten got stuck in? Well, I got into real trouble with that tree—this time, with a chainsaw.

Hurricane Gloria decided to wallop Maine. I quit work early to button up the house in preparation for the storm. I noticed that there was a really BIG dead elm tree, right where it would smash my bedroom if it came down. And I saw that I needed to drop that live white ash first; otherwise the elm would bounce and probably hit my bedroom. The ash was in the stone wall and, as I'd already discovered when I rescued the kitten; my arm span would not reach even halfway around the tree.

I started up the big chainsaw that Harry had bought for himself a number of years before. It was definitely not sized for me, but I would not have admitted that fact to anyone for the world. The 18" blade was so long, that I had to stand on tiptoes to keep the blade from hitting the ground when I started it. It took everything I had—and then some—to get it going.

Since the tree was leaning out from the woods to reach the sun in my yard, the natural center of gravity would make it fall on my side of the stone wall. To prevent this, I cut a large wedge in the tree to drop it on my neighbor's side of the wall. He lived about a mile away on another road entirely.

The hurricane came—and went—doing no damage to my property.

So far, so good.

A few weeks later my neighbor, Walter, arrived and said, "I heah ya cut my tree."

I reply, "Yes, I did. It would have fallen right on my bedroom if I hadn't."

"Why dint ya ask me ta cut it?"

"I didn't have time. It was right before the storm hit."

"That's some valabul tree. It's a white ash an worth lotsa money"

"I didn't steal your tree. The wood's still there. You can get it out"

"S' gonna be real hawd gitt'n it out."

"You can come across my lawn to get it. That should be easy enough."

"Nope, ya'll jes sue me fah damages to ya lawn.

"I wouldn't do that," I said. Beginning to realize this situation was not going to resolve easily, I added, "I could bring the wood on down to your house in my truck."

"I don wan it fa fawood. It'll git me moah money as a log down ta the mill."

"How much do you think its worth?"

"Bout five hundrit."

"Yikes, I don't have that kind of money."

"That's whata wan."

"Would you take two barbeque pigs instead?" I was raising pigs and they were worth something (Maybe not $500, though).

"Don't wan no pigs. Alla wan is the money—or I'll sue."

"Well, I don't have it," I said, "so you'll just have to sue me then."

Walter was a journeyman electrician working for his brother's electrical contracting company. His brother had the masters for their business and here I was, not only a master electrician, but with my own company. His nose was out of joint about this—Big Time. He wanted to take me down a peg or two. That's what this was all about.

Sure enough, I got the summons to come to court. He brought the president of the State Bar Association as his lawyer. I couldn't afford a lawyer so I threw myself on the mercy of the court.

The judge listened to my argument that the tree was a 'line tree', and as such we both owned it.

Then he asked, "Did you have to step on his property to cut it?"

I said, "Yes, it was really big."

The judge responded, "That eliminates it as a line tree." Then he added, "I'm really sorry but Stumpage Law states that if a person cuts down someone else's tree, they *will* be charged three times the value of the tree."

He added, "This law does not say you *may* be charged for the tree. It gives me *no* discretion in the matter, so I *do* have to charge you for three times the value of the tree."

Then the judge asked Walter, "Do you have the estimate for the tree?"

"Eh yuh, I got it right heah."

The judge said, "The tree is valued at three hundred so that will be nine hundred total."

"Wait jesa minit Judge, how 'bout my pain an sufferen?"

"What suffering?"

"I lay up ah night, worren 'bout what she'll do next."

The judged smiled slightly, "I don't think so," he said. "Nine hundred it is."

This was my first venture into our judicial system and in my estimation, justice did not happen. Work was a much more satisfactory experience.

Another outfit I worked for was Women Unlimited, the brainchild of the state treasurer Dale McCormack. Her idea was to get women exposed to trades as one way to get them off welfare. The subjects taught were carpentry, electrical, plumbing, trucking, etc. They gave me complete freedom to build my own course which was a refreshing change from my public school teaching experience. I was finally able to use some of the things I learned when I got my teaching degree; teaching plans, testing, etc. (Not to say I wasn't constantly teaching on the job when I was training new helpers.)

One problem I had with the public school system when I was doing my student teaching was the team teaching system the school used at that time. We were locked into coordinating with other team members, which left no time for individual digressions into other areas. My teaching style was much looser. Plus, I was great with digressions! A better spin on it would be to say I liked teaching patterns and connections.

In contrast, Women Unlimited gave me the freedom to teach my own way, which was exciting. Plus, they paid me $25 per hour, which was $5 more than I was making as an electrician. I designed a course that covered basic home wiring. I also built a demonstration board with single-pole switches, 3-way switches, lights, and receptacles on it. I could plug this demo board into a power outlet and it would energize everything. With those outlets I could demonstrate how to make the proper wire connections, so everything would work. This concrete visual aid was probably more instructive than the book I had ordered for the class.

I taught my sixteen week program at the Central Maine Vocational Technical School in Auburn, half an hour away. I also taught at Southern Maine Technical School in Portland, one hour away; and at Bath Iron Works, where they build ships for the Navy, almost two hours away.

I did this for two years before I realized I was *losing* money, not making it. First of all, there was no way I could schedule electrical work on the day I was teaching. Then there was all the time spent in preparation, grading, travel time, not to mention the cost for the travel time. The final straw was when Dale wanted me to find jobs for the graduates of the course. It was hard enough for *me* to get work, much less recommend someone whose work ethic I was unfamiliar with.

Work ethic is the operative phrase here. From all these women I never accomplished the goal of adding another woman electrician to the workforce. These women knew a good thing when they saw it; Maine is famous for having the best welfare system in the USA. Immigrants come to our freezing state just for that reason; even people from desert, tropical, and impoverished countries.

I did have hopes for one girl, though, and hired her for a big job I got at a boys summer camp on Lake Thompson. That winter there was a really big storm. Their electric power had been fastened to live trees, and the storm had taken many of them down. When the power company came to repair the lines, they wouldn't, because the new code did not allow hooking to live trees.

The camp needed all these bunk-room buildings to be powered up according to current code. This was going to be a big job, and I needed more helpers. Besides the top girl from my class, I hired two other helpers: an older licensed journeyman electrician and an unlicensed young student whose background was in electronics. Harry also helped, as much as he could.

The reason for the big push was the camp needed to open in three more weeks. Rather than go overhead, we went underground. I had to truck over my tractor/backhoe to dig the trenches.

As far as my helpers were concerned, the licensed journeyman was the one I had to watch the closest. He put everything in slap-dash, and on to the next. His work simply wasn't neat enough. I had to have him go back and redo "how" he did it. The electronics student wanted the "why", so I wasted a lot of unnecessary time explaining the code requirements that were involved. The girl from my class just asked me what needed to be done, then did it with no fuss and no bother. Even Harry said she was the best of the lot.

But she didn't become an electrician. She went into the Department of Transportation (DOT). She wanted to become an engineer and if she was accepted by the DOT, their schooling program would help her accomplish that. Even though my hopes were dashed, I couldn't fault her ambition. So much for Women Unlimited, (in spite of their promising name.)

The camp job, where I used the one and only girl from Women Unlimited, was the reason why I had my second run-in with the judicial system. It happened like this. The camp maintenance man wanted to rent my tractor with its backhoe for some additional work at the camp, but never brought it back to us. He just called and tersely said, "The tractor broke down and we left it over at the John Deere place to get it fixed."

After three weeks of hearing nothing further, I went down to the repair shop, myself. My tractor was still sitting outside, unrepaired. The front bucket was bent and the clutch was kaput.

When I asked why they hadn't worked on it, they said the camp owner hadn't paid his last bill, and they weren't going to do any work for him until he did. I told them that tractor belonged to me and I needed it repaired right away. I said I would pay for the work and settle up with the camp owner later. Wouldn't you know, the camp owner refused to pay the bill, so I reluctantly took him to court. What a joke that was! The same president of the Bar Association was the lawyer for the camp. I again did not have a lawyer (stupidly, not having learned my lesson yet).

The judge said, "You can sue for liability or for 'tort'."

Since I didn't know what 'tort' was, I said, "Liability?"

The camp owner's lawyer said, "They had heard a funny noise in the tractor so they told Harry, but he didn't hear anything and told them they could go ahead and use it."

Harry had been losing his hearing which they knew about, because they spoke louder when they talked to him. But by Harry saying it was ok to run, their liability was removed. The judge ruled in their favor. He informed me, "If you had chosen 'tort,' they would be paying for the bill now."

I asked, "Can I change to 'tort' now, since I didn't know what tort meant?"

"It's too late now, the judge said, "I've already ruled on it. You should have had a lawyer,"

"So, you are going to penalize me for not having a lawyer?" I asked.

"No, you are penalizing yourself," he replied.

When I got home I looked up what tort was in the dictionary. It is a wrongful act in which the injured person is owed compensation. That's exactly what I was looking for. Locking the barn door after the horse is stolen is about as useful as my belated knowledge.

Dear reader. Let this be a lesson to you. If you ever have to go to court, GET A LAWYER! That is their work and they are good at it.

In the late 1980s, my work came to a grinding halt. Harry had become physically unable to work, due to illness. Leaving me as the only source of income for the three of us—and we were hurting.

A large part of our food came from the "pig run." I fed my pigs by daily picking up what the local supermarket threw out. I didn't actually remove all their trash. That was done by another person who understood hard times, so he let me pick through the trash for anything the pigs and my family could use. For my part of the bargain, I gave him a pig for a pig roast every year.

Barter is great, and this pig run was *really* great. The supermarket threw out tons of perfectly good stuff, like boxes of bananas that had started to get just a few brown spots. It seemed a shame to have the pigs the only beneficiaries of this largess, so I'd leave some of the bananas out by the road for the neighbors. I got a dehydrator and made banana chips. I also made lots of banana eggnogs for breakfast. Emma got so sick of them, she refused to have any for many years.

Other things the store threw out were cheeses, greens, and all kinds of really ripe fruit. I learned to appreciate avocados, mangos and other expensive fruit I had never tried. By the time the store threw out this fruit it was at the peak of ripeness so we really chowed down. Deli sandwiches were our downfall, and I think we got food poisoning three or four times, at least.

The pig run wasn't the only help we had. Half our heat was from wood, so I cleared my two acres of most of its trees. The goats helped by stripping the bark from the trees. By the time I took those trees down they had been standing dead-wood for quite awhile, perfect for winter heat. I got pretty good at dropping a tree where I wanted it to go. But, my ship was still sinking no matter how hard I bailed.

I tried hiring out to other electricians but they were in the same boat I was. I even applied to get a job reading meters for the utility company. They said I was too old! Would you believe fifty was too old? Here I am at seventy+, and still going . . . (well, maybe not quite as strong).

I did get a job at a paper mill, in Jay an hour's drive north of us. The pay was $15 an hour, which was really good for that time. I learned a lot about complying with Occupational Safety and Health Organization (OSHA) regulations for safety, harnessing up and buckling in just to climb a six foot ladder. What a pain! I discovered why we got paid the big bucks, though.

There is a by-product of the papermaking process, which is chlorine gas; you know, the poison gas from the war. They had all sorts of sensors and alarms so we wouldn't be exposed to it. I caught a whiff of the chlorine gas that wasn't even enough to set the sensors off. For half an hour I tried to heave my stomach out my mouth, my eyes and nose streaming. All the guys split their sides laughing. Fortunately, I didn't get enough to need medical attention. Good thing I was only temporary help.

By the time I was done there, my own work had started to pick up. Rather than run two separate households, Harry and I decided to fix up his place as a rental. He would move over to my place and all the electrical stock would come also.

Now I was to experience a strange disparity. Harry granted me equality on the job, and yet, as soon as we walked through the front door after work, inequality set in. He would plunk himself down in a chair, get a newspaper out, and expect me to get dinner ready immediately. I was *not* impressed. What I usually ended up doing was going down to the barn and getting the goats fed and milked; then there were the pigs, chickens, cows, etc. Now *he* was not impressed.

We had a meeting of minds on the next action he took. While we were living at the Little Red House, Harry found a 50-foot trailer we were able to buy cheaply. We moved it down to the middle of the 20 acres I had previously purchased. I wasn't happy with the whole trailer thing, so decided to build an add-on closed entry room. As I was drawing out the plans for this room, my ideas kept getting grander and grander.

Financing this project was the next hurdle. I sold half my land and Harry mortgaged his house. With the joint money, we built the septic, foundation and driveway. Then we began building a nice 30' by 40' three-story house butted right up to the trailer. Unfortunately, the trailer was sitting on a rock ledge. Joining the addition and the trailer together, entailed blasting into the hill the trailer sat on. It was a tricky business pulling it off without damaging the trailer. Many beautiful huge granite chunks resulted from this, and we piled them up for later use in rock-wall building.

Sadly, we ran out of money before we could finish the building. The trailer was livable though. The one inconvenience was no well. I needed $3,000 for that and couldn't seem to save that amount.

Meanwhile, my youngest son, Timmy, had come back to live with us while he worked downtown at the paper. I was so happy to have him around that it just bubbled out of me. Timmy had a wonderful sense of humor and kept us in stitches with his mime routines. My two favorites were Flossing Teeth While Driving and Unseen Wave. All this focus on Timmy didn't go over very well with Harry. He thought I was paying more attention to my son than to him, (which, actually, I may have been doing).

One evening I mistakenly put the first plate of food down in front of Timmy. Harry thought he should have gotten it, and accused me of showing preference to Timmy. "It's either him or me," Harry said. As he stomped out the door, he added, "I'm never coming back." Down he went to the trailer. And he was right about not returning. Since he was even more adamant than I am, he lived in the trailer until he died, joining us only for dinners, showers, and such.

Yet again, I did something I deeply regret, when I told Timmy, "My life is with Harry. You are going to be making your own life soon, and I'll be having no part of that. You need to be the one to go." His quiet acceptance of that was to come back and bite me later. Thirty years down the road he chose his wife over his family back east. How can I fault him for the same thing I did?

Still hurts, though.

Although weathering the storms in my life should have weakened me, the reverse happened. It was something like the tempering of metal. It strengthened my character.

My body, however, was a different story. Work was achieving the inevitable wear and tear. Injuries never healed to the original condition. Joints stiffened and other areas softened. Grey hair appeared and teeth loosened. It was actually kind of funny, how you disintegrated. Who needs pride, anyway?

I learned some valuable things from my work experience such as: confidence and belief in myself.

Working for myself gave me the flexibility for personal days such as visits to the dentist.

It also gave me independence: nobody could tell me what I should be doing, except maybe the code enforcement officer.

Work also gave me authority, because electricians are the most respected of the construction trades.

Some practical things I learned are:

1. have a second source of income to cushion the feast /famine of electrical work

2. study taxes and/or hire a good bookkeeper

3. stay healthy because medical insurance is outrageously expensive

4. hire a helper because teamwork is more efficient than working alone.

Why do I work? Not to make a ton of money—but to have a place where I can root and flourish and be in contact with the natural world. I work to provide for my family and to be of service to those who are in need. I work because it is who I am.

The bottom line is—in spite of the wear and tear, work has been good *for* me and *to* me.

10 GRAFTING
(New Branch on Wild Root)

The bandwagon of feminism I had jumped on with such charged enthusiasm earlier in my life was beginning to run amok. Equality had morphed into Female Power. I got a lot of my ideas from Betty Frieden's *The Feminine Mystique* and Margaret Mead's, *Coming of Age in Samoa*, and *Male and Female.* These books showed how interchangeable the gender roles could be, and I (of course) was drawn to strong matriarchal societies.

I didn't exactly burn my bra, but I *did* take it off. Having my breasts loose also loosened other strictures. I regained the confidence and resolve I had as a young child. Independence and self-sufficiency became my highest priority.

As a true feminist, my choice of Harry as both my lover and partner did not include the convention of marriage. By this time I had gone back to my birth name, and wanted to take no man's name, much less have him dictate the choices I should be making. I wanted to decide things for myself. I needed to be the one in control.

I had a real wake-up call about my choices at that point. I was doing some work at a pastor's house, and what he had to say about his ministry really drew me. I went to his church a few times and I realized that I wanted to make God more of a part of my life. The way to do that seemed to be by getting baptized. I approached him with this request, but unexpectedly he said, "I'm not going to be able to do that because of your relationship with Harry."

I said, "There's no adultery involved, neither of us are married.

The pastor said, "That's right, but what you are doing is considered fornication."

I was so blindsided by the ugliness of that word I started to cry.
Buck up, Pat.
Now he's going to put you in the weeping woman category!

Come on. My beautiful relationship with Harry couldn't ever be described with that hideous word.

I got up and stormed out. Plus, I stopped going to Church.

The next thing that happened was getting sick with large fibroids in my uterus. The doctor said I needed a hysterectomy, but I was afraid of what would happen to Emma if I died in surgery. I had almost died when she was born, so it seemed quite possible it might happen with this surgery. If the worst happened, Emma would end up in foster care because I had chosen to not name Harry as her father. For her sake, I reluctantly married Harry, though I did not yield to him my head of household status, nor did I take his name.

Since our wedding ceremony was almost nonexistent, a good friend of Harry's, he called Doc, and his wife, Lynn offered to have the reception in their house. The only other people at the ceremony were my boys and Emma-Rose so the reception was small. But Lynn had her house beautifully decorated with pine boughs and she made the occasion special with champagne and other goodies.

Our honeymoon was a trip to view Niagara Falls. Although some might categorize this as a trite choice, I prefer to call it classic—and it really was. The vibration in your bones caused by the massive water as it thundered down made it much more than an eye-pleasing sight. Nothing can really convey how awesome this natural wonder is. It has the power to make us realize how puny we humans really are.

When we got back from the trip I underwent the surgery, and sailed through it without a hiccup, thanks to the time the surgeon took to allay my anxiety (plus his excellent competency).

Harry and I enjoyed our honeymoon so much that we took another trip the following year to Pulaski, New York, where went salmon fishing. Unfortunately, we didn't catch anything. Being skunked like that resulted in my overwhelming desire to catch one. I chased one up the river, flinging my line in front of it, but to no avail. I almost threw myself down to grab it with my hands, or swat it out of the water. The adrenalin of the chase brought me close to the edge of unacceptable behavior (game wardens don't allow catching fish like grizzly bears).

My sister Stephie came to take care of Emma when Harry and I went on the trip. When we got back, Steph said, "I'm NEVER going to have a child."

"Why not?" I asked.

"Taking care of a kid is hard. I don't know how you do it".

"It's not that hard," I said. "You just have to pace yourself".

"Wait 'til you see her hair," Stephie said.

When I saw Emma's long hair was a mass of snarls, I asked, "Why did you let it get like that?"

"I could barely get a comb through the top two inches," Stephie said. "Then it would all ball up."

"The method is to start on the bottom," I said. "Get that clear before moving higher on the length of hair. Bit by bit it can be done".

"Why didn't you tell me that?" Stephie retorted.

"I didn't think you needed to be told. It seemed obvious." She hung her head.

"Oh, Steph, I'm sorry," I said. "I should have given you better directions." Now I felt bad too: She was right. She never did have children. I think that her decision not to do so was partly my fault. I feel even worse about that.

The next trip Harry and I took involved a local babysitter. We went white-water rafting on the East Branch of the Penobscot River. It was classed as a 4+ category (drop of five feet), with one section classed as a 5 (drop of 10 feet). Actually, my oldest daughter, Lee, invited us to go with her group at work. We were able to get a reduced price for the run, but spent more to get the DVD of the trip. The photographer was on the shore and the only way you can tell the video was of us was because of my perennial visor. So the money for the DVD was waste, but the trip itself? It was adrenaline the whole time.

In spite of being newly married, our day-to-day living arrangement remained the same. Emma and I lived in the little red house and Harry continued to live in the trailer. Because of the lack of a well there, I'd bring water to him from the well at the red house. I'd fill the back of my pickup with 30 buckets, fill them with the hose, then line them up in the hallway in front of his bathroom. That worked for the toilet. When he needed a shower, he'd use ours.

When Harry and I came home from work, I'd drop him off at the trailer, then go home to do chores. I'd call him when supper was ready, and if he didn't like the vegetarian food I was fixing, he'd cook his own meal, southern style. It was an odd marriage, but it worked for us.

Since I was now married, I decided to go back to church, but I chose a different one from where I had been hit with that ugly 'F' word.

I heard my first altar call there. The congregation was singing the hymn "Just as I Am," (which is a beautiful song, by the way). The Pastor was walking back and forth, begging people to surrender to God. He was practically crying, saying, "You will be lost if you don't choose God. The door is open now. All you have to do is walk in."

After every verse he would stop the singing and plead some more.

He continued, "I wasn't always a religious man. I used to do drugs and alcohol when I was a teenager. I know how low you can go. I was once there, too."

Another verse would be sung, and then he would begin again.

"Please, leave all your burdens on Jesus. How wonderful that would be. But, the door won't always be open, and you should make your choice for Jesus now, before it's too late. If you don't choose Him, it will be the same as choosing Satan."

I really wanted to come forward and kneel at the cross, but I wasn't sure if that was the correct procedure. Finally, a person in my own pew got up and walked forward.

Oh, good. This is what's supposed to happen.

I gratefully popped up and followed him to the front. I knelt there crying my heart out with the intensity of my surrender. Soon there were lots of people there. I felt two people come stand behind me and gently put their hands on my shoulders.

Finally, the Pastor finished the praying. I got off my knees and asked for a tissue. I had snot running all down my face

This is really embarrassing.

The two people behind me were the pig farmers that lived down the road from me. They hugged me and gave me lots of tissues, which I really needed. I was as limp as a wet dishrag with the enormity of what had just happened. And to have people I hardly knew come up and touch me, supporting me in the choice I had made, just blew me away.

I started studying the Bible with an older woman in the church by the name of Goldy Welch. She was intelligent, knowledgable, sensitive and tender. I couldn't have had a better mentor.

My spiritual dimension started growing like it was on steroids. I now accepted absolute right and wrong; which is actually a very difficult and exacting concept. No more 'situation ethics', like I had before. Let me tell you what I mean by that.

Situation ethics means your concept of the right thing to do would depend on the situation. For example, although situation ethics would make it OK to steal some bread if you were starving, absolute right and wrong would not allow that.

Let me propose several real-life situations that involve making an ethical choice. The first involves the choice of lying, if it is for a good purpose.

During the Second World War, some Germans were hiding some Jews. The Gestapo came to the door and asked if they were hiding any Jews. The homeowner, who was a Christian, was torn about how to reply. If he replied honestly, the Jews would be killed. However, lying would be an immoral choice. He opened his mouth and the following words came out. "Do you think I would be so stupid as to have done that?" The amazing thing was, the soldiers accepted that and didn't search the house. God honored that unwillingness to lie by allowing the soldiers to accept that answer.

These situations don't always have an ending we are aware of. Let me give you an example. This one happened in the missionary field, where a person was tempted to lie because of the greater good that might result by doing so.

A person was smuggling some Bibles into a Muslim country that was closed to Christianity. He was stopped at the border and asked if he had any Bibles. If he lied, the Bibles would get into the country where they might do some good. If he declared them, they would be confiscated. That is what he did, and they were taken from him.

It sounds like a defeat, but who knew what God's plan was for those Bibles. Maybe they would be stored someplace where somebody would pick one up and be converted as a result. Even if it was only one person, it would be enough to make the whole effort a success.

The final example of an extremely difficult choice is not for the faint-hearted. A missionary family in Africa was invaded by a band of guerilla boy soldiers. They were going to conscript the family's teenage boy for their army. If the parents didn't let him go, the soldiers would kill him. What would be the right thing to do? Let your son join and have him commit murder and who knows what else? Or refuse and surely die?

This real life choice was made and their son was shot and killed.

What is the good in this awful result? His parents knew that to die as a Christian was to live eternally. But to live as a guerilla soldier would most likely result in eternal death.

Would I have the moral fiber to make the right choice here? I don't know.

Did I learn that right and wrong are written in stone, and never shaded into something different because of the situation?

Absolutely!

But the best thing I learned was that if I had Jesus, God wouldn't see my failures. He would see Jesus in front of me, and I would be accepted.

How about That!

Once I incorporated the new ethics, I lost that sense of being bad I had carried within me for such a long time. I knew I needed constant vigilance to keep from going over the line (somewhat like quitting smoking) but at least I knew where the line was—and—it wasn't constantly shifting.

Additionally, something (the Holy Spirit) began to leave impressions on my mind. The first one was that I needed to take Harry's name. When I told him about that he cried, with happiness, I think. I had no idea how much I had hurt him with my stubborn independence/refusal.

Ultimately, I was able to to suspend my distrust of authority in general so I could accept the authority of God over me. It basically came down to trust. I knew God loved me in spite of all my weakness, and more than that, He knew what was best for me. My idea of what was best for me was definitely inferior.

Believe me, this was no lightening strike of insight. It has taken me years to come to this conclusion. Talk about a slow learner.

What convinced me?

Demonstration after demonstration of God stepping in and providing what I needed in answer to prayer And then, sometimes when it didn't even occur to me that I needed to pray. Having experienced life without His blessings, I could see the difference plain as could be.

I learned that God places his hand of protection over His children, many times averting real disaster.

Not long ago, we had a tornado come through our property, cutting an eleven mile swath of destruction. It tossed huge pine trees fifty feet; it tore off the front of a barn and ended up moving a house ten feet off its foundation.

Emma's boyfriend was the only one at home when the tornado hit. He was asleep because he had been working nights. He woke up to the terrible roar and the whole house shaking. He jumped up to grab the air conditioner which was being sucked out of the window. After twenty seconds it had passed by. He went down stairs and called Emma who was trucking over the road.

I was out on a job also, thinking this was just another summer storm. She immediately called me and said, "You better get up to the house. A tornado just came through and all the trees are down. The dogs are all tangled up in the pines and I don't know if they are hurt or not."

I jumped into my truck and raced up the hill with lightning and thunder crashing all around, and the light that weird scary yellow that happens in a storm. It was only a five minute trip but it seemed twice as long, my heart in my mouth the whole time. I wouldn't ordinarily have been in the middle of it, but I was afraid for my animals.

I was relieved to see the horses were alright, and Chris had already gotten the dogs in. Everything had blown off the porch, and my little lawn cart was wrapped around a tree. But none of the vehicles were damaged, nor the house. All my beautiful big white pines were uprooted and piled around like tiddley winks. I lost about sixty trees both pine, fruit and hardwood.

The amazing thing was that the damage was on both sides of the house, so it seemed the funnel split to go around the house. I think God cupped His hand around my house so I got off easy.

See what I mean by God intervening?

Unfortunately, Emma wasn't having that kind of intervention when she was in middle school. I couldn't understand why she was angry all the time until I experienced the provocation she had to cope with on a daily basis. I was waiting at school to pick her up for her fiddle lesson. When she approached the car from one direction, a boy came the other way.

He yelled, "Hey, cross-eyed geek, running home to mama?"

My temper flared. I wanted to jump out of the car and grab him by the neck, but restrained myself.

When Emma got in the car I said, "That's awful. How do you stand it?"

She responded, "I get that all the time. You ought to hear some of the other stuff they call me."

Thus, I was not surprised when the principal called me up a few weeks later and said, "You won't believe this, but I've got Emma in the office here for fighting. Apparently she threw someone into the lockers."

No, I wasn't surprised.

I understood completely why she had done it. The only trouble was I didn't want her to get the idea that was the adult way to deal with her difficulties.

I was thinking a church school might be a good possibility for her, but I wasn't sure of the quality of education she would get there. I knew they would be teaching the creation story from the Bible rather than evolution. I didn't want her disadvantaged in the world by learning some inaccurate biblical myth of creation rather than the scientific facts everyone of reasonable education and intelligence accepts. (That's what I thought back then).

When I was a teenager, I didn't question the science I was taught. I took it on faith that the teachers knew more than I did and it was my job to absorb it all, not to question whether it was true or not.

I *wanted* to believe everything in the Bible, but all I had learned in public school, college, and even on the discovery channel stood in opposition to it.

So, to reconcile these two oppositional ideas, I started researching creation vs. evolution. I began to see the flaws in Darwin's Theory and in the science that supports it.

I was taught that life began from a (so called) simple cell that had arisen from a primordal soup of watery chemicals that had been struck by lightening, possibly near a volcano that was spewing out the heavier elements. AND, there was a scientist who had duplicated these conditions and been able to form something like an organic compound from these non-living elements. Note: an organic compound is comprised of elements found in living (or formerly living) plants or animals.

However, this scientist was unable to go any further, i.e. create life from these compounds. The very most insurmountable problem was the complexity of the elaborate machine, formerly known as the simple cell. With the introduction of the electron microscope, what looked like a simple one-celled organism like an amoeba, was actually a highly complex inter-dependant set of systems like respiration, locomotion, reproduction, food absorption, elimination, growth etc., all necessary for life to exist.

Look at the ever changing shape of the amoeba as it moves. The cell wall has to change shape as the inside of the animal flows from one area to another. The cell wall thins on the side it is moving toward, and thickens on the side it is coming from. It is almost as if it is pushing against the back wall of the organism. In spite of all this pressure the edge doesn't rupture.

The cell wall is an amazing semi-permeable membrane that allows some elements like food enter the cell, and other elements like waste products to leave the cell. Plus, it doesn't get the two mixed up.

Let's examine the possibility that all these inter-related systems could have arisen by chance, but I'll simplify by only considering the reproductive system. In addition, I'll say there are only 100 protein combinations in the DNA chain when there are actually tens of thousands. Since there are twenty amino acids in a protein, finding the correct order that would result in reproduction would be one chance in the following number: 1,000,000,000,000,000,000,000,000,000,000,000,000,000,000,000,000,000,000,000,000,000,000,000,000,000,000,000,000,000,000,000,000,000,000,000,000,000,000,000,000,000,000,000,000,000. That is 1 followed by 130 zeros.

Remember, this is only for 100 proteins, not tens of thousands.

You might as well say there isn't enough time in the universe for life to arrive spontaneously.

Let's consider a more concrete example of something complicated arising from chance. How about a monkey with a typewriter? How long would it take him to write the complete works of Shakespeare, assuming he could live forever? How about just one of his plays? The answer is—it wouldn't happen.

If you don't like that example, how about another?

What happens when an explosion on a plane happens? The plane is destroyed.

Would the reverse happen if there was a junkyard that had all the components of the airplane included within it? Of course an airplane wouldn't result from the explosion.

This demonstrates the second law of thermodynamics, also called the law of entropy. This law very simply states that energy can only go from an ordered state to a disordered state. In other words, things don't get better, they get worse. You might even call this the Law of Disorder.

Order and design just doesn't happen by chance. It requires an intelligent designer. To me, when I look at the natural world design is an obvious fact, as much as when I look at the manufactured products that man has made.

Evolution says that change from one form of creature to another, was a result of survival of the fitest. The most fit to survive would survive longer, breed for a longer period of time and eventually outnumber the less fit.

This adaptation to the surroundings or even selection by humans for a specific purpose, such as the difference between a lap dog or a racing dog can result in great variety, but a beetle can't evolve into a bat. The difference between kinds of plants or animals are there because they were designed that way.

Incorporated into design is the principle that, "nothing works unless everything works." When a gas stove is built and all the elements work perfectly except for the igniter, the stove won't work. You could substitute for the flaw by putting a match to it, but the point I'm making is the appliance won't work unless everything works.

Let me give you some natural examples of this principle.

A complex structure like the human eye couldn't have evolved because there was no survival advantage to the intermediate but not yet functioning eye.

The second example is much more interesting. It is the Bombardier Beetle. This bug has a defense system similar to a skunk, but much more elaborate. He squirts boiling hot, bad smelling fluid right into his attacker's face. The fluid is the result of two chemicals, hydrogen peroxide and hydroquinone, combining together to make an explosive reaction which he can direct at the target.

First the beetle needs to store these two inert chemicals in different chambers so they won't react together. Then the combining chamber has to be heavily insulated and strong enough to contain and direct the spray.

A single chemical would have no survival advantage. Having both chemicals but without the combining chamber, there wouldn't be an advantage either. If the combining chamber was poorly insulated the bug would incinerate himself. Then the pointing mechanism should be in place, otherwise he could completely miss his opponent.

The end result . . . no defense unless everything worked. All this could not have happened by adaptation because there was no advantage to having one or two of the elements The only explanation is that the beetle was designed that way.

Nature supports evidence of design. And if there is design, there needs to be an intelligent designer. As a side note, we can learn something about this mastermind just by observing his creation. He could have made a generic flower, tree, or seashell.

Instead he chose variety. Was this beauty just for him, or did he put it there for our enjoyment, also?

How about humor in our creator? If you look at a moose or a camel, they are certainly funny looking. Then there is the Duck-billed Platypus. I think God made that animal just to confound the taxonomist (one who names and classifies).

The flawed theory of evolution is not only based on natural selection and adaptation, but also on the existence of missing links.

First, the missing links can't be found. When Darwin proposed his theory, he expected the missing links to eventually appear. They never did, even though paleontologists have been searching for over 150 years. The missing links between birds and reptiles, between man and ape, and between fish and amphibians simply haven't been found. And the list goes on.

Let's look at the fish that has stiff bottom fins that enable it to walk on dry land for short periods of time (probably to get food). Evolutionists say, that fish is an intermediate life form between fish and amphibians. In actuality, it has no characteristics of an amphibian other that being able to walk on land. Does a duck become a fish just because it seeks food in anothers habitat? Does the flying fish become a bird because it can leap out of the water and glide to escape its enemies?

What about Neanderthal man as a missing link? His legs were bowed and misshaped because he had rickets, a nutritional deficiency disease which causes those exact deformations. He is considered fully human now.

Piltdown man turned out to be a hoax based on the combination of a human skull with the jaw of an orangutan.

Lucy was probably a pygmy chimpanzee.

When Darwin first proposed his theory, he himself called the missing links the weakest part of his hypothesis. He fully expected that the future would bring forth many examples of missing links. That hasn't happened.

Whenever a new find is discovered, there is great excitement, but they eventually fade into oblivion because they don't stand the test of time.

Mutations have been offered as another way for an animal to become more adapted to their surroundings. Unfortunately, mutations are mal-adaptive because they result in downgrading the organism. A mutated rooster without feathers lacks protection from the elements. Plus, he can't breed because he has no wing feathers to steady himself in his position.

As far as crossbreeding between species is concerned, the result is sterile. A donkey bred to a horse becomes a non-breeding mule. The Bible is very specific that each animal would only bear (off-spring) "after its own kind."

Let's look at another Bible reference, the flood in Noah's day. The geology of the earth supports evidence of a world wide flood. I have personally seen the result of extreme flooding on the roads in my area. Overnight, washed out roads have developed into deep ravines. Gradual erosion didn't create them. It was sudden violent flooding. The Grand Canyon is a standing witness to cataclysmic flooding, not eons of erosion.

The old age of the earth is another bulwark of science which is in opposition to the biblical young age of the earth.

According to the first chapter in the Bible, in the beginning the earth was "without form and void." It could have been created with the rest of the universe long ago, and only six thousand years ago terra-formed to make a world suitable for man.

Radioactive carbon dating is done by measuring the amount of decay in the radioactive carbon that is within the material. This procedure has several flaws. One is that the premise it is based on may be incorrect Scientists assume because the rate of decay seems to be constant now, it must have always been that way. What if the dacay rate was more like rolling down a steep hill? That would mean that a lot of decay would have occurred in the beginning, with the slower amount happening now 'on the flat', so to speak. This rate would account for the young age of the earth.

Another problem with carbon dating is the inconsistent results. There are many instances of items measured as being very old when in fact they are known to have a currant age. Sometimes the reverse is true. When a prehistoric skull was carbon dated, the results weren't accepted because it was too old! Humans weren't around then was the explanation.

Would I like to base my support of science on such an unreliable source?

Actually, it all comes down to faith. Do I believe in the presuppositions of science which are the product of man's thought? Granted, these men of science are probably much more intelligent that I am, definitely more educated and experienced in their fields. But, none of them have been able to create anything living.

My answer to that question is an unequivocal and resounding, no!

I choose to believe in the incredibly superior being who is the Creator of everything, living and non-living, known and unknown.

Once I accepted the accuracy of the whole Bible, and shelved the things I didn't understand for later study, I was ready to enroll Emma in the church school. But was she interested? This was right around Christmas time, right in the middle of the school year; perhaps a difficult time to insert her into an established class.

I asked Emma if she would consider going to the church school, maybe just try it for a few days to see if she liked it.

She was willing to give it a try.

I immediately called up the prayer chain to ask for the school to be a good fit for Emma. When I picked her up after school, I didn't want to rush her, so I kept quiet to see what she would offer. That little rascal didn't say anything at first. Then she said. "I didn't like it," (long pause) "I loved it! (She was picking up teasing techniques from her father.)

I went back to the ladies and gave them the praise report for answered prayer. Then I asked if they could continue praying, because now I needed to come up with the tuition money, and work had slowed down to a standstill because of the winter. Three hours later I opened my bank bag and found $350 dollars I had tucked away and forgotten about. I had not only the tuition money, but enough to go down to the thrift shop to get her some skirts (dress code, you know).

Now, a skeptic would say, "You see, nothing manufactured that money for you. You just forgot about it." Yes, but money was so tight at that time I would have missed not having it available, and would have searched high and low for it. Somehow, God provided enough work so I didn't miss it; then He made me forget about it, (and my memory was much better back then). Why would I suddenly remember it, if He hadn't put it in my mind. The timing of the whole thing is what makes me believe that it was answered prayer.

I began going to the Sunday school for adults at the church, which was a new experience for me. I thought Sunday school was only for children. But I soon found out how much I didn't know.

The very first question I asked has continued to bother me down the years, even though I got a satisfactory answer then. The question was, "What about the salvation of the Jews? Are they forever lost because they don't have Jesus?"

The answer was, "Yes and no."

Wouldn't you know, not a straight answer!

They continued. "Yes. Collectively, the Jews as the chosen ones are lost. But individually they may be saved. It all depends on their relationship with God. And in regard to the pagans, those who had no opportunity to know Jesus, they will be judged by the light they had been shown."

There, that set my heart at ease. The whole concept of people being lost still bothers me though.

As I forged ahead gaining ground in the spiritual dimension, I left Harry behind. He wasn't one bit interested in going to church with me. Not only that, Harry began to lose ground in the physical department

Diabetes raised its ugly head in Harry's life. An associated problem was the loss of peripheral circulation. Many of the activities he enjoyed became more difficult, but in spite of that we went ice-fishing one winter. It was a lot of fun, especially because Emma came with us. We watched a bald eagle swoop down and snatch the bait fish we threw on the ice.

That was a sight!

We caught some huge pickerel. And—Harry caught frostbite in his toes. It really wasn't that cold, but because of his poor circulation, it happened. He went to the doctors twice to have the dead tissue removed, because his toes had become gangrenous, but the situation did not improve.

I decided to try alternative medicine and so we went to Poland Spring Health Institute, where Dr. Hansen surprised me by asking if we minded if he began with a word of prayer. Startled, I said, "Of course not." What a pleasant surprise to find a doctor that didn't think *he* was god.

Then he showed us how to do Hydrotherapy (a kind of water treatment). This entailed soaking his feet, first in hot water for three minutes, then cold water for thirty seconds; repeating this five times, ending with the cold water. I think the contrasting temperature was designed to increase the circulation and stimulate the body to heal itself. We were to do these four times a day, but the best we could do was twice. In spite of that, his toes finally healed. This kind of alternative healing was right down my alley.

Harry began to stay home more and more. He also spent a lot of time down at the coffee shop and on the motorcycle. We had a great big Honda Aspencade touring bike (1500 cc) just fine for the two of us, but a little too big for just one person. Because of his diabetes he began to get neuropathy in his legs. As he lost feeling, the motorcycle became much more dangerous. Sure enough, he dropped it, pinning himself to the ground. It was twenty minutes before our neighbor heard his cries for help, and came to lift the motorcycle off him. The roll-bar kept Harry from hurting anything, except perhaps his pride. Do you think that stopped him? Not at all.

Another time I came home to find the motorcycle in the cellar where we usually kept it, only it was on its side crammed underneath the stairs. Even though Harry was OK this time also, I was able to talk him into selling it. I drove it myself and didn't really want to see it go but that was the only way to keep him from killing himself on it. We practically gave it away, because I was so anxious to have it gone, no longer a temptation for him.

With the money from the sale of the motorcycle we finished paying off the original loan. Plus, there was a little left over for Harry to console himself with. He bought three guns and some re-loading equipment, which kept him busy for awhile.

Then a new gun appeared. I asked him, "Where did you get the money for that?"

He said, "I'm still capable of going out on a job myself."

I knew differently, and asked, "Where did you go?"

"Down to the variety store," was his answer.

"What did you do there?"

"I hooked up a water pump"

I was getting really tired of the many lies that surrounded Harry, so decided to finally confront him. But first, I needed to find out if my gut-feeling was a certainty. I drove down to the store and said, "I think my husband may have left his linesman's pliers here when he was hooking up the water pump."

"What water pump?" they said, "We're on town water."

Oh, boy. Now I look like a jerk.
I recovered. "I'm sorry. It must have been a different store."
I beat a hasty retreat.
All right, now I knew for sure.
I went back to Harry and said, "I know for a fact you didn't work down at the store, so where did you get the money for the gun?"

His shoulders sagged when he answered, "I endorsed one of your checks."

Strangely, I did not become furious. Instead, a sort of understanding took its place. All I said was, "I needed that money to pay the taxes." Now that I knew Harry was a liar, other inconsistencies began to make sense, like his claim to having attended college.

I also later discovered that his claim to be a childless bachelor was another big lie. When the three of us went down to visit his family, my father-in-law let the cat out of the bag, when he asked if I wanted to see pictures of Harry's grandsons. Totally floored, all I could do was say weakly, "Of course." Both boys looked like younger versions of Harry, just as handsome, and with his stunning smile.

Later I asked Harry why he had told me he had no children when it was so obviously untrue. His answer was his wife had been unfaithful and his so-called son wasn't really his. I accepted his answer but in my heart I knew that Emma had a half brother she would never get a chance to know and hoped she would change that once she got older, (which she has).

Oddly, none of this new knowledge about Harry's untruthfulness affected my love for him. I knew that he loved me and never looked at another woman after we met. The discovery about his lies only lessened my respect for his character. Secondly, I no longer took his distrust of my faithfulness quite so personally because I knew I wasn't the only woman he didn't trust.

The amazing root of Harry's attitude was didn't even trust his own mother! He revealed that he heard his father accuse his mother of the fact that Harry was not his own son. The only son his father was completely sure was his, was Harry's younger brother. There even was a time Harry was sent away to live with relatives because his mother was so concerned about his safety. I guess his father had beaten him pretty badly on numerous occasions. Strangely, Harry put the blame on his mother, not his father. Harry said, "If his own mother was unfaithful, how could he trust any woman?" In the light of all this, Harry's behavior with me made a lot more sense. The really inconsistent thing was how he fawned over his father as an adult instead of rejecting him. I guess that sometimes happens with abused children; they cling to the abuser.

Did I cling to my abuser? Perhaps I did. I know I didn't want to turn him in, and in that I failed my younger sisters.

Unlike Harry, I trust my body to heal. He viewed his body as unreliable and even as an enemy. As his health began to go downhill he considered himself a victim and just moaned about his misfortune. He didn't take responsibility for his diabetes, and I had little sympathy with his attitude. Emma became the one to cater to him. I was too busy earning a living for all of us.

Eventually, because of Harry's continued indulgence in the wrong foods, his kidneys failed. As he got sicker I had to move down to the trailer to be with him. Emma stayed up in the little red house (which she thought was a great idea.) Harry did not want to go through dialysis, and had lost his will to live. As his kidneys failed, his skin made a valiant effort to get rid of the poisons built up in his blood. He began to itch all over and dug himself raw. Although we tried all kinds of skin creams, even prescribed ones, nothing helped.

His ability to metabolize protein stressed his kidneys. All he wanted to eat was zucchini and yellow squash, which I had plenty of in my garden. Actually, squash was really good for him, being low in protein. I couldn't believe it would keep him alive but he ate only that for three months. Eventually, even that was too much and he began throwing up. I had been caring for Harry for three years, but his vomiting had gotten to the point where I had to have nurses come in when it was time to do chores. He was so weak I couldn't leave him alone for even that length of time.

Eventually, Harry became too weak to walk. When some friends came to visit, they said they'd get him to church if he wanted to go. Surprisingly, he accepted. We got a wheelchair for him and because there was no handicapped entrance, the men carried him in. This turned out to be a Pentecostal church and I was quite distracted by all the noise and movement. Someone came and brought Harry to the front and the pastor knelt down beside him. I couldn't hear them because of all that noise, but I did see Harry raise his hand. This was monumental. Then they brought him back to me because he had started throwing-up again, and I took him home.

I began to see God knew what was going to happen all along, and the nursing home experience was intended just for this purpose—to prepare me for taking care of Harry. So, I was planning to nurse Harry for years. But the home health nurses that came in to help said I needed to tell Harry it "was all right to let go." I strongly objected, "I can't tell him that, and it's *not* all right."

I was in denial, I guess.

But they kept after me and so I obliquely talked about his death by asking him what he wanted done for his funeral. I still could not say the words, "It's all right to let go." Three days before he died, he asked Emma not to visit anymore, which hurt her deeply. I think he wanted to spare her his dying, which was pretty gruesome.

The last words he said to me were, "I love you." A few hours later he stopped making eye contact and every breath became a moan, even though he was getting morphine. That night, as he gurgled his last breaths, he died in my arms.

My grief was noisy. I did not weep, I wailed. I groaned. I howled. The sound would stop only when I didn't have any air left in my lungs, but my stomach would still compress for long seconds after. My grief was guttural. And deep.

Although I saved this kind of grief for private times, embarrassingly, I wept throughout the whole funeral.

So much for my stony stoicism.

What didn't help was I had a friend play "Meditations from Thais" by Massenet, on his violin. That's a tearjerker all by itself.

One last curious experience occurred when I dreamt that Harry was standing at the end of a long corridor. He was backlit so I couldn't see his face, but I knew it was him and ran to him. He wrapped his big arms around me and said, "How'ya doing kid?" I felt desolate. All I could do was cry, because I knew he was gone and this was only a dream. It took two years for the bitterness of my grief to abate.

It is my hope that I will see him again for real—and that the eighteen years I had with him will become an eternity.

The new branch that God grafted on my wild root was taking hold. I could feel His spirit moving in me.

11 RAMPANT GROWTH: (Stewart)

After Harry died work was slow to pick up because of the long break I had to take while he was sick. I was in heavy grief. I almost stopped eating and weight just fell off me. I lost enough to take up tennis again, and not having electrical work allowed me to play two or three times a week. I couldn't bear to hang around the house: just too many memories.

On those days when I did have some work, when I had returned home, I would hop on my bicycle and take the long 23-mile loop around South Paris, West Paris, and Norway. I was doing the very same thing I'd done when Mom died. Back then, I had strapped on cross-country skis and expelled some of the pain in that manner, so at least I was being consistent.

Without Harry as a buffer, and before I took on another man in my life, I discovered a curious convergence of my work life and my animal husbandry. I call these stories, "Pat the Bat" and "The Hooked Loon."

I was working way out in the country in a house that had been bought by two teachers, Victor Coal and his wife Cynthia. They were from the suburban area of Connecticut but they loved everything about Maine. Because of their young children, they were very safety conscious. Cynthia had a unique way of talking to her children which included phrases like, "That's 'A Sharp', be careful." This was in reference to a screwdriver her six-year old was getting for her father. Victor was up in the peak of the house attaching an outdoor light. He said, "Do bats make a rattling noise?" he asked. "Every time I hammer, something rattles."

Then, their 12-year old boy screeched, "There's a bat on my wall!" Victor was having none of it and came down the ladder in a hurry.

Cynthia entered the room where I was working and asked, "Do you know anything about bats? I was thinking of throwing this over it." I turned to see what "this" was, and saw her with a sheet covering her arms and hands.

Suppressing a smile I said, "Get me a blanket. I'm pretty sure a bat can bite through a sheet." I couldn't resist adding, "They can be rabid, you know."

"Wait a minute," Cynthia said. "I'm going to get something on my head." She came back with a safari hat on. She was afraid the bat would get in her hair but she was there to help me save it anyway. I could have hugged her.

I carefully put my hand over the bat and he *was* rattling. It must have been his warning noise, much lower in pitch than his hunting sounds. I took him to the window and let him fly away. Bats can fly in the day just fine. Their preference for dusk is because that is prime hunting time for moths etc.

The Coal children began chanting. "Pat saved the bat." Then they decided they were going to name it, Pat the bat. I got a real kick out of going down in history as Pat the bat.

The Hooked Loon occasion happened when I was working for a summer camp. I was outside when I noticed a loon slowly swimming close to shore and acting strangely. He kept dipping his head to the side as if he were falling asleep. As he approached some rowboats that were tied to the trees on the shore, I decided to catch him and see what was wrong with him. I kicked my sneakers off and quietly slid into the water, using the boats to conceal my approach. Knowing how ungainly loons are on land, I wanted to get between him and the open water so I could chase him up on land. The scene played out just like I anticipated—until I grabbed him and was surprised at how BIG loons are. Having seen them only in the distance, I thought they were the size of crows. Wrong! He was as big as a goose. He muckled onto my arm with his beak. Hard. My arm felt as if it were in a vise.

This was when I saw the fishing line wrapped around the bird's neck and going into his mouth. He had grabbed a minnow someone had been using for bait and was well hooked. The line was so tight it was cutting off his circulation and he was probably drifting in and out of consciousness. I put him in the cellar of the place where I was working and asked someone in their office call the fish and game people. Because I didn't want to continue working in wet clothes, I then went home. When I returned the next day, the loon was gone. I hoped they were able to get that hook out. Having things like this happen when you work makes for variety, and you simply don't ever get bored.

Work is actually fun.

But, I needed more than work in my life. I was fifty-four years old when Harry died. We had a good marriage, so I now had a pretty good opinion of the institution. I thought it might be possible to find someone else to partner with, both in the work arena and in my personal life. However, I had no idea of how to accomplish that.

Most single people seem to go to bars to meet other singles, but that was not my cup of tea. What to do? My solution was to go down to the nearest dance hall. A*nother one of my brilliant moves?*

Although the place didn't serve drinks, it was BYOB, so some people were drinking. My first time there, I met someone too old. His idea of exercise was walking and I knew he wouldn't be able to keep up with me. The second time, I met someone who was too young, plus he smoked. The third time I met someone who was just trolling for flesh.

This wasn't working out very well.

The fourth time there I met Stew (not his real name). I was talking with someone about my geese. When he wandered off, Stew, who was standing next to him, spoke up. He said he used to have geese, so the ice was broken, and the conversation took off from there. He told me he was a Frenchman from Lewiston and he had just a hint of accent in his voice. His shoulder-length curly hair and moustache, fit perfectly with the leather hat he wore. The brim was smaller than a cowboy hat, more like a backwoodsman's hat.

His height was not impressive, but he was big and burly. More importantly, he didn't ricochet when I bumped into him. Naturally, I thought he was good looking. This was his first time at a dance hall since his wife kicked him out six months earlier.

Stew asked me if I was Indian. I was wearing my hair loose and it was halfway down my back; I also wore a skirt and sandals, which probably added to the picture. The next thing he said struck me with its perception. He said, "You look like a hurtin' unit." I was surprised because I was having a good time and that was what should have been showing. Actually, Harry had died only four months before, so I guess my grief was still apparent on my face.

Because it didn't look like he was ever going to get around to it, I asked him to dance. He was a little taller than I, and we fit comfortably against each other. It seemed as if we had known each other for years. I could see that he didn't smoke and he *said* he didn't drink, so we hit it off famously. Having someone wrap their arms around you when you are in pain is very comforting.

After that night Stew came to my town three times before he caught up with me again. I was either out on the bike or playing tennis. His persistence was gratifying.

During his first week of visiting, I asked him if he wanted to go on a bike ride. "Sure," he said and hopped on Emma's 18-speed mountain bike. I lived on a hill and as a former bike racer, I pedal, not coast downhill. Stew was behind me as I flew down the hill, so I didn't see it when he almost lost it, but he caught up with me quickly. After the 23-mile loop, he sprinted back up the hill. I was suitably impressed. He admitted to me later that he could barely walk the next day, and I found that frankness appealing.

He also told me he *used* to drink which is why his wife threw him out. But since her boyfriend moved in the very next night, he figured she just wanted to be with the new guy. He hadn't had a drink for six months and he really liked having a clear head. Not having learned my lesson with Harry, I took everything he said at face value.

Because I was still grieving, I continued talking about Harry, and Stew talked about his wife. I began to see that he and I had the potential to be good partners, but I didn't want to be number-two woman. I told him this, and added that until he figured out whether I would be number-one, we were all done.

That weekend I went to the dance hall again. I met one of Stew's friends there. "Where's Stew," he asked, to which I responded, "We're all done."

Apparently the friend reported back to Stew because a few days later he called up and said, "What's this about our being all done? I spent the night with my wife to see if there was anything there and even though she wore her 'teddy' I felt so uncomfortable, I slept with the children. I want to be with you not her." This conversation convinced me that I *was* number one woman, so we picked up where we'd left off.

I had told Stew we couldn't be intimate until we were married (the new ethics), so the pressure was on. The Pastor at the church I was going to refused to marry us. Since I was a widow it was all right for me to marry, but because Stew still had a living wife, (even though she had divorced him by then) we couldn't get married.

I decided to leave that church. I found another that seemed to be more liberal, and started bringing the family there. I waited for a decent interval (one month) and then asked the pastor for pastoral counseling in preparation for marriage.

Basically, I wanted Stew to become born again into a new relationship to God, because he was a lapsed catholic and had little interest in going to church.

The pastor agreed, and we got through two sessions. We had three more to go when the pastor said, "I'm sorry but I can't marry you, either. I've prayed about it, and I just don't have peace in my heart about it."

You've got to be kidding!

I answered, "Why on earth not?"

"First, you haven't grieved long enough, and second, Stew is an alcoholic and you can't trust an alcoholic. I know because I used to be one."

*First, that should be **my** judgment whether I've grieved long enough, not yours. And second, you shouldn't be prejudiced against alcoholics especially since you were one once.*

Did I say all that to him?

Nope.

It wouldn't have changed his mind.

Hindsight tells me his counsel was better than mine.

We decided to marry ourselves on top of Hawk Mountain, a secret place no tourists knew about. Emma had described it to me because she went up there when her boyfriend used the cliff to practice his rock climbing. Following her directions, we teetered up a river bed in my Nissan 4-wheel drive pick-up. Once we got to the top we parked the truck and followed a path out to the face of the cliff.

The mountain lived up to its name. Although birds soaring in the rising thermals might have been turkey vultures rather than hawks, the view was breath-taking. The hills were sharply delineated and we could see so far that distant mountains melted into the clouds. It was hard to distinguish where mountains left off and sky began. All we could see was trees, no towns or cities. We both just sat there speechless for a long time. This was the perfect place for our vows; stunningly beautiful with the added bonus of rare solitude. We solemnly exchanged our vows with only Stew's son there as our necessary witness. It was a precious gem of a wedding.

Our honeymoon was a salmon-fishing trip to Lake Erie. It was close to where Harry and I had gone many years ago. This was a much more successful trip. We chartered a boat to go on the lake, and the captain knew right where to take us. Each of us caught a huge salmon. Fighting to reel it in was so exciting that we lost track of time; it seemed like only five minutes when in actuality it was more like a half hour. Since mine was bigger, we left it to be stuffed and shipped to us. The other one we brought back to eat. It was awful, dry and tasteless, and the cat got most of it.

Stew was a truck driver working for someone else when I met him. Soon after his divorce he came to me with a question, "If I come to work for you, could you pay me enough to keep up with my child support?"

"Sure, I can manage that."

"Great, I always wanted to do something intelligent."

Stew quit his job, and I had a helper again. Although it took almost a year for him to get the hang of electrical, but once he turned the corner and understood the concept, he was a really big help. We made great progress, both on the job and out in the gardens. We were a good team. I had been carrying the whole load for such a long time and was truly ready for some relief.

I was living in the little red house in South Paris, Maine when Stew first met me. But when his two children came to live with us, we really didn't have enough room, and the move to the trailer became necessary. Unfortunately, the lack of water there had to be addressed. My godfather Bart came to the rescue, post mortem. When he died I received $3,000 from his estate, so I was finally able to put in a well. I was extremely grateful for that, but also a tad troubled.

Bart had left the bulk of his estate to the Society for the Prevention of Cruelty to Children. Why had he done that? What had his childhood been like? Had he suffered some terrible abuse? It made me wish I could have explored this with him, maybe help heal the hurt of his possible abuse. I know I had gotten way past the damage I had received many years ago by understanding and forgiving, and was now in a much better place for having done that. I would have liked to have shared this with Bart.

Stew was definitely in a better place. He was going to learn a new trade, and was optimistic and elated. He began his electrical apprenticeship with the wiring of the new addition to the trailer, more accurately described as Chantrel. Actually, Emma was more help because she was already an electrician, having learned it as a youngster.

Emma had discovered that living alone up in the little red house wasn't so great and I wasn't that keen on it either. Stew helped me to fix up the little house so it could be rented, and Emma moved over to be with us in the trailer. Soon, her boyfriend Nate joined us. Now, six of us were on top of each other and completely in each others hair! The push was really on to get Chantrel completed.

Emma and I did the insulating because the men couldn't tolerate the itching it caused. The next task was installing the beautiful knotty pine on the walls and ceilings. I did the cutting on the chop-saw and Stew did the application. The most dramatic knotty whorls we placed in the middle of the walls where they could be displayed to advantage. Because I paid cash for everything, it took a few years to get that completed. I was fiscally very conservative, remembering all too well the hard times of the last recession.

I held off moving into Chantrel because I knew how much harder it would be to finish with all of us in it. We laid the hardwood floor, got someone to do the chimney, and even though the walls weren't done, we couldn't wait any longer. Emma and Nate moved upstairs where they had their own little apartment. Stew and I had the bedroom right under theirs and we soon learned what a poor design that was!

About this time Emma and Stew began to butt heads. It came to a boil and they were toe-to-toe "Fu—you"-ing each other. When Stew said she had to go, I was devastated and cried for a week (where nobody could see me, of course). I'd expected that she would live upstairs indefinitely, but gradually saw that Stew was right: she needed to get her own place. God provided the perfect place which was next door in the Apple house I'd bought a few years before. The tenants there were divorcing so the house had become available. It was the best solution because Emma didn't go far, yet she was mistress of her own house.

Emma also decided that she didn't want to take the time to get her electrical license, which would have taken almost two years of school, plus work. Instead, she got a job driving dump truck with the class A license she had gotten in high school.

When summer construction and dump trucking stopped for the season she went to work for another company driving tractor trailers cross-country. Emma's next step was to get her own tractor, rent a trailer, and drive for herself. She had seen a junked Freightliner and poured herself into it getting it back on the road. She started talking this whole new language of engines and trucks. A flatbed trailer was a skate board, a car-hauling trailer was a parking lot, a sanding truck was called a saltshaker, a tanker was called a thermos, and a refrigerated truck was called a reefer.

Emma expanded her horizon from Maine to New England, then to all of the east coast. Getting past the Mississippi was the next hurdle. Finally, desert driving was the last uncomfortable part. Not knowing whether to drive across during the day if her air conditioner was acting up or where the truck stops were going to be took some getting used to, but she kept on pushing.

What we didn't realize was Stew's nose was getting wicked out of joint about Emma's getting her own truck and working for herself before she was 30, while he was 50 plus and still working for others. This was going to come back and haunt Emma and me later.

In the meantime, Stew and I shared many activities. I taught him to play tennis and we enjoyed that. He also learned to play chess and we were fairly evenly matched. I developed the ability to lose and still enjoy playing. Unfortunately, Stew would not only stop playing if he lost, he would sweep the pieces off the board to the floor. I would think (but not say) "How juvenile!"

We had conflict in several areas, some trivial and others not. The most minor was about the toothpick Stew kept in his mouth. It was very distracting while I was talking to him, to see that toothpick moving around as he adjusted its position. He couldn't seem to get the picture that it was an ugly habit and it drove me nuts.

More serious was his chewing tobacco. He was always spitting and that was not only difficult to observe, but damaging his health. In addition, his behavior was copied by his children. They both spat after they said something, as a technique of emphasis. I tried to explain to him the effect of his little daughter spitting and how negatively it affected the image others had of her. I was more successful with this effort.

The most serious area of conflict was about his children. I tried to do small things like remind Rachel (not her real name) to wash her ears because she was getting big blackheads in them. She resented my suggestion and went to her father. I was baldly told to leave them alone.

I was the bad step-mom and that never changed for the whole thirteen years Stew and I were together.

Stew was not one for "Manuel Labor," as he called it. I could get his help in the landscaping only if it involved operating a machine. We used the tractor to build the rock-wall terrace with the huge chunks left from the blasting of the ledge. The tractor was a good-sized 950 John Deere with a bucket in front and a backhoe on the back, but it really wasn't an excavator. Nonetheless, we moved some monster rocks. I would rig chains around the rock, which was challenging to do on an essentially round object. If Stew and the tractor could lift it a bit off the ground, it could be positioned just right.

The first year, we built the lowest of the three tiers. We began with the biggest chunks, and then filled in with progressively smaller rocks, being very careful to link together two rocks below with a rock spanning the gap between and above them. Staggering the rocks this way made the seams less vulnerable and the wall stronger. Another important point was to lean the wall into the bank instead of having it perfectly perpendicular. The wall then had more ability to hold back the weight of the earth behind it.

On the top layer we put the most stunning rocks, crystal quartz or glittering mica or mossy-layered rocks. We didn't use strings or a plumb line to get perfection. What I wanted was more casual and organic. It was as much a work of art as any of a more conventional sort. Stew wouldn't stick around for the final placing of the top layer. He had no patience with my trying one rock after another, flipping it one way, then turning it back. The whole wall was 30 feet long, so the project took us three years—one year for each tier.

We also planted over 50 fruit trees. Stew was against the idea. He said, "We are too old to be planting trees. We'll never see the harvest." The first tree we planted is now 35 feet high. It is a flowering crab tree that has apples that are almost edible, if you like a very tart flavor. The inside has white flesh shot with red. The best use of these apples is for astringency in an apple wine mix.

Some of the other apples trees are Sweet Sixteen which I got for Emma because it is a low acid apple. Regular apples make her stomach ache. I have a Black Oxford which was developed here in Oxford County. My particular interest is the heirloom apples like Baldwin, Russets, Cox's Orange Pippen, Winesap, and Winter Banana. Some of the other varieties are especially for cider or more common hard and crisp types. I got a Macaon just because someone described it as being so juicy when you bit into it, the juice ran right down your elbow. Unhappily, because I won't spray pesticides, the apple production is flawed. I don't get the perfect fruit you see in the supermarket, but it still tastes good.

The peach production is much closer to store standard, but peach trees do best in a zone five (warmer weather) while we are a zone four right here. Since our winters are colder, I have lost half of my peach trees and don't know whether I will replant new ones. I've had about six years of good production from them and really hate to see them fail.

The pear trees didn't produce anything until I read that there are two classes of pear trees. They can successfully pollinate each other only if a class A is beside a class B. Since I didn't remember which pear trees were which by this time, I just planted one of each next to each group I already had. Now the pear production is coming along nicely.

Absolutely the worst effort was the Bing Cherries. I have hopefully planted year after year, with no harvest yet. The problem is probably the same as the peaches, just not suitable for the climate.

The most successful of the fruit trees were the plums: green, yellow, red, and black. For the first five years I got blossoms, but no fruit. Finally, I read that for pollination, the branches of one tree should intertwine with another. So, I planted a new plum tree between each of the original. Then I had to wait five years for them to get old enough to bear. Now I get so many plums I invite my friends to come help by taking some home.

Stew's involvement with the fruit trees was digging the holes with the backhoe; then I'd place the tree. The only problem then, was the hours getting the lawn cleaned up where the backhoe had ripped it to pieces. He did very much enjoy the fruit once they started bearing. Every fall evening after work he would take a 'walk about', eating fruit as he went.

I also used Stew's backhoe expertise to help me build a grape arbor, the last big project he was willing to help with. What I had in mind was to build an outdoor room, which had a dual purpose as a large grape arbor. I got the idea from Nana, my maternal grandmother. I never forgot the time she had us over for a Sunday dinner when I was quite little. To my surprise, the fancy china and sterling silver didn't come out. *We* went out—to her grape arbor. She had set up a beautiful table with a white cloth, but we had picnic stuff on the table, plastic plates and utensils. Bompa had built the arbor kind of small so she could reach the grapes, and we had to hunch to get in, but it was great fun; a grown-up version of an outdoor tea party.

What I wanted at Chantrel was something similar but much bigger. My plan was to set six separate fifteen-foot cedar poles in the ground three feet deep. The footprint of the arbor was 10'x15'. I had traded some electrical work for the poles and they were on the site. All Stew had to do was dig the holes with the backhoe; I'd tip the poles into the holes, and then hand-shovel the dirt back in around them. Because of all the waiting between holes, Stew got bored and thought he would have a little fun. While I was resting, propping up a pole next to a hole, he tapped the pole with the bucket. I stepped back as the pole went over, but, tripped over the dirt piled behind me. I fell backwards really scared as I pictured my leg bones snapping under this great log. Once I hit the ground, I was able to yank my legs out just in time. There I was, on my back with my feet in the air, just like a beetle. My first reaction was relief that I didn't get hurt. My second one was to get mad at Stew for his dangerous horsing around. He was laughing so hard he almost fell off the tractor, and his hilarity was so contagious, I started laughing too. Good thing I had on loose shorts, because I almost wet my pants. I ripped them down, my bare butt waving in the air as I relieved myself. It must have been quite a sight. Backwoods country living certainly has its moments.

I'd never heard of a hyperbaric chamber until I learned about it from someone I was doing electrical work for. He was getting treatments in one for his multiple sclerosis. He said the chamber accelerated healing because it gave him more oxygen than is found in ordinary air. That started me thinking.

I had learned in high school biology class about transpiration of plants, the action of a plant as it breathes in carbon dioxide and releases oxygen. I thought a grape arbor built as an outdoor room would be the ideal place to experience this kind of transpiration, like a natural hyperbaric chamber A place where the grape leaves would give you super-oxygenated air. The shade from the vines overhead and the heady oxygen from the leaves would make it a wonderful place to rest in the summer. Plus, after the first frost the grapes have sweetened up, and that harvest is available, right at your fingertips. My grape arbor fulfilled all these hopes.

I also experienced the chemistry that is involved in gardening. Apparently our bodies have a positive charge (seeking to find free electrons to bring us into balance). The earth has a negative charge (seeking to give away free electrons). When we walk barefoot, like down to the beach, or put our hands into the earth (without gloves) for weeding or planting, we get the free electrons we need to put us in balance. This is one big reason why it is *so* refreshing to be near water or to work barehanded in a garden.

Stew would help in the garden first thing in the spring when it involved using the roto-tiller, but forget any planting or weeding. Occasionally he would weed-whack with the trimmer. And sometimes he would mow with the riding lawnmower. I was grateful for what he did do. But over the years he did less and less.

Exactly the opposite happened when we did electrical work. He wanted more and more money. In the beginning all he wanted was for me to pay his child support. Soon it was $20 for pocket money. Then it was $50 a day. The next step was $100 a day. He finally was getting $200 when I was doing a big service. I tried not to begrudge him that because he *was* a big help, and I loved him.

The last unusual job Stew helped me with was the Ice Storm of '98. We were without power for 11 days. Some people were out for more than 20 days. As an electrician, I was well-equipped with backup power, but many others were unprepared. Because I had lights, heat, water from my own well, and hot water from propane, several neighbors got water from my house.

Stew and I went crazy, getting alternate power for those who managed to find a generator. There was a real run on them. People were driving down south, bringing them north, and selling them off the backs of their trucks. Unfortunately, there was a lot of price-gouging going on instead of everyone pulling together.

I had a long list of people to take care of, and as I got them set up, more would come in. I had friends that would call, and because they were friends, I would put them at the head of the list. I got really stressed out about changing the order of appointments from what it really should have been. Giving preference to friends seemed right because that's what friends do. But being unfair to strangers wasn't right either. Classic dilemma.

The ice storm itself was a surrealistic experience. We drove down roads where we had to weave back and forth from one side of the road to another just to get around the hanging branches of ice-laden trees, barely able to sneak under some. It was incredibly beautiful, while at the same time being so hazardous. The sun had come out from after the storm and the dazzling crystals were almost blinding. Also, the slight breeze made them natural wind chimes. It was gorgeous. We would creep down the road probably only doing five miles an hour with our windows rolled down, heads hanging out the window exclaiming, "Wow, unbelievable!" Not very original but we were almost struck dumb by the beauty. Perfect Kodak moment, but no camera, of course.

Because we were working long hours, sometimes as much as eighteen straight, we started to get punchy; you know, staggering around, acting stupid. I even drove off from the job and left my cordless drill on the back of the truck. (At least, I think that's what happened to it.)

We'd "Rube Goldberg" (jury-rig) the hookup to the generator, just to get people going, then return later and do it right, according to code.

One ice-storm job, especially, sticks in my mind. I had never done work for this man, but he got to me with the plight of his family freezing because they had no backup wood heat. He was a doctor from Pakistan, lived in the classiest area of town. and he wanted to put the generator in the cellar instead of out on his porch. I explained it was much safer out in the open air, but he would have none of that. He said he'd put towels along the doorjamb of the cellar door and that would be protection enough. Basically, he didn't want to go outside in the cold to refill the gas tank. He was so sure that it would be all right there, and HE was not going to take the advice of a lowly woman electrician.

I had mixed feelings when I heard he had checked his whole family into the emergency room for carbon monoxide poisoning that night. They were fine the next day. In spite of that, he still asked me come back and put his generator on the porch. He had his wife pay me, though. He probably didn't want to chance me telling him, "I told you so."

One of the dividends from the ice storm was all the wood on the side of the road free for the taking. Stew got really pumped about all this free wood and we worked hard loading, cutting, and splitting. I think we got about three winters' worth of wood from that ice storm.

The best thing about the ice storm was the hot water baseboard heat we were able to get with all the money we made. We were living in Chantrel, and for two years our only source of heat was wood, and we were going through a lot of it. The total for the new heating system cost almost $6,000 and the ice storm paid for it completely!

Not half bad.

Now that I'm on the subject of money, working for yourself, you have the option of adjusting your prices according to whatever seems right. Rather than tell little old ladies on a fixed income that I'll do their work for nothing, I'll charge them $20 instead of my usual $50. They don't know the difference—and can keep their dignity.

Another turning point in my life happened when a friend of mine from Hebron, invited me to attend a series of evangelistic meetings at the Seventh-Day Adventist Church in Oxford, Dwight Nelson's Net '98.

The convincing session was titled the Broken Goblet, and it concerned the Fourth commandment, which is the keeping of the Sabbath on Saturday as designated by God, versus changing worship to Sunday as the Catholics and most Protestants do today.

Breaking the Fourth commandment is no big deal, as long as you worship some day. Who cares which day is The Day.

Guess what, God cares.

If I chose one of seven brothers to marry, would I be happy if a different one of them jumped into the get-away car with me instead of the one I had just married?

Dwight gave the example of how breaking just that one commandment is the same as breaking them all.

He said, "This crystal goblet is going to represent the Ten Commandments." Then he took a hammer and said, "I'm going to break just a little piece of this goblet, representing the breaking of the Fourth."

He tapped the lip of the goblet and the whole thing shattered.

"You break one, you break them all," he said.

This visual image convinced me, and I started going to the Seventh-Day Adventist Church, which I still attend.

You are wondering how this applies to Stew? Well, I managed to drag him to church occasionally, and he began to grow spiritually, as did I. This growth developed into the conviction that I wasn't really married to Stew. I was filing taxes as if we were not married because the benefits were better. Saying we were married on the one hand, and not married on another, was not exactly truthful. Truth needs to be a reliable constant, even if it has unpleasant consequences. The awesome result of this constant is the security of standing on solid ground rather than shifting sand. By the way, this certainty is very freeing. Although Stew didn't understand the importance of getting legally married in a church right away, he gradually came around to my way of thinking.

My caution led me to set up a prenuptial agreement. It stated that everything I owned prior to the marriage would remain mine and would pass to my children when I died. Everything acquired during our marriage would become jointly owned. Stew signed it, but now I see this as the turning point in *his* life. He somehow expected that all my property would become his in spite of the prenuptial. But I still did not trust him enough to turn all my property over to him, and that was just the way it was. Time confirmed the correctness of my intuition.

In 2000, Stew and I were married in the church with Emma-Rose the only family member present. None of Stew's family came to the wedding, which hurt him deeply. They had the idea that Seventh-Day Adventists were a cult. Unfortunately, it polarized the two of us completely. The church and I were on one side, while he and his family were on the other. Actually, Stew was caught in the middle. In the beginning he was with me, but eventually he chose his family instead.

The inner voice that kept after me about the dishonesty of my do-it-yourself marriage to Stew then turned to another area of dishonesty in my life. I was having a problem with screws. When I was working, I would sometimes help myself to the screws that had actually been bought by the carpenter. I wouldn't take very many, only a handful or two. I had not bought those screws, so I shouldn't be using them. In actuality, I was stealing from the carpenter. I realized I was going to lose my salvation over a handful of screws I could very well provide for myself. This would be the ultimate in stupidity (you could say I was *really* screwing myself). I changed my behavior. And felt better.

In 2003 Stew brought me proposition. (You'd think I was old enough by now to be wary of men with propositions). Since he was having difficulty breathing with the sheetrock dust and insulation, he said why not start up a trucking business? This would not only be something he could do, but also we would have two incomes and be on Easy Street. He said the truck would gross $100,000 a year, and he would be able to pay the loan off quickly. It turned out, however, with the high cost of fuel, the trucking business only netted about $30,000, but it would have paid off the loan eventually.

Well, I had relaxed my vigilance by now and begun to trust Stew. So, I threw my natural caution to the winds (mistake). We went to the bank and increased my home equity loan from $12,000 to $150,000. Stew bought a 2002 Volvo tri-axle dump truck for $90,000.

Then we went on an ENORMOUS spending spree (next mistake): a camper, two motorcycles, two snowmobiles, three four-wheelers, another work truck for me, Lasik eye surgery for Stew, an SUV for me, a new Chevy Silverado pickup with plow for Stew, a car for his daughter, and helped Emma get an SUV. Emma also found an old junk Freightliner cab for an 18 wheeler truck and fixed it up to put on the road for cross-country hauling. All of this stuff came from the enlarged home equity loan, which both Stew and I signed. Together we were responsible for the payback of that loan. Not once did I have a quiver of concern.

Un-be-live-able!

Of all these toys, the four-wheelers were the most fun. We could connect with snowmobile trails right from our backyard. We would go roaring through the woods exploring, climbing river beds, and getting stuck in mud. We had motorized winches to get ourselves out, but that was part of the fun.

After a few years, once we had mastered all the woods trails and they had gotten boring, the motorcycles became the most fun. We toured around Mount Washington, stopping for an overnight at a bed and breakfast, and took several fall foliage trips on the Kangamangus Highway. But our major use of the motorcycles was searching out vintage cider apples in local orchards because we were pressing our own apples for cider. Actually, because we added sugar to the apples it was really apple wine.

Making this wine turned out to be disastrous. I didn't realize that Stew was a barely-in-control alcoholic. All that easily available wine proved to be too much for him, and he began drinking heavily, even going to his family with a gallon of wine while I was at church. When he came home he'd vomit in the yard before coming into the house, reeling and reeking. I was appalled, drew away from him, and our marriage began to really fall apart.

Stew's character seemed to shrink, too. Emma and I learned that he had been bad-mouthing her to other truckers, saying she was too young for the responsibility of her own truck, and would fall flat on her face. Not only that, when she returned to summer construction dump trucking, he organized a threatened walkout if Emma kept getting work when he and his group did not. When I knew him earlier, he seemed much more generous than what he had become; a bitter and spiteful man.

It was about this time that I noticed the reappearance of the toothpick chewing. This was a mystery to me then, but began to make sense later. Another noticeable change was Stew completely stopped helping around the house. I really missed his cheerful dishwashing but I didn't want to nag him so I just let it be. I was mystified by his attitude, but the next event finally communicated to me his change of heart.

Emma's old jungle gym was a thorn in Stew's side when he mowed the lawn. He wanted it gone; I wanted it to stay. I was expecting my grandchildren would enjoy it just as much as Emma had, and therefore I prevailed (or so I thought). When a huge popple tree had blown down in the yard, I asked Stew to cut it up. The next thing I knew, another perfectly fine big popple was down, right across the bone of contention. I went out and asked him, "Why did you do that?"

"It was dying and would be down in the next big storm, anyway," he answered.

"Awful lot of green leaves here for a dying tree," I said. "And how come it's on top of the jungle gym? You can drop a tree better than that."

"The wind took it."

"What wind?" I asked. "There hasn't been a breath of wind today."

"No, really!" Stew protested. "The wind came up just for a bit."

What could I say after that protestation of innocence?

Later I went out and looked at the cut in the stump. It was totally lined up with the jungle gym. Stew had put the tree right where he wanted to. At that moment, I realized we were no longer on the same page. I no longer had a friend. I had an antagonist, *and* I was married to him. I was deeply saddened, and began to review in my mind whether I wanted to stay married to him. Due to Stew's health (so he said.), there had been no conjugal relations for quite some time And, since I still had a strong libido, adjusting to this lack took some very firm work on my part. My final decision was based on "A promise is a promise, for better or for worse." So, I recommitted to our marriage—such as it was.

Stew's health took a nosedive when he developed colon cancer. At this point I realized he needed me close; to be a support for him during his medical crisis. Emma also pitched in to help, quitting her job so she could keep his truck going during the summer when construction was at its peak.

The VA hospital in Togus, Maine, gave Stew radiation and chemotherapy. Then we went to Boston for the colostomy.

I spent nights with my older sister Barbara in her very posh suburb half an hour from Boston. That way I could be with Stew during the day as he was recuperating. The treatments were completely successful, and Stew was declared cancer free.

Not long after this, Stew blindsided me when he announced, "I'm tired of working for you and your daughter. I want to work for myself and my children. I've worked all these years and I have nothing to give them."

I realized he had a legitimate point, because we were a family, so I said, "I know they should get something, but I just can't figure out how to do it."

Stew rolled his eyes and answered, "I've been after you and after you, to make out a will, but you never seem to get around to it."

"I would if I could be sure that they wouldn't just burn the houses down for the insurance money," I said. This was a very real fear because Stew had already suggested it twice: once for the red house and once for the Bridgton rental property we had acquired. "You know Emma and I have a strong sentimental attachment to our property. It was the first house I owned and where she grew up. There are a lot of good memories associated with it."

Stew's voice got louder. "It's not fair that she gets everything, and you know it."

Suddenly, I was struck with the solution, and said, "All they really want is the money so why don't we just take out a big insurance policy so they can have that?"

That's not good enough," Stew answered. "I want them to get half the property."

Wearily I replied, "That's just not going to happen."

I was exhausted by all the stress of things that had been happening. I just didn't have anymore struggle left in me.

Now he was *really* shouting. "Since there's nothing here for me, I'm leaving!"

My answer was really original. I said, "Go ahead and go."

A great sword came down and severed my tie to Stew. It was strange. I felt nothing—except cold and dead. Silence reigned for a few moments.

I pictured him getting into bed with me later. That was simply not possible. I said, "You can forget about sleeping in my bed tonight. You can sleep upstairs."

"No, I'm not."

"Yes, you are" Voices escalated.

"No, I'm not!"

"Yes, you are!"

Stew's eyes started to throw sparks. "No, I'm not."

I couldn't believe our relationship had disintegrated to this. I pulled out my trump card, "Whose house is this?"

That was the end of the conversation—and the marriage!

The next morning, I couldn't get him out the door fast enough. The only problem was he refused to repay the loan and I was stuck with $150,000 debt. All my careful planning was for naught. This was the back-stabbing by a Frenchman that Harry had warned me against a long time ago.

I felt really bad that Emma was going to inherit the debt my poor choices had incurred. However the financial disaster had one positive outcome. My whole life had been driven by the goal of self-sufficiency and independence. Now I realized there was no way I could manage this burden by myself. I was just not sufficient to the task.

Do you know what God did? He provided me with children that help as they can.

My oldest daughter Lee employed me to do $10,000 worth of work on her house. My son Nick helps me with a monthly check of $250. And my youngest daughter Emma Rose moved in with me to shovel roofs, plow, get wood etc. She and her boyfriend Chris Seeley have made it possible for me to continue to live here in my beloved Chantrel.

I do what I can, but I also rest in God's provision. He had been leading me to that realization for a long time. I had been screaming at the top of my voice, "I can do it myself!" just like the toddler I was. Now I knew differently.

Let me give you another example of God's provision.

One winter I had a tenant that owed me for two months rent. The problem was I couldn't be at home at that time. Emma had told me earlier that she was going to be home working on her motorcycle, so I told my tenant to leave the money with my daughter. Unfortunately, I didn't tell Emma about the money being dropped off, and she left to go downtown.

That left nobody home when my tenant arrived. Her solution was to leave the money in the mailbox, in a white envelope. Plus she didn't close the lid tightly.

When I came home six hours later (after dark), the money was nowhere to be found. I immediately called my tenant to see if she had left it. She said she had, and rather than leave money she had gotten a money order.

Well, a check would have been fine, because it could have been canceled. But a money order was the same as cash. There was no way it could be refunded. Plus the wind was blowing and there was snow on the ground.

This was not looking good.

Next I called Emma to tell her what happened. She felt terrible, that somehow she had been at fault. She went right out with a flashlight.

I didn't have a quiver of doubt. I knew God wouldn't let me down. Or, if the money order couldn't be found, He would provide in some other way, maybe by sending me more work.

What I did was immediately start praying. I asked God to show Emma that He will answer prayer. Three seconds after I finished praying, she called me from her cell. Her jubilant voice sang out, "I found it!"

"Thank you, sweetheart."

"You know, I've been praying ever since you left the door?"

"I know, Mom."

Thank you, Jesus.

Besides standing on the solid ground of truth, I could now count on the security of God's provision for me. No more nightmares or sleepless nights.

God provided in another profound, but totally different way.

I had been studying a book about the Holy Spirit by Dennis Smith. I knew it was my Christian duty to forgive those who have hurt us, but I strongly resisted. I was very comfortable hating Stew for what he had done to me. I hung on with tenacity, to my bitterness, hostility, and anger. I *didn't* want to pray for a forgiving spirit.

Finally, a few weeks later, after reading about the Holy Spirit's power, I yielded. But, it was a grudging prayer.

Oh, all right God.

Please give me YOUR spirit of forgiveness, because I'm certainly not accomplishing it on my own.

I didn't feel any different after the prayer, but I knew God heard me. This was very different from the uncertainty I felt a long time ago when I prayed about my son's cancer. My faith was a lot stronger now. Positive answers to prayer over the years had confirmed that connection.

Then, I got a check in the mail for Stew from the State of Maine. I'm afraid to say the 'old me' opened up someone else's envelope. Inside was a check for $27. My first impulse was to throw it in the trash, but my better judgement stopped me.

Do unto others what you would have them do unto you
OK God. I'll try to get it to him.

But how was I going to reach him when I did't know his address? Plus, he wouldn't take my calls.

Incredibly, Emma and Stew were both driving dump trucks on the same construction site. I asked Emma if she could get his address so I could mail the check to him.

The next thing I knew, Stew was on the phone talking to me. This was the first I had heard his voice in two years. I felt a warmth envelope me and it was directed toward Stew. I spoke with him about where to mail the check, his health, and his upcoming operation.

I was completely amazed. The 'old me' would have been icy, stern, and clipped. I experienced God in me and it was flooding my heart with joy.

Why do I refer to my time with Stewart as rampant growth? Does unbridled and incautious growth make more sense? I should never have brought him into my life. After Harry died, it would have been much better in the long run to have cut out the desire for a man to share my life with, because I had to do it after Stew left, anyway. Should have been done sooner rather than later.

Life's lessons can be very painful, *and* very expensive.

12 PART I
STEWARDSHIP AT THE LITTLE RED HOUSE—Small Animals

The dictionary defines 'stewardship' as the responsibility and management of something that doesn't belong to you. We are not owners of Earth, just managers. This idea is very close to the Native American relationship to the land. No wonder our Indian tribes were so easily persuaded to sell their (supposed) property. They didn't consider they owned it!

Stewardship is a value that threaded itself through almost every phase of my life. My first experience with stewardship was at Waterlily when I was quite young. It began with the doomed effort to keep baby minks alive in a cage. My next effort was the transplanting of bullfrogs from the swamp to my own habitat, a fast-running brook, also unsuccessful. Then there was the horrible experience of the snapping turtle. He would have been much better off left in the swamp where he was meant to be.

The first successful animal responsibility was the stray black cat, Cinder, and her son, Rumpelstilskin. Of course our dogs always did well, (unless someone tried to get them to climb ladders.)

The plant world can also be included in the scope of this concept of stewardship. At Waterlily, I learned to keep the lawn trimmed and the aggressive green and white bishops' weed contained enough to keep it from choking out the tall old-fashioned pink phlox. The vegetable garden was a poor effort because of the choice to put it in the shade of some tall trees. But that too, was a learning experience.

In Marblehead, Massachusetts, the aquatic world drew me, and my effort to duplicate a microcosm of this world through the marine aquarium in my room was somewhat successful.

I also learned stewardship by caring for my younger sisters. The common denominators here are love, nurturing, and responsibility.

Babysitting was another way I learned stewardship. My first heavy duty job was when a couple took a three-day weekend trip, and left me with three children. The two older children, eight and ten, were easy. The problem was the baby. I was initially quite pleased that he didn't have number two in his diapers. By the second day when he still had no BM's I started to get worried. The morning of the third day, I found one small marble of poop in his diaper. Boy, was I relieved! I struggled with myself about whether to admit to my failure in childcare, but once they arrived, I babbled about my concern over the baby's bodily function. The mother asked me, "How much water did you give him?"

"What water? You didn't say anything about giving him water."

"You're right," she said. "I didn't tell you about that. Don't worry about it. No harm done."

I still see that as a faulty execution of the responsibility given to me, and you can be sure to this day, I give very detailed notes to caregivers.

My early years as a young mother similarly amount to a negative balance because I walked out on the marriage to their father. I have asked each of my children to forgive me for this, but what I cannot seem to do is forgive myself. That someone else raised my children is my biggest sorrow.

When Michael left for Massachusetts taking the children with him, my consolation was the long-haired black family dog, Isaac. He got me into my own place. When my landlady sold her house to a man who was afraid of Isaac, my new landlord said, "Either the dog goes, or you do." You probably know me well enough by now to predict which one I chose.

Harry helped me out by telling me of a couple he knew who had left the state because they couldn't pay their mortgage. He tracked them down, and I offered to pay the five-month debt in exchange for their signing the mortgage over to me. All I had to offer them was their improved credit score with the debt paid off. They almost did not accept the offer. They wanted more money over and above, but I simply did not have it. Surprisingly, they accepted my offer. On top of that, with what I have learned recently about how banks operate, there was no reason the bank would have allowed me to assume the mortgage. My credit was nonexistent. So what made the bank suspend their rules? Was I lucky, or was I being blessed? I chose the latter.

The little red house I bought had started life as a garage: The former owner, (who was also a drunk), added on a room here and a room there.

Everything was cobbled together, off center, out of plumb, and not square. Even the doors hinges were put in upside down, which caused the pins to fall out every few months. The hot and cold water were reversed, which doesn't sound bad, but the problem inherent in that arose when you used someone else's plumbing. The ingrained habit resulted in turning on the hot water when you wanted a cold drink. It was very annoying. The other side of the house I used for storage. Technically, the house was a duplex with separately metered power; but I couldn't bear having someone live that close to me, so I didn't rent out the other side until I moved into Chantrel.

Finally, I had my *own* roof over my head (such as it was). The mortgage payment was exactly what I was paying for rent before. Of course, I had to find money for utilities, taxes, and insurance, but that looked do-able. The best part was no one could throw me out. Mom and Dad had sold Waterlily a while back, so besides the family farm, I sank my roots deep into my own two little acres and ramshackle home.

Now I had room for Nick, Tim, and Lee to come up and visit. The boys came once or twice a year but it was difficult for all of us. Not because we were uncomfortable with each other, but because it just reopened the wound of severance.

I got a wonderful letter from Tim about 10 years ago, apologizing for not calling more frequently when he was growing up with his father. His reason was the pain of being unable to have me around daily. I, too, had difficulty contacting the children—for the very same reason. Isn't that amazing—*him* apologizing to *me*? Tim is my right-brain youngest son. He is very tall and the spitting image of his father, quite handsome, also. He is artistic, has a hilarious self-deprecating sense of humor, and can make you laugh with his actor's flair for body language. And he is musical, with a wonderful tenor voice. Because he lives in Oregon, I only get to see him infrequently.

Nick, my oldest son, is very left-brain. He graduated from Rensselaer Polytechnic Institute as an electrical engineer and is into computers. As opposed to Tim, who lets it all hang out, Nick is a clam with his emotions and his life. Nick also resembles his father strongly. I get to see him yearly because he comes up to Maine from Hawaii to hunt deer with his best friend Frank, whom he has known from childhood. Nick only recently married so I don't expect grandchildren from him (except the steps) or Tim either.

My first child, Lee, is more of a combination of both her parents. Being female, her right and left brains are more balanced. She graduated from Massachusetts Institute of Technology with a degree in material science, and has used an electron microscope in her work (of which I am quite envious). She became quite a city girl and came to Maine to visit only a few times, giving as her reason that she hates the state. She met her husband, Jonathon, at her work in the computer field, and they have an entrancing six-year-old son named Matthew. She heroically delivered him at the advanced age of 43—quite an accomplishment! She has only just gone back to work part-time, but is doing a super job raising her son with the best possible kind of start in life.

A number of years ago, before she married, Lee drove up to Maine to visit. She brought a replacement headlight and a puny screwdriver and asked me if I would (not could) change it for her. She said, she couldn't get the screws out, but she knew I would be able to do it.

I gulped because I knew I wasn't as strong as she thought, but said I'd try. My first attempt told me that I might end up disappointing her. I got a bigger and better screwdriver that hopefully would have more torque. The second attempt was similar to the first. For the third try I dug deep and put everything I had into it (including the accompanying, "Gr-r-r-r-r-r-r." It finally broke loose. I don't know if Lee realized how close I came to being unable to do it.

Why am I including this story? I absolutely could not disappoint her again. What I had done to her, by walking out on my marriage to her father, was already too much. So, accomplishing this small job symbolized far more to me than Lee ever knew.

There is one child I did not fail and that is my youngest daughter Emma-Rose. She is a rugged country girl, very good looking with thick long blond hair that is usually somewhere between her knees and her waist. Even though she is almost six feet tall, there is no apologetic slump to her. She is a good electrician, although unlicensed. Having her work with me taught her all she needed to be a journeyman, so when she started taking the courses required for licensure she was bored out of her mind. As a result, she didn't stick with it.

When she was less than ten, I would take her to the fields we were haying. Because she wasn't big enough to toss the bales up into the back of the pickup, I had her drive the truck and I pitched them. That experience gave her a taste for driving that ended up with her becoming a class A truck driver. Her work now is driving 18 wheelers cross-country. Actually, there isn't much she can't do, from plumbing and carpentry to engine repair. Cooking came a little slower but she does all right there.

Sadly, Emma feels very alienated from her siblings, saying her blue-collar life is incompatible with their education and professions. She also feels censure for some of the life choices she has made: not going to college, becoming a truck driver, boyfriends etc. She has a huge heart and is always there to help anyone. I am extremely blessed to have her so close, and I consider her not only my daughter, but also my best friend (poor girl).

When I first bought the little red house, I had to go up on the roof to fix some leaks. The next thing I knew Emma was up there with me—at the age of 18 months! This was typical of her life: if I did something, she would follow. In spite of this pattern, she is extremely independent and her choices are hers alone. I have very little impact on those choices. But then, perhaps I modeled that independence for her also.

Of all my four children, I have the closest relationship with Emma, which is only logical because she is the one I spent the most time with. Plus, she has the same deep attachment to our home here in Maine that I have, so we are on the same page.

Behind our first home I put in a small garden with two flats of tomatoes that produced prodigiously. I canned 98 quarts of tomato sauce that summer, and it took me ten years to use it all up. Not surprisingly, I haven't canned since!

My first farm project was raising rabbits. Harry said that rabbit meat was a low cholesterol meat which he needed because his cholesterol count was over 350. I got some female New Zealand White rabbits from my neighbor Percy, and someone else gave us a wild male Cottontail they had trapped because it was marauding in their garden. The rabbits did their thing, which was multiply.

When it came time to prepare the rabbit for the table, Harry refused to be involved, which mystified me, even though he had been hunting and field-dressing wild rabbits for years. Thus, it became necessary to overcome my aversion to killing. I got a book and read how to kill a rabbit. It involved snapping its neck with your thumb. I tried but my hands were too small, so I hit it over the head with a hammer. The only thing that happened was the eyes popped out! This was *much* worse than throwing eggs against the wall, which I had done as a child. I had to string up the rabbit and cut its neck to bleed it out. Once it was dead, the process got easier. I gutted, skinned, cooked, and served it to Harry. I was totally exhausted. This rabbit had cost me a huge price.

Harry's response was to ask me, "Did the rabbit smile at you when you took him out of the cage?" I was so mad I could have strangled him; I didn't. I just opened the cage doors and let all the rabbits run wild.

Well, they were half-wild anyway.

My next farm project was goats. In Bridgton, I had been introduced to a couple of huge goats that still had their horns. When new people came to visit them, the goats ran to the stall door and clunked their hard hooves on top of the half-door. With their 2 foot horns reaching almost to the ceiling, they were very intimidating. But, I wanted goat milk for Emma because she was having trouble with cow's milk.

On the way to town one day, I spotted a mostly black Nubian mother goat and her baby. The mother's long, white, speckled ears hung halfway down her neck. This, along with her Roman nose and long, elegant neck, gave her a regal air. Her udder was so big it almost dragged on the ground. To my untutored eyes she looked like a good source of milk.

I bought her and the baby, and then discovered I didn't know how to milk. Mama's udder kept getting harder and harder. I went down to the grain store and bought a book on how to raise goats, but the milking section wasn't descriptive enough to be of any help. That poor goat missed three milkings before I desperately muckled onto those teats and was able to squeeze milk from her.

Big Mama was my first and biggest goat because Nubian goats are a type that combines the skinny dairy-conformation with a more solid build for meat production. Because of her bulk she ruled over the other dairy-type goats I had. She was my foundation doe and naming her Big Mama was inevitable.

I also bought a Toggenburg doe that we called Flower. She was fawn-colored with the breed's typical white streaks down her face. I took her to be bred to a grand champion Alpine buck. His genes dominated and the black and white baby was very strongly Alpine (a small Swiss mountain goat). I let Emma name the baby and her choice was (interestingly) Patricia. This goat was my best milker, giving more than a gallon a day.

I needed to get rid of the milk I couldn't use, so I sold it to people that came to my door. If they brought their own containers for milk I could legally bypass all the government regulations.

Because the market for goat's milk was so small, I began to make goat cheese. I sent away to a cheese making supply house for the liquid rennet that coagulates milk. Would you believe rennet comes from the lining of a cow's stomach?

The simplest kind of cheese to make was cottage cheese. I warmed up the milk, added the rennet, stirred, and then let it set up into curds (solid pieces of custardy protein) and whey (the watery other stuff.) At that point, I could pour the kettle of curds and whey into a strainer, put a little salt in, and now it was cottage cheese.

A better cheese was Feta, which started like cottage cheese, but got wrapped in cheese cloth and put in a press, to squeeze the last bit of whey out of it. I made my own cheese press using cloth-covered bricks. Sometimes I would add dill or Crazy Salt (seasoned salt) to make a different version. The best cheese was Edam. My only problem was, even though it was refrigerated, mold would form on it in several weeks. I sent away for some red beeswax to cover it, but the mold would grow under the wax.

I realized that all those government regulations had a good purpose. I should have had a stainless steel kitchen, with walls that could be sprayed down with disinfectant. What I had was a nice country knotty-pine kitchen. The open pores of the wood harbored the mold that would get on my cheese. My farmhouse production wasn't up to snuff, so I just made it for my own use.

When I went back to Bompa's farm for one of the annual summer meetings, I told my Uncle Sumner about my efforts at cheese making. He said, "I have something you might appreciate," then took me out into his barn and showed me a huge cheese press for making big wheels of cheddar. "You can have it if you want it," he said. Then he went upstairs and came down with a beautiful wooden butter-mold. He said, "This belonged to Aunt Emma and I want you to have it also." I was so blown away by his generosity I could hardly speak. I must have managed to say something, but it was probably totally lame. I wasn't lame about getting the new treasures quickly settled into my car, though!

Goats are one of the smarter domesticated animals and they have beautifully elegant and expressive bodies. It was quite easy to learn their language. (No need for Dr. Doolittle here.) Plus, they were of a size and temperament that a pre-school Emma could manage, even as young as she was.

I started going to the local fairs and learned that, "udders dragging on the ground," is not considered good conformation in dairy goats. Apparently, "high and tight" is as desirable in goats, as in women!

I needed to do something about the udder problem, but I had absolutely no money available, SO—I sold Mom's treasured sterling silver to buy a white Nubian buckling. I had seen him advertized in a goat magazine as coming from a long line of outstanding milkers with beautiful udders, and had fallen in love with him: AND—I had enough money to have him flown in from California. I named him Sheffield, which was the brand name of Mother's very expensive sterling silver. I was probably the only one who got that reference. Come to think of it, my older sister Barbara might know what I was referring to, but she would have been horrified at the exchange. I can hear her now, "Mother's silver for a GOAT!" Interestingly, Sheffield's offspring were sometimes a silver/pewter color from the combination of their white and black parents.

Unfortunately, the older bucks get, the more aggressive they become. When a buck rears up on his hind legs to bring his hard head crashing down on you, it can cause major damage. For this reason, it is vital to occasionally establish your dominance over them for safe herd management. The way I did that was to grab a long Nubian ear and spin the buck around until I got him on the ground. Then I would put my knee on his shoulder and hold him there for a few seconds before I let him up again. This made me the dominant buck and peace would reign—for about two months.

The longest I kept a buck was five years. By that time it was difficult to prevent inbreeding with the accompanying faults like under-shot jaws. So I would need to get a new breeding line. I would sell the old bucks to the Jamaican apple-pickers who prized these males for their "prairie oysters." Apparently, the oldest white-haired man among them was given these choice parts to make up for any male diminishment he may have had. There was much giggling and rib-poking as they served it to him. The reason I know this, is because I asked to be at the dinner when they cooked the goat. I'd never eaten one of my own goats and I wanted to see how it tasted. The Jamaicans put so much curry in the stew to overcome the unsavory buck odor that I never did discover how goat meat tasted.

Bucks are extremely smelly with disgusting habits that are not fit for sensitive stomachs. Unfortunately, the school bus would drive right by the pasture and all the boys would be hanging out the window to get a good look. Then they would say awful things to Emma about the nasty relationships they imagined she was having with the bucks and pigs. Children can be so unbelievably cruel to each other.

We had to bottle-feed baby goats with a powdered milk-replacer so we could get the fresh milk we wanted from the mothers. This also bonded the babies to us and made them more like pets than 'dumb' animals.

The happier side of having goats is the milking of them. I would go down to the barn after a hard day at work and lean up against a grassy-smelling doe. I would put my cold hands on her warm soft udder and harvest sweet milk. It was not a chore but a therapeutic unwinding of the day's tension.

Unfortunately, the goodness of the milk could be seriously affected if we had kept the buck and his smelly, nasty habits anywhere near the does. So the buck had to be segregated from his sweethearts for the months we were milking the does. This didn't help moderate his bad behaviors. Because of all that, my small operation could only handle one buck at a time (and that was more than enough).

Another negative of raising goats is keeping them inside a fence. They are really good at spotting a weak area and getting out. I was a serious trial to my neighbors with my wayward animals.

The necessity of castrating the bucklings was another issue. It wasn't that bad because I had an Elastrator which put a very tight rubber band around the sac. The constriction of the rubber-band cut off the blood supply to the area, so it would die and fall off, somewhat like the umbilical cord. The hardest part was keeping them still enough to accomplish the job. Even with Emma's help, it was difficult.

The absolute worst thing I had to do was burn off the horns of both male and female kids (baby goats) so they wouldn't hurt each other as they got older. The specter of a punctured udder was very real because goats can be very bossy, sometimes even bullying to each other. I built a long narrow kid-sized box with a hinged lid and a "V" for the neck and head to stick out. Putting the kid in that made dehorning a one person job. I had to heat up an electric dehorning iron for about 10 minutes to get it hot enough to burn quickly. It took about 20 seconds to get the first layer off, and another 20 to sear the tissue around the base. If this isn't thorough enough, ugly horn spurs can grow. The baby goats scream and stick their tongue out. The acrid smell of burning hair and horn is so pungent I'd have to breathe through my mouth, and even then, it makes your eyes water. Doing this takes great fortitude, especially if you love your animals. I still dehorn for one farmer and one pediatrician, even though I don't have goats myself anymore.

I also had to learn to be my own veterinarian. I gave shots of antibiotics IM (intra-muscular) which wasn't too bad, but sometimes I'd have to put an animal down. Somehow, this procedure seemed easier than the dehorning because there wasn't the screaming and kicking. The leaden finality of it was more oppressive, though. After giving birth, one of my third-generation does developed a brain condition which was a form of encephalitis. She couldn't get up because she had lost the pathway from her brain to her muscles. I had to put her down. By this time I had learned a few things to make it easier for her. I got a very sharp knife and cut her carotid artery. I had her facing down-hill so she didn't get covered in blood. She just closed her eyes and in one minute it was over—without any struggle

The final goat negative, is culling, sending surplus and/or genetically flawed goats to market. This isn't as bad as dehorning but still can be emotionally trying.

My responsibility for these animals wasn't always a one-way street. One day Emma and I went into the pasture where it was more open, where we could lie down and gaze up at the clouds. We wanted to see what images we could find in the different shapes. Patricia, my favorite goat, came over and plunked her front feet on one side of me and her hind feet on the other side. Then she lowered her head and glared at the other animals that had come over to see what was going on. I think she thought something bad had happened to us because we were lying on the ground like that; and *she* was going to protect *us*. Amazing!

I honed my carpentry skills on goat projects by building a nice milking stand so I didn't have to stoop down so low to milk. I also made that special box to hold the baby goats for dehorning. I built mangers, stalls and cages for the rabbits. I made doors, windows, gates. I had a ton of fun building and growing things. And, being a true blue Yankee I strongly believed in the old saying, "Use it up, wear it out, fix it up, or do without." I was truly my grandfather's granddaughter. (Not nearly as accomplished, though).

Someone gave us some guinea hens and one guinea rooster. They were almost wild and could fly and roost high up in the trees. The rooster was very aggressive (which is probably why they were given to us). He would attack three-year-old Emma, who wasn't much bigger than he was. I showed her how to carry a stick to hit him with, and she would lift it way over her head to bring it down on the rooster, but he would duck in under and still get in some good bites. You would have thought she might have developed a phobia about birds, not Emma.

Once people learn you have a farm, you get all kinds of unwanted animals. Bantam chickens arrived this way, and they were complete escape artists. No matter how thoroughly I closed up all the little holes in the hen house, they still managed to get out and roost in the cedars across the road. When Emma was older I had her climb the trees at night when they were roosting and hand them down to me. Into the pen they would go, only to find a way the next day. I finally gave up and just let them do their thing. What was their thing? Eating ticks and being as varied and beautiful as flowers.

We even had people drop off baby kittens, figuring there would always be rats and mice around a barn. One group of three kittens we found after dark, when we went out to do chores. It was raining and we heard the babies crying, soaking wet, and in the woods, not in our barn. Remarkably, we were able to keep them all alive.

The last animals given to us were attack geese. They tolerated us once we were able to establish dominance, but forget it if you were a stranger. They would run at people, wings outspread, head down with beaks open, and honking like crazy. With their wings spread they seemed as big as condors. When they caught you, they would grab hold with their beaks, meanwhile furiously beating you with their bruising wings. It was not fun to be on the receiving end, but it was lots of fun to see them chasing people. We got quite a kick out of it, but those on the receiving end were not amused at all.

It became apparent that that all I had were grey ganders so I went to a neighbor to see if he would part with any of his female white geese. He was amused at my matchmaking but willing to give me some. Now that the geese were paired, they quieted down and integrated themselves into the menagerie. I started getting lovely huge goose eggs that were mostly yolk (great if you like yolks). They looked like big tangerines sitting on your plate. I also turned some of these monsters into Pyzanski (elaborately decorated Ukrainian Easter Eggs). My Russian mother-in-law had shown me how to do that many years ago.

I got my first pig when I was in the middle of town on an electrical job. When I went out to my truck to get some material, I saw this little white pig running around loose on people's lawns. He was all scratched up and looked totally out of place. I asked who might have pigs in the area and no one could think of anyone. So—I sprang into action, threw myself on the ground, and grabbed for legs.

By gum, I caught it!

The only reason I knew how to catch a pig was because Harry had described it to me one day. We were talking about the pig scramble at the fair and I asked how that was done. There were usually three separate age groups so the older kids don't get all the pigs, 7-8 is one class, 9-10 is the next, and 11-12 is the last. Harry said the kids can just jump on top of the piglets. But it's quite a bit different when an adult needs to catch a loose pig. Basically you have to land on the ground next to the piglet so it's not crushed. Sounded like something I should remember and it did come in handy.

I put the pig into the front seat of my truck, brought it right up to my farm, and put it into the tool shed. I knew nothing about pigs, so I went down to good old Paris Farmers Union and got a book on raising pigs. I left my name and number there for anyone looking for a lost pig. I also came back with a bag of grain. That pig kept getting longer and longer, until he could barely turn around in the tool shed.

I asked my neighbor, George, to come up to give me a price on some foundation work for my house. I knew he also had pigs, so I took him down to look at Big Pig. He took one look at my pig and said, "That looks just like Old Boy."

"How long has he been missing?" I asked, guardedly.

"Oh, he's not missing," said George. "Yours just looks like Old Boy"

Relieved that he was not going to claim my pig, I told him the story of catching the pig at my advanced age of "over forty," and having only heard verbal descriptions of how to catch a pig. He was suitably impressed that this city girl managed to catch a pig, so we hit it off famously. He told me that he donated ten of Old Boy's babies to the fair for the pig scramble, but when it came time for the event only nine were in the pen. He said he had already given them away so he didn't want the pig returned. Big Pig had already started to grow these great long tusks and they were truly awesome. I asked him if he would castrate the pig and he agreed. Getting Big Pig tied down to do that job was quite an interesting chore.

Big Pig soon outgrew the tool shed, and because he was nearly blind, I was able to let him wander at will within the goat area. Somehow, he could sense the electric charge in the fence, so he carefully stayed away from that. Because he was my first pig he was a pet and I kept him for many years.

Unfortunately, because I grained Big Pig, he couldn't keep up with the over-supply of milk from my goats. My Yankee frugality wouldn't let me waste any of that ambrosia, so I got some more pigs. But, I needed a place to put them.

A carpenter was able to help me out. He had called me to repair his electric service because a visitor had knocked his pole over. He didn't have the money to pay me, and I needed a separate pig house, so we bartered. His name was Hank, and he did a very nice job. Now I had room for the additional pigs. I electrified a large enclosure with fiberglass rods and 'string' with wire in it. The area was big enough for them to be able to keep one corner for defecation. Surprisingly, pigs are quite clean if given the opportunity. I never realized that the mud they like on themselves is a deliberate application for insect repellant, rather than carelessness of where they lie down.

Learning a pig's body language is a lot more difficult because of their thick stumpy immovable trunks, but I learned to find subtle clues. I bought an already bred black and white sow (female pig). When it came time for her to farrow (have babies), I was warned that as a first time mother she might freak-out and kill her babies, thinking they were rats. I guess sometimes they might, but I never had that happen. I brought a bucket into her pig house and sat with her while she farrowed the first five piglets. I'd take some of the slime off and let her sniff them before I put them on a teat. They were ready to nurse immediately. After the fifth piglet, she rose up on her front legs, leaned her head against me, resting for a few minutes. Then she lay down and had eleven more. I think having me there helped her, kept her from panicking. We trusted each other. She understood that I was there to help her, and I understood she wasn't going to panic and start thrashing around or eating her babies.

That birth went so smoothly I decided to get another sow, and a male pig to keep for breeding. I built a super strong pig crate I could wrap with chains and lift up with the bucket end of my tractor and put it into the back of my pickup, pig and all. Now I had a traveling boar I could take to other farmers that had sows. In exchange for the breeding I would take two babies.

Pretty soon I had bunches of babies and I really couldn't afford to have a vet come and castrate that amount of babies. It would have been an astronomical bill. So I decided to do it myself, having seen George do it before. Basically the testicle sac is attached to the back leg so all you do is cut a slit in the back of the leg and then pop the sac out. Instead, when I did that, a loop of intestine popped out.

"That shouldn't have happened."

I jumped into my truck holding the baby pig up by the back legs with the loop of intestine still hanging out. I used the other hand to shift and steer and—'whoomp,'—the truck lurched over something. I didn't hear anybody screaming (although I am inside) so I didn't stop. I drove down to Percy's, another pig farmer next door on the other side of me. Fortunately, he was home and after a quick look, he says the same thing, "That shouldn't have happened."

"Can you come and do the rest of these and show me what I'm doing wrong?"

He agreed and I headed back to my house. On the way I saw that it was my "Garden Way" cart I ran over. I was sad about that. It was a really great cart.

Percy arrived right behind me, whipped out his knife, and cut. Another loop of intestine popped out. "That shouldn't have happened," we both said in unison. I stuffed the intestines back in and hoped for the best.

The next two males go smoothly. Percy said, "Something is wrong with this sow genetically. You better not keep her."

Sadly, I had to sell all her baby pigs for summer pig-roasts and mother pig went to the meat man shortly after. One of the malformed little males didn't make it—the other one did. After that disastrous beginning, I manage castrating the other litters just fine.

By this time, my pig enterprise subsisted on the 'pig run' which I had at the supermarket. This was the daily pickup of the discarded produce and outdated deli meats they threw out. It wasn't rotten food, just overly ripe or bruised fruit, etc. Because of all that free food I didn't have to feed my pigs grain. They didn't even know what it was. My traveling boar met his demise because of this deprivation.

I'll have to tell you about that one. I got a call from a hobby farmer that wanted his two sows bred. He was recently retired and seemed to have a fair amount of money available because he had every kind of farm equipment imaginable, and it was all brand-new with no sign of having ever been used at all. His two sows were in the cleanest pen I ever saw. He had removed the separating wall between two 12x12 horse stalls, so their pen was now 12x24. It was belly-deep in loose shavings and the pigs were the cleanest pinkish-white I had ever seen. Not only that, they bore a striking resemblance to ones I'd seen in children's picture books! They had a full trough of free choice grain that was kept topped-off at all times. My boar must have thought he had died and gone to hog heaven.

It was about six weeks before the gentleman farmer finally called and said, "You might as well come get your pig now."

"I guess he finally got the job done," I answered.

"I don't think so," the man said.

"Why not?" I asked.

"Come take a look," he said.

When I arrived there, immediately I could see why he couldn't get those sows bred. I didn't even recognize my own boar. He had swelled up like the Pillsbury Dough Boy. There is no way he could heave himself on the backs of those sows—and if he could have, they surely would have collapsed. I almost couldn't get him in the crate. I had to push with my foot to get him to hunch over before I could close the door. When I did, the top of the crate rubbed his back raw.

Knowing I'd never get him back in the crate again, I drove directly down to the meat-packing plant to pay to have him ground up into sausage. I figured that might help the boar toughness of the meat and the spices might cut the boar odor. I was wrong on both counts. Bottom line? I had the most expensive dog food you ever saw.

My turn came to help my neighbor Percy as he had helped me. His daughter, Nellie, my daughter's best friend, came running up to our house one day, saying their boar had gotten loose and her mother was afraid to go near him.

No big deal.

I went down to see their boar grunting and slavering at the mouth. He'd wedged into a corner between two cars, his back almost as high as the car hoods. He had wild eyes and his sides were heaving. He didn't look anything like my nice calm boar, but I decided to go for it.

One thing I learned with pigs is you can't drive them because they will go in a completely different direction than what you want. The best thing is to lead them. I asked for some grain, scooped out a handful and let him slup a nibble from my hand. Then I held the grain out in front of his mouth, backing up into his pen, and he walked right in. Whew!

Two hours later, Nellie returned and said, "He's out again." Just as I arrived at their house, Percy shows up. "I can take care of him," he says. He gets a 2x6, winds up, and clobbers the pig across the head. No wonder the boar was acting so weird!

Percy's animals were afraid of him, and rightly so.

Fearful animals are unpredictable and if they are large they can be dangerous. Granted, you need to establish authority and dominance, but this can be done with love and respect. It is a two-way street. And it's exactly the same as with people—love and respect are foundational to a relationship.

12 PART II
STEWARDSHIP AT THE LITTLE RED HOUSE—Large Animals

There I was, standing in the middle of my small animal farm, when I was struck with an epiphany. I remembered my lifelong desire to have a horse, and I said to myself, "nobody is going to magically give you a horse. If you want one, go get it yourself." The confidence and resolution I had as a runaway three-year-old was back.

But, I was embarrassed by the self-centeredness of that thought so I decided, if my daughter was the least little bit interested in having a pony, that would be the excuse I needed to have the horses I'd always wanted. Emma was about nine and a little young to be responsible for the care of one, but I couldn't wait.

Practically the next day I saw a little black pony, strangely running up the middle of Elm Hill Road. I stopped at the bottom of the hill and the first person I asked said yes, that was her pony, and not to worry about it. The pony was just going up the hill to join Harley's horses, eating in his good pasture because all she had was a little dirt yard. I was shocked with her indifference and managed to persuade her into selling the pony to me. The mare turned out to have very bad manners. She bit and kicked and I couldn't trust her behavior around Emma so I gave her back.

The next two ponies I got were a lovely quiet white mare called Miss Winnabet, and a gorgeous paint gelding called Scout. He was mostly white with splashes of brown, and a mane that was halfway down his shoulders, and the proverbial tail that swept the ground. However, his beauty was only skin deep. He thought the goats should be driven off, so he would run at them with his head down and his mouth open. Sometimes he was successful and managed to get a chunk. He didn't stay very long either. Sadly Miss Winnabet developed 'moon blindness,' which is a milky white covering on the eyes causing loss of sight. The vet was not very optimistic about successful treatment. Because of that, she had to go also. I was not having very good luck with ponies, but I didn't give up easily.

My next try was much more of a success. I found a pair of matched chestnut driving ponies that were for sale. Gloria Hadley had a team of eight small ponies she drove, but wanted to work with larger Haflingers. So, she was selling her smaller ponies, which were about twelve hands high, (one hand equals 4.5 inches.) I asked her how much they had been ridden and she said her niece had ridden them and they were quite well-mannered. By this time I knew the correct procedure was to definitely 'look the gift horse in the mouth'. I got on them to see how well they responded to leg cues. (I'm sure it must have been quite a sight with my legs almost scraping the ground). They were as good as she said, so I brought them home. The mare was named Nutmeg and the gelding was called Bill.

Emma had a grand time with them. Her friend Nellie would come to play and they would hop onto the ponies and ride bareback *and* with no bridle! They didn't do this when I was likely to see, because the ponies would try to shake them off by running and turning suddenly, or coming to a screeching halt. Emma said that she and Nellie would laugh themselves silly when they were doing that. Sometimes they *would* fall off and there were good sized rocks in the field. One time Nellie did get a good bump on her head (I just learned this recently). At their age I was running around snorting and pawing, pretending I was a horse. I figured I was able to give them an improvement on my childhood lack of equine enjoyment.

Emma and Nellie managed to survive my lack of supervision because they were tough country girls. But they had horses every day. Their desire for something different to do on a special day like a birthday was to go to an amusement park like Aquaboggin in Saco. I enjoyed those rides almost as much as they did. After we had done that a few years, the next choice was Fun Town. I was not one speck interested in any of those rides, so I brought two books; making sure not to run out of reading material. I managed to get through the day just fine. What I didn't find out until many years later was the impression I made on Emma: That is, how far I was willing to go, to do something she really wanted to do.

To get back to the farm, since Bill and Nutmeg were driving ponies, I thought I would get their help to smooth out the lumps and bumps in the pasture. I bought an old horse-drawn harrow for that purpose. It took some time to figure out how to get that complicated harness on Bill, but he stood patiently. The next hurdle was to get him hooked to the harrow. Once I did that I clucked to Bill to get him going. As soon as he heard that harrow rattling and clanking behind him, he freaked-out and bolted. I was standing behind him, so letting go of the reins was easy. Bill tore around frightening all the other animals into pandemonium. I watched helplessly as he careened around trees, the harrow crashing into rocks until he finally broke loose of it. Once he was free of the harrow, he turned around, fixed his eye on it, and blew through his nose as if to say, "You're not going to chase *me* anymore."

It was clear. These would only be riding ponies, not driving ponies.

In two years Emma's legs had gotten so long she was ready for a horse. I asked the Mel Olson, the carpenter who was building Chantrel, if he could find a horse for me, because he was an animal dealer and went to the animal auctions every week. He said he'd look, and a few weeks later he told me he'd found a nice two-year old colt, a handsome Palomino Appaloosa. His mane and tail were white and he had a white blaze on his face. His appaloosa white rump faded into speckles on the gold of his main coat. He was absolutely beautiful.

The only problem was, he was covered in sweat. I told the carpenter that I'd pay his price of $200, even though I had misgivings about the horse's health. I had the vet check him out and sure enough he had shipping fever. I had to give him a shot of antibiotic deep into his neck muscle every day for a month. That cost me another $200. When I told my carpenter about the sickness he said, "What do you expect for such a cheap price?" Horse Traders!

The horse turned out to be a wonderful find though, so I shouldn't complain. Because he looked like he belonged out west, I briefly considered naming him Nevada, but that sounded like a name for the Marlboro Man, so I ended up calling him Arizona. He had what was called a "kind eye." It's hard to describe what that is except to say the expression in his body and face was soft. There was no tension of muscle or alarmed spookiness. He was a small quarter-horse with the big rear-end for the powerhouse drive. Actually, I think he favored his pony background more because he was such an easy-keeper. I could only give him a handful of grain, otherwise he chubbed right out into a beer-barrel belly.

His pony smarts made him alert in the pasture, playful with things, and attentive to people. When I lifted the shade on the window in the morning, he looked up at the house to see if someone was coming out. He could recognize the rattle of my work truck and would have his head up to get the first glimpse of me as I came down the hill. Also, he would briskly trot over from the far pasture when I called, even when he couldn't see me. He was all I could ever have wanted in a horse.

Because he was only two he hadn't been ridden yet. I didn't want to risk Emma on an untrained horse, so I asked my farrier (horseshoeing person) if she would train him to saddle. She brought him over to her barn and spent a month on him. She called me towards the end of that month and asked me to come over. She saddled him and showed me how well he behaved under the saddle. Then she took me to her barn and showed me the stall she had kept him in. I was baffled by the reason for the tour. Then she hit me with the bad news. She explained, "Just a few days ago, I found him hanging over the stall door. His front half was on the floor but he had gotten his hind quarters stuck, one leg on the inside of the door, the other leg on the outside."

"Oh, no!" I breathed. "He's never been in a stall before. He must have been frantic to get outside. I should have told you that."

"I think his back leg was injured where it gouged against the top of the door," she said. "I don't know how long he was like that, maybe the whole night at worst, or a few hours at best."

"How come you didn't keep the top of the door closed?" I asked.

"I did keep it closed for the first three weeks but I thought he would be comfortable in there by now," she said.

"How badly do you think he's injured?" I questioned.

"It's kind of hard to tell. He doesn't really limp, so it may not be all that permanent. I feel so badly about it, I don't want you to pay me for the training."

"No, your time is worth money," I said. "I'll still pay you."

I brought Arizona home and told Emma what had happened. She said, "You know Mom, you really didn't have to take him over there. I've been riding him for a long time."

"What do you mean?" I questioned.

Emma said, "When you were gone I would get on his back and we would walk around. He was very careful with me. Whenever I wanted to stop I would lean sideways, like I was going to fall off, and he would stop."

Wouldn't you know!

I took Emma down to the horse supplier and got some nice English riding equipment. Soon she was charging around the pasture full speed.

One day, I was watching from the kitchen window when I saw her tumble off the horse and Arizona almost fell to his knees as he ran over her. I flew out of the house to see how badly she was injured. She got up and said, "I'm fine, Mom."

"How could you be?" I asked, "I saw you go under his feet."

"He stepped on me," she said "but as soon as he felt me, he picked his weight off that foot. That's why he almost fell. If you don't believe me, look at my pants."

I looked at her pants and the binding piece between both legs was ripped from crotch to leg. Unbelievable!

That's what you can have in the animal world, the return in kind of the attention, love, nurturing, and responsibility you give to them.

Emma was not enthusiastic about the English riding saddle so I got her a western saddle. Plus, earlier I had noticed blood at the corner of Arizona's mouth, not because Emma was sawing on his mouth, but because his mouth was so tender, so I also bought a hackamore bridle (which was just a nose band with no bit through the mouth.)

Emma did other things with Arizona than just ride around the farm with him. I have a picture of her in a parade on her horse, wearing a western skirt and a cowboy hat. Also, she would go to the county fair and enter Arizona into the games they had with horses, like musical grain bags or barrel racing. Arizona's leg injury cropped up at this point when he turned to pivot around the barrel on his bad side. He was never going to be in the top ranks but Emma had fun riding him, which is all that really counts. I have a very small picture of her going around the barrels but my camera was a joke and you can hardly even tell it's Emma. Stephie took the best picture of her riding Arizona. It was from the back so you'd think it was another lousy picture, but it's actually great. Emma's waist length hair is the exact match, in color and length, of Arizona's flaxen tail.

Emma's only complaint was she had no one to go riding with, now that Nellie had also outgrown the ponies. I saw we needed another horse. A farm I was doing some electrical work at was pasturing a few standard-bred race horses for the off-season. They asked me if I knew anyone that wanted a horse, and explained that the owners had come to pick up the horses expecting to find them in good condition. But one big Bay (deep brown with black mane, tail, and legs) was pretty ragged. The dominant horse had kept him away from the hay so he had lost, not gained condition. Since he was eleven years old, the owners said find a home for him or the meat man will come get him.

Any doubt what my response was?

I brought him back with me and because he was so homely I considered calling him Homer. He had that high Hambiltonian hump in his withers (where his neck and back joined). His neck was swaybacked, his coat was dull, and he was skin and bones. It took 16 quarts of grain a day to get him back into condition. Then he began to look like his racing name, High Eagle, especially when he was in motion. At a trot he would spring off his feet, floating airborne above the ground, while Arizona had to canter to keep up with him. Eventually, I was able to drop his grain intake down to eight quarts a day.

I'm going to digress a little bit here to give you some history of the horse. Thoroughbred (racing) horses are descendants of three foundational sires imported to England; the Byerley Turk in 1680, the Godolphin Arabian in 1729, and the Darley Arabian in1780. They were considered hot-blooded because they had a fiery temperament with great speed and agility. These stallions were bred to cold-blooded English mares that were more placid but also more durable. Messenger, a grey thoroughbred stallion was imported to America just after the American Revolution. His grandson was a fine, fast horse called Abdullah. Hambeltonian, a son of Abdulla, was born in 1849 in New York to a man called Seeley. As a colt, with that weird hump, Seeley did not consider him a promising prospect. As a matter of fact, he thought the colt was worthless.

One of Seeley's hired hands, a man named Rysdek, thought differently. He believed in the gawky colt and was able to buy both the mother and colt for $125. At six months the colt started to grow into his promise so Rysdek entered him in a show class at the county fair. At two years the horse had precociously bred four mares. There was another, older son of Abdullah called Abdullah Chief that was the local popular stud horse. His owner had great contempt for Hambiltonian, saying he was only a show horse, not a trotter. A match race was organized which Hambeltonian won by seven seconds. That's a crushing dominance! Passing this ability on to his foals is another strength entirely. Hambeltonian impressed his genes on his offspring, and sired over 1,300 foals, earning Rysdek a small fortune.

The foals with the hump proved to be just as fast as their sire. I think that Hambeltonian Hump allowed for greater area of attachment for the driving front-end of these horses. They became known as standard-bred horses, ones that raced in harness pulling a cart, or later a sulky. Almost all successful standard bred racers can trace their lineage back to Hambeltonian.

My horse, High Eagle, was a successful pacer that had earned his keep as a racer for the eleven years before I got him. The pacing gait moves both legs on the same side (front and back) at the same time. This results in a rolling side-winding effect that is difficult to sit on and ride. Trotters alternate moving right front and left rear together, and then left front and right rear together. The result here is a smooth level back that is easy to ride. Both gaits are natural, with trotting being the most common and favored by the horse out in the pasture. Since pacing is actually faster than trotting, 80% of standard bred racers are pacers.

Now we had two terrific horses. I was in seventh heaven. And, Emma had Nellie as a riding companion again. I rode occasionally and Emma and I established the tradition of going out on a Mother's Day ride together. We would go into our neighbor's woodlot which had a nice trail down amongst great huge pines. It was always a transcendent experience.

When my younger sister Stephanie came to visit, we took the horses out. I saw that she was doing all right on her horse, so we picked up the speed on the return trip. Emma had stayed home to wash her waist-length hair leaving it loose to dry. She was curious about how we were doing, so she was running up the back side of the same hill Steph and I were cantering up. We all met at the top of the hill. When the horses saw Emma with the great wings of her hair spread out by her running, they dug their front feet into the ground and came to a dead halt. Steph and I both went flying over the horses' heads. I somersaulted through the air and landed on my rear end, which wasn't too bad. I popped back up, grabbed reins, and saw Steph on the ground moaning, "My back, my back."

Emma jumped on Arizona and raced back home to get someone to bring the truck to us, while I stay with Steph. By the time the truck arrived, Steph had improved and she wobbled into the truck. We were all shaken by the experience—including the horses. Fortunately, Steph was only rattled, not seriously injured.

I told Steph that falling off a horse is no big deal. The more you ride, the more you'll fall off. It's not a dying matter. I compared it to the times I get hit with electricity in my job. People think if you get electrocuted, you die. But that's not been my experience. I get "bit" about once a month, but mostly it's my tools that show the damage. The same thing applies to horseback riding. The more you ride the more you fall. Knowing how to fall off a horse is almost as important as learning how to stay on a horse. It's all survivable.

I found the dynamics between the horses interesting. High Eagle was the bigger horse and the more dominant but he had spent his whole life in a stall. He knew nothing about living in a pasture. He would let Arizona decide where they would go, and when. Arizona would lead, High Eagle would follow. But as soon as food entered the picture, the dynamics of the relationship changed. High Eagle would establish the food was his and chase Arizona away. That only lasted for about five minutes though. Arizona would sneak slowly back, pretending to graze nearby until High Eagle got so used to his closeness he wouldn't bother defending his food anymore.

The first winter that we had ice on the side hill (instead of deep snow) I looked out the kitchen window to see High Eagle with his legs locked, sliding slowly down the hill. His head was up and the whites of his eyes were showing. He looked terrified. I called out to Emma and we rushed out and put our feet on the downhill side of his feet, Emma in the front and me in the back. Once he saw his feet stopped sliding, he would take one step, and then we would brace at the new position. We slowly walked him off the ice that way. Then Arizona goes 'trip-trip-trip' over the ice, showing High Eagle, "This is the way you do it."

Arizona was still a stud horse and he bred our pony mare, Nutmeg. I didn't know when it happened so I didn't know exactly when the baby was due. One morning I heard some anxious whinnying, looked out the window, and saw Nutmeg run as close to the fence as she can get and holler for me. Then she wheeled around and ran down behind the barn.

Oh, no!

My heart hits the floor.

I tore out of the house and found Nutmeg standing over her unmoving baby, pleading in her face. The baby was a little palomino. The amniotic sac was over his nostrils, so he was never able to take his first breath. He was stone cold, so I didn't try to resuscitate him.

I felt absolutely horrible. It was a real life enactment of a nightmare I used to have. Basically the dream was something was dying because I had forgotten about it: sometimes it was an animal, sometimes it was a child.

To get back on a better note, I really needed more pasture space than my measly two acres because I had so many animals by this time. My next door neighbor had an old apple storage barn they had converted into a summer house. It sat on 20 acres they had fenced in for the replacement heifers they raised there.

What is a replacement heifer, you ask?

Well, a milking cow's production is so unnaturally extended beyond the period of time it would take to raise her calf, that the mother is worn out and broken down in four years. A replacement is needed for her. That is what my neighbor was doing, raising replacement heifers for those poor used-up milk cows.

My neighbor died and his widow had set a price of $35,000 for the property. I told her I was interested but I wasn't making much money at that time. Lots of people came to look at the property but with both Percy's pig farm and mine right near it, nobody made an offer. I negotiated with her for the following three years, and finally bought it for $23,000.

Boy, was I a happy camper! (So were my animals, also). Now I could really expand my farm enterprise.

Down at the feed store I heard about the 4-H program for farm children and it seemed like a good idea for my ten-year-old daughter, Emma-Rose. I got her a young Hereford named Champagne Lady for her project, and she halter trained it in preparation for the Oxford Fair. It's a good thing she had the people in 4-H showing her what to do, because washing and clipping is quite a production, about which I knew nothing. Emma did quite well at the show, with one minor struggle to get the heifer in position to stand for the judges. Someone snapped a picture of her and sent it in to the newspaper. Imagine my surprise when my Uncle called me up to say he had seen her in the Boston Herald!

This was an encouraging beginning, and since the whole 20 acres was already fenced, getting more beef cattle seemed the next step. I bought three purebred, white-faced, cinnamon-colored Hereford cows for $850 each. I read about artificial insemination, but it seemed too complicated with the liquid-nitrogen storage tanks and the whole process itself. So, I bought a Grand Champion Bull for $1,800 and let him run with the cows. He was of the dark mahogany-colored variety and a Big Boy. His shoulders were higher than my mine! I got a clamp-on nose ring to lead him around but when he was out grazing it had to come off. Otherwise he might get it caught in something and possibly rip it out. It wasn't too long before I found the flaw in that practice.

One day I came home from work to find my bull and my neighbor Percy's squared up in Percy's pasture and going at each other. I grabbed the nose ring hanging in the barn, a bucket of grain, and climbed over the fence. Fortunately, my bull is a chow hound so he left off the battle to come for the grain. When he put his head down into the grain, I clipped the nose ring in, but made a mistake by not having the lead line already hooked to the ring. The bull became wary of letting me get close to the ring with the line, but I finally snagged it and picked his head up to follow me. Percy had just come home and didn't say a word to me, just opened the gate so I could bring my bull home. I then settled down to fixing my fence. Robert Frost said, "Good fences make good neighbors." He was right.

All the cows had their babies unsupervised except one wild first-time heifer. There's a really good medical word for her, primapara (first-pregnancy). She had never been handled when she was young so she wouldn't let me get near her. She was in labor but she should have been bred to a smaller bull. The calf was too big for her tight virginal birth canal. I could see the calf's foot sticking out, but that was as far as it got. I chased her around 10 acres of pasture before she lay down about three hours later, too exhausted to push.

I called up Emma's 4-H leader who was a dairy farmer and asked if he could help. He came over right away, and asked for some baling twine, which he wrapped around the hoof. He pulled, but couldn't get a good grip on the twine. I got a stick and wrapped the twine around it. He gave a good pull and the twine broke. I ran to get a stronger nylon rope. He wrapped this around the hoof and stick. This time when he pulled, the stick broke. So I got a small log which he wrapped the rope around and when he pulled nothing broke—but the calf didn't budge either. I got on the other side of the log handle and we lay down and braced our feet against the mother. Together we managed to drag the bloody calf out. But he just laid there, a slippery, grey, unmoving piece of meat.

I was *not* going to lose another baby. He was too big to do mouth-to-mouth, or hang upside-down and hit on the back. I did the only thing that seemed possible. I threw him over my shoulder which was difficult because he wanted to just slide through my hands. His body was so long his face almost hit the ground. I started jumping up and down. By gum, the calf started coughing!

The farmer asked, "Where did you learn to do that?"

"Nowhere," I said. "It just seemed the right thing to do."

He said, "I'm going to have to remember that."

The final unhappy development was the mother refused to let the baby nurse. I had to milk her, and she could kick sideways. After a few days of trying to milk her and getting kicked, I gave up and fed the calf goat milk. He thrived beautifully.

Animal husbandry or raising farm animals is much more than having pets. Hard decisions have to be made regarding safe herd management, culling undesirable animals, becoming your own veterinarian, reproductive (or anti-reproductive) procedures, and fencing, and housing facilities.

Although sentiment may be a factor in these choices, it can't be the primary influence. Toughness is a very real requirement.

13 STEWARDSHIP AT CHANTREL

Mel, the carpenter who was framing up the big new house (Chantrel) was an animal dealer, and his tongue was hanging out for my seven Herefords. And, I was getting pretty fed up with the many hours I was spending taking care of animals. It was beginning to cut into the time I needed to earn a living. But, I didn't really want to sell them, so I (mostly) doubled the price I had spent on each of the animals. I told him I wanted $3,000 for the bull, $1600 for each of the cows, and $350 for the babies (which I hadn't paid for anyway). He met my price without blinking. I think I underpriced them. I should have researched it better.

With the sale of the Herefords reducing the labor cost of the building Chantrel by one-half, my eyes were opened to the monetary value of my animals. But that had not been my motivation in acquiring them. Was loneliness my motivation? Perhaps, in part.

Chantrel was a house that evolved. It began with the placement of the trailer on my "Angry Hill," in the middle of the pasture. When I got angry, I'd go there to cool off. It was on a knoll and had about ten big white pines around it. I would lie down and hear the wind in the pines and my pain would just drain out of me and into the warm ground. On the backside of the hill were Chanterelle mushrooms that came up in the late summer. That's where my name for the house came from.

By the way, sadly, I destroyed that patch of mushrooms with the installation of the septic system.

The concept for the building had begun one winter when I decided to put an outside entry room on the trailer. I got some graph paper and started drawing. The room kept getting bigger and bigger until I had a 30'x40', three-story house with a full drive-in cellar. I oriented it so the long side of the house had southern exposure. I meant to keep the north wall un-penetrated by windows or doors (because of our cold winters). But, once it was built I couldn't stand how dark it was, so I added windows on that north side.

Stew had salvaged two beautiful antique stained-glass windows that were being replaced by vinyl combination windows. The workers were throwing them in the dumpster. He knew what I would think of them, so he grabbed the only two unbroken ones. I took them down to a glass store and they created a six-inch frame around them that would fit in our wall. The old lead had started to gap allowing cold air to come in, so I had them put insulated glass on the outside behind the stained-glass. I thought the "Victorian fancy" of the windows wouldn't fit with the rough barn look of the living room, but surprisingly, they were not out of place.

Chantrel has a wrap-around porch and natural cedar clapboard siding with barn red trim (except for a "slut red" roof, thanks to Stew). Let me tell you how *that* happened. My husband's nephew was a roofer. Stew said we could get a good metal roof installed at a cheap price through him. I agreed to the project, requiring only that the roof match the barn red we had for the shutters and trim. On the day of the job, I left to do some electrical work, and Stew stayed to give them a hand with the roof. When I got home I was horrified to see the roof was scarlet! This was definitely not the nice quiet country color I had in mind It was slut red. I told Stew how upset I was and how important color is to a woman. I'm afraid to say, I was almost crying. Stew asked if I wanted them to take it off. I couldn't make them do that, but it has been ten years and I still haven't gotten used to the color. Hopefully fading will make it more presentable—unless it becomes pink!

The knoll the trailer and addition sat on turned out to be deep ledge rock which had to be dynamited to butt the cellar of the new building right up to the existing trailer above. On the south side, we built a three-tier terrace from the pieces of blasted rock, and filled it with roses and other perennials. I wanted to be able to smell the fragrance of the Damask roses from my open bedroom window. On the north side I built a long roofed wood shed that held ten cords of wood, a wood splitter and the four-wheelers.

Inside, Chantrel is all knotty pine floors, walls and ceiling, plus big barn beams, so the end result is an amiable blending of log cabin and barn. I'm not a great housekeeper so the effect is more "casual comfort" than "studied elegance." The wrap-around roofed porch provides access to the kitchen, bedroom and front entryway which has glass side lights beside the heavy wooden door. The transition from inside to outside living is smooth, making participation in bird study, weather, and animal antics possible.

Some of Bompa's old tools adorn the walls and an exact duplicate of Aunt Emma's wood cook-stove gets the big living area warm and cozy. In winter, I keep a pot of water with cinnamon sticks in it on the stove so it usually smells good. The times it doesn't would be due to skunk, or wet dog, or Brussels sprouts.

Unfortunately, the skunk problem was aggravated by me, and would you believe it all began with woodchucks? When Stew couldn't keep up with the elimination of all the woodchucks marauding in the garden, I taught my longhaired German Shephard (named Sawyer) to kill them. I brought one of the woodchucks Stew had shot over to Sawyer. I threw it down on the ground, started kicking it, and growled at it, saying, "Bad woodchuck. Bad". Sawyer got into the spirit of it, picked it up, and started shaking it. I took it away after a bit. It wasn't long after that I heard his high excited bark. He had a woodchuck cornered, so I told him to "Go get 'em." Sawyer grabbed it, shook it to snap its neck and that woodchuck was history. The next woodchuck he went and got himself. So far, so good.

The next year, Sawyer started barking his high bark and digging in the rock pile where the woodchucks lived. I said, "Go get 'em," so he kept digging. Because of the rocks, he was unsuccessful. That evening, I got a good blast of skunk and Sawyer came in loaded with it. The next morning I found a dead skunk laid out in the driveway. Apparently, a family of skunks had taken up residence in the rock pile and I had told Sawyer to "go get 'em." Now I not only had a skunk killer, I was the one that told him to do it!

I tried all the 'old wives ways' of getting rid of skunk smell. Tomato juice didn't work and it made him look like he'd just slaughtered a deer. What *did* work was vinegar—lots of it.

Sawyer was willful and hardheaded. He had to be in close eye-contact with me, otherwise, he'd take off into the woods. He'd hear me calling but would stubbornly refuse to come back. During hunting season, that would put him in jeopardy with the game wardens or even hunters. They would shoot him on sight. I'd get furious with him, especially when he would look back at me, decide he was out of my range, and just keep going. But, once he returned, my anger melted. Eventually, because of age and sickness, he had to be put down. I couldn't do it, but Emma was able to—with one shot. The grit that girl has is unbelievable. He is buried here at home.

My relationship to this dog showed me an aspect of God I could understand better. God isn't just love. He gets as angry with continued stiff-necked disobedience as I did with my dog. As much as I was tempted to shoot the critter, I didn't. Then when he turned around and came back, my anger just melted, as if it never existed.

But to get back to my narrative, skunks were the more benign animals my dogs tangled with. Porcupines were much worse, and Emma was part of this procedure also. It is fortunate she has a real knack with dogs because I don't know how many times she has had to de-quill a dog; you know—taking porcupine quills out of dogs. Not too long ago, I witnessed a three hour session she spent taking forty quills out of my dog's mouth, nose, and legs. The dog didn't get the quills in her legs by pouncing on the porcupine, but by pawing at her mouth trying to get the quills out. All she did was drive them deeper.

I tried to help by holding the dog but I could only last ten minutes. Chris helped also, but he only lasted maybe fifteen minutes. Emma hung in there wrestling with the dog as she took them out, one-by-one. When there was no one left to help, Emma backed the dog into the corner of the kitchen cabinets and held with her legs. My dog would get so worn out she would just give up for a few minutes. That gave Emma the opportunity to go for the more difficult areas like the gums. The break only lasted for a few minutes and then it was back to the struggle again. The whole ordeal lasted three hours. The astonishing part of this was the dog never once tried to bite her, and it wasn't even her dog! Emma didn't give up until the quills were all out. Two quills had broken off and the area swelled up, leaking pus for almost two months before they were finally absorbed. My dog would have died from that many quills if they hadn't been removed.

This dog had a brother, and the pair of them would run together when they got loose. Because of the first painful three hour battle to remove quills, that particular female dog developed a fierce hatred of porcupines and whenever she could, she would hunt for porcupines and try taking a big chunk out of them. Her brother would join right in and he would get quilled also. The first time they both got quilled, they had been gone for two days. I was spending hours searching for them. I actually found two different people who had seen them running, but then the trail got cold. I finally called the animal control officer, and he relayed calls to me of people who had sighted the dogs. One woman had tried to approach them, but by the time I got there they had run back into the woods. Finally, someone called who said the dogs had collapsed on his lawn looking badly hurt. He was staying clear of them because he didn't want to spook them back into the woods. When I got to them they were in so much pain they growled at me, until I got close enough for them to smell me. The female tried to kill the porky, and was so quilled she couldn't close her mouth, and was drooling big time. Again, she had pawed at her face and gotten quills all over her legs. The male was smart enough not to bite. He must have tried to tap it with his foot, and then collapsed on the porky because he had quills driven into his chest. He couldn't walk and getting them in the car was dicey.

Even though it was late at night, I drove right to the vet's, who was willing to de-quill them. Actually, he put them under and we both pulled quills for about two hours. There was a cold fall rain that evening. I doubt they would have survived if they hadn't been found. Animals can get themselves into some pretty pickles, bless their little hearts.

My whole life has been accompanied by dogs, sometimes pure-bred, sometimes cross-breeds. Harry had a German Short-haired Pointer called Dave for a hunting dog. I had never experienced what is called a "soft mouth" in a dog before, but I was soon to learn.

I was at work (as usual) when I got a frantic call from Harry. He said, "You better come down here because I think Dave killed the kitten."

I said, "It'll take me about twenty minutes to get there, but I'm leaving right now," I pulled up to the trailer and ran inside. "Where is it?

Harry was sitting in the chair and waved limply towards the bed. "He ran under there, but Dave wouldn't let me get near it. He must have had it in his mouth for a half-an-hour so it's surely dead."

I looked under the bed and saw a bedraggled clump with wide-open eyes staring at me. I reached in and carefully pulled out the gummiest saliva-soaked lump of fur you could ever imagine. I examined the kitten closely, but he seemed just fine; without a single mark. Astonishing!!

The next Dave incident happened when I offered my neighbor Myra, an unused dog house I had. She came down to collect it, bringing her eight-year-old son with her. I opened the door to speak to them, but Dave was a German dog, selected for protectiveness, as most German breeds are. He pushed past me, barking aggressively. Myra screamed and threw her hands up in the air. Her son turned and ran away. Dave took off after the boy. I took off after Dave, and Emma was a half-step behind me. Myra was still on the stairs screaming her bloody head off. The boy tripped and fell and Dave muckeled onto his butt. Emma grabbed Dave and got him back in the house. I ripped the boy's pants down to see the damage my dog had done. There wasn't a mark on him! I couldn't believe it. Apparently, Dave just pinned him to the ground with his mouth. The soft mouth of a bird dog had no crunch in it. Thank goodness!

Looking back on this now, I'm appalled I took such liberty with another woman's child. My only excuse is, in the heat of the moment, people do strange things. I was fortunate Myra didn't take exception to the whole thing.

Another dog we had was Tang a young male Rottweiler/Mastiff combination. He was big and intimidating, although he was quite gentle. We also had a young female called Zoey, who was a Boxer/Rottweiler combination. They were beautiful dogs.

Late during their first winter with us, they disappeared. Emma was devastated. She was sure someone had picked them up because they loved to go for rides and might have been lured into a car. Another alternative was they may have decided to go woods running. The concern there was the pack of coyotes we could hear singing at night in those very woods. These young dogs were tender meat and not used to defending themselves. I was afraid they were goners. We looked for days, canvassing neighborhoods. We had some reports of sightings of them, but nothing recent.

We finally decided to criss-cross the valley from Crockett Ridge to our Elm Hill. Emma was to start at our house and head to Crockett Ridge. I was to start there and head for the house. Bird Brook was in the valley between the two ridges. I called and whistled the whole time, partly to call the dogs, and partly to let any of the other woods denizens (bears) know that a human was around.

Since there was still crusty snow on the ground, I was surprised to find the brook free of ice. Not to be daunted, I took off my jeans, shoes, and socks to cross the brook. My feet directly felt, not stones, but hard slippery ice which had just sunk. I realized that the only way to cross was to go three-legged with a cane to steady myself on the bottom ice. At this point I stopped making noise because I didn't want to draw attention to myself, in case anybody else was in the woods, and me in my underpants. I managed to wobble across with my clothes clutched in one hand and a wooden stick holding me up in the other.

Boy, did I get my clothes on fast when I got to the other side! After about an hour and a half, I trudged up to the house feeling very depressed our plan hadn't worked. I saw something dark on the front stoop. I squinted but I still couldn't make it out. Suddenly it barked—threateningly.

"Zoey! Is that you? I yelped. "What are you barking at me for? You know me."

Her ears went down and her butt wiggled as she came to me. She looked apologetic. Whether it was because she didn't recognize me coming up from the woods that way, or because she knew she was bad to have run off, was a toss-up.

Emma and I were jubilant. But where was Tang? We tried not to think about that. Maybe, being male, the coyotes had taken him down, but had spared Zoey because she was female and more interesting.

Two hours later, a woman called and said, "We think we found your dog." I went roaring off in the car and sure enough, it was Tang. He was in the caller's pickup and growled when I approached, until I said his name. Then he gingerly got out of the truck and into my vehicle.

The Lady said they saw him laying on the side of the dirt road when they went out for their morning walk. He growled at them so they didn't approach. That afternoon when he was still in the road they thought he may have been hurt, so they carefully approached. They managed to get to his collar which had our phone number on it. The rest was just happiness.

Emma and I tried to reconstruct what had happened. We think Tang got sore feet from the crusty snow since he was heavier and probably kept breaking through. Zoey, being lighter, stayed on top so it didn't bother her feet as much. When Tang gave up and refused to go any farther, she decided to go back home and get help. They knew all the time how to get home. They just were having so much fun they didn't want to. Don't tell me dogs aren't smart.

They also have very human feelings. Remember Dave, the German shorthaired pointer? He had a unique way of showing love. He would nibble softly with his small front teeth, the ones in front of his canines. When he got old and eventually died, our other dog we had, called Tang, grieved Big Time. He moped around not eating and refusing to play. Then Tang started doing an interesting thing. He began giving little nibble kisses the way Dave used to. Tang had never done that before Dave died.

But now, it seemed as if he was remembering his old friend when he did this. Dogs really *do* experience grief.

My concept of animal stewardship was the reverse of Stew's predatory drive. He loved to hunt—and it really didn't matter what it was, when it was, or how many it was. He was a big-time poacher, (although not as bad as some I know). I tried to keep him from blatantly breaking the hunting laws, but he would just hunt in other areas where I couldn't keep track of him. My son Nick wouldn't hunt with him for that reason, but that didn't bother Stew. He had his family to hunt with.

However, Stew was afraid if a game warden got a warrant to look in our freezer, we would be caught with the evidence of many different deer in there. Because Stew was not keeping the law he was enslaved by fear of getting caught. If he had kept the law he would have been free from that fear. The ethic here is one that I've only come to realize recently. I used to think that law abiding was not only confining, it was bondage. I now see that law keeping is actually freedom. Furthermore, peace and serenity are the natural consequence of that choice.

A good example of this can be seen in traffic laws. Going the speed limit is not namby-pamby slavery. It frees you from constantly looking over your shoulder to see if there is a policeman around. How much the quality of life improves by realizing where freedom exists!

To get back to farm life, we had never eaten any of our own beef. The Herefords were sold before we decided we wanted to try homegrown beef, so I decided to buy a beef critter from my neighbor down the hill. He had a meaty dark-red breed called Limousine. We bought it as a spring calf and let it range on the pasture for the summer. That fall we put a hundred pounds of grain into it over the next three months and then took it to the slaughter house. That meat was unbelievably good—tender and tasty. There just wasn't enough of it!

The next year we got a Black Angus from the same neighbor. Stew decided we would save money by slaughtering it ourselves. Then we could cut it up, package, and label the meat the same way we did his deer. Sounded like a good plan but the execution of it left a lot to be desired. Stew's first shot between the heifer's eyes just went through the nasal cavity. She started spraying blood and took off through the pasture, snorting and shaking her head. Stew's son Mark, who was about eleven, took off also, screaming bloody murder and high stepping (due to uneven terrain?) out of the pasture. He was convinced the heifer was charging him when all she was thinking about was getting the pain out of her nose. Stew managed to catch up with the heifer and he had to put three more shots into her before she was dead.

Why on earth did we think we could do this? I wondered.

The skinning and cutting of the meat was a much bigger job than Stew expected. Mark helped with the cutting, and I thought his avid interest in handling the meat it was just a reaction to his earlier fright, but learned differently later. I had no interest in meat cutting but helped by packaging and labeling. All this effort was for naught. The meat was tougher than an old bull. The frenzy of that heifer's death tightened up all her muscles to the point of inedibility.

The responsibility we owed to the animals we acquired definitely broke down here. We didn't raise any more beef critters, but I still can't get that debacle out of my mind.

Eventually, I became aware that my farm animal population was over seventy head, so I put the brakes on and began to reverse the trend. When I moved down to Chantrel where there was no barn, I sold the pigs, goats, and everything else except the horses and chickens. They continue to bring me great joy. Very few people understand the connection I have to them

The gift of stewardship of animals is not the only area of responsibility. It also includes plant life. My first vegetable garden at Waterlily was a total failure, and the effort in Marblehead was not much better. I did manage to put in a decent perennial garden for Mother a few years before she died. But the tomatoes I planted at the red house almost overwhelmed me with their success. I began to be drawn in that direction.

At Chantrel, I began to paint with my gardens. I had a blue and silver herb garden (cool tones), a yellow, orange, and red garden (warm tones), old fashioned roses, and more modern hybrids. I planted many different varieties of fruit trees; plum, pear, peach, cherry, and apple. Berries included, strawberries, blueberries, raspberries, and gooseberries were planted. The vegetable garden was liberally enriched with manure from my horses and was abundantly prolific.

I raised free-range chickens for bug control, (no pesticides allowed.) Unfortunately my chicken population had many predators. The bantam hens were really good about setting on their eggs so they would hatch out a bunch of chicks at least twice a year. You would think that would have increased the population, but that wasn't what was happening. I had chicken hawks carry off a few. Skunks would chomp on a setting hen because she wouldn't leave her eggs. Twice, Stew and I got rousted out of bed by a screaming mother hen. Stew managed to shoot one skunk with the pistol we kept by the bed.

I began to search out the setting hens so I could pick them up and put them in the hen house, which I shut up at night. But this didn't improve the situation any. One night I heard a racket in the hen house and ran out to discover a skunk in one of the nesting boxes on the floor with half a chicken in his jaws. I shut the door and went to get Stew and he shot that one, also, making the place smell twice as bad (and it doesn't smell that good to begin with).

My next effort at chicken preservation was to put the nesting boxes up on cement blocks where the skunks couldn't reach them. Again I hear crash-bang out in the hen house. This time, it's a whole family of raccoons—and they can climb. I lost three more chickens that night. My neighbor's dogs got some, until she started reliably tying them up. And, my own dogs were responsible for the loss of a few more.

Finally this winter, with my chicken population down from thirty to four, I ordered twelve more baby chicks at the feed store. My only legitimate reasons for building the chicken population back up is for bug control and their delectable eggs. The other reasons for enjoying them are not at all practical, but they are completely valid—to me, anyway.

I kept bees for pollination of all the fruit trees. I had as many as three hives going and I got three gallons of honey from them. Sadly, I got that brood die-off, a new disease that made national news in 2010, and so I haven't restocked the bees. I'm hoping the wild bees will do the job, although I'm sure the fruit production won't be as plentiful.

Another garden activity was building lots of rock walls. They provided a setting for the various groups of perennials and the greyness of the rocks was as much of an artistic statement as the flowers themselves. I would echo the rocks with Silver King or Silver Mound, varieties of the perennial Artemisia. I've even used Dusty Miller, although I don't usually put in annuals.

I also keep bird feeders going summer and winter. I've seen about twenty different kinds of birds at the feeders and another twenty that are in the vicinity. 'Peterson's Field Guide to Birds,' is an indispensible reference for identification. The best sight was the woodpecker mother bringing her baby to the feeder. She would stuff the suet in his mouth. It took almost a week before he could get it for himself. He turned into a completely spoiled-brat butterball. When I accidentally let the suet run out, he squawks up a storm, madly emptying the whole feeder of the black oil sunflower seeds. They get strewn all over the porch completely uneaten. Crazy baby woodpecker.

On the days off from electrical work that I took for garden work, I didn't even stop when it rained. I guess that makes me a fanatic. (No big surprise). I had about four acres of fields to mow and you would think it was a monumental burden to take care of, but actually the opposite was true. I would come in the house after working ten hours in the gardens, pouring sweat, and covered in dirt from head to toe. I would get in my old-fashioned claw-foot bathtub, fill it up to the brim and feel such peace and happiness it could only be described as joy.

The last area of responsibility I want to cover is in regard to people. During my school years, I chose to turn away from the study of medicine because I didn't want my possibly inferior ability or training to result in lives being lost.

My chosen vocation doesn't have such high stakes, but the commitment to excellence still needs to be there. An electrical job needs to be done in a workman-like manner that will continue to provide reliable and safe operation for a maximum number of years. Adding to that would be the aesthetics of neatness and style. Also there is the service aspect, which is where people enter the picture.

I would like to give you an example of how an electrician can be of service. I went to work in the cellar of a young couple who were finishing off their basement as an apartment for their parents. The young mother looked really dragged down. She brought two toddlers down cellar with her while she wearily folded laundry. I was standing up in front of a switch trying to figure out what her husband had done when he put the wires in. I asked her what the rooms were for, partly to assist in the trouble shooting, and partly because I was curious. She told me the new living space was for her mother who had cancer and her step-father who had Parkinson's disease. She said she didn't want them to have to go into a nursing home.

I felt the tug of the Holy Spirit to give them a break on the price for the job. But I thought Stew would never go for this idea.

Nothing ventured, nothing gained.

So, I checked with Stew to see if he would go along with it. Much to my surprise, he did.

But still, I didn't feel peace with this decision. Then, I got the impression that what God wanted was to give them the whole job.

Amazingly, Stew agreed to that also!

Thank you, God, for softening his heart.

When the job was done and I told her that she didn't owe anything, she broke down and cried. She apologized and said, "The stress of everything was really getting me down, but to have that burden lifted really is a miracle."

That whole experience gave us such joy, we were cruising for hours. To be in the center of God's will, as He is blessing someone, is qiute a high.

Later I got a really nice thank-you note from her. She said I was an angel. Well, I knew I wasn't an angel, but being God's agent was pretty darn good.

Another one of those areas of responsibility that was given to me was Stew's children. Mark, the oldest, came to live with us when he was five years old. A year later his younger sister Rachel joined us. I felt I had dropped the ball with my children from my first marriage and this would be an opportunity to do a better job of child-rearing.

Mark had difficulty learning to read but we applied to get some private tutoring at school. He finally caught on by the third grade. His reading interest was in the narrow area of science fiction, and especially dark fantasy. I had a few books of sword and sorcery in my science fiction collection he was interested in. That was something I could share with him. What I couldn't understand was his attraction to dead things. When he went fishing with his father he would hold the dead fish in his hand for about five minutes, jiggling it and watching it flop. It was very unnerving. It reminded me of his fascination with the butchering of the dead cow. I was so spooked by his behavior I had Stew put a lock on the gun cabinet, but that was a joke. It was one of those tiny locks that were more decorative than functional. Plus, he never kept it locked. That didn't help my anxiety level any.

To top it all off Stew gave Mark a pellet gun for his birthday. Boys and pellet guns are a volatile mixture that my horses, dogs, cats, chickens, and song birds felt the brunt of. Ironically, it was Rachel that inflicted the only damage I was aware of. She shot through one of the windows, supposedly "by accident."

Later Mark went into a gothic phase where he wore all black with chains and sweeping long coats. His fascination with death extended into satanic black magic.

Mark's other main interest was Nintendo with games of combat. His father spent hours with him playing those games also. Eventually, Stew would go watch a sports program but Mark would keep on playing, hour after hour. He was able to convince his father to buy him new games that were labeled with an "M" (for middle years, Mark said). "M" was actually for mature so these games were filled with blood and gore.

I tried to get him interested in outdoor things. I remembered how much I loved my tree house at his age so I got the whole family to help make a tree house. It was even bigger than the one I had (which isn't saying much). Neither of the kids ever used it.

One winter, I made an effort to get him out in the yard with me on cross-country skis. That went over like a lead balloon. He went out once but that was it.

I liked classical music, Mark liked heavy metal, and Rachel liked country. About the only thing we all enjoyed was careening through the woods on the four wheelers. Other than that, there was no common ground. I was an alien. Stew didn't help because he said they were *his* children and he didn't want me to have anything to do with them. I wasn't to get them to clean up their rooms or make any suggestions at all.

Rachel was a little Barbie doll, extremely focused on her body and her style. She had a lot of friends that were always visiting. Part of it was her fear of being alone. She would have the dog come upstairs with her at night if she didn't have a visitor staying with her; the strange thing about her fear was she was allowed to go to the most gruesome horror movies you could imagine. I went with her to one and never went again. If I had a steady diet of that, I might be afraid of the dark, too.

Rachel and her friend came with us on a Father's Day visit to a sushi restaurant in Portland. After we had spent quite a bit of money we went outside only to discover that Rachel and her friend had thrown it all up. They said they had started laughing but ended up puking. I suspected it was induced because Rachel was extremely thin, but Stew didn't want to hear of my concern.

Another area of disagreement was they all thought farting was great fun and would even raise their leg to squeeze it out. I was not impressed. Since whatever I am thinking appears on my face, I'm sure Rachel was aware of my disapproval. Her response was to be very antagonistic to me, so I was pretty much out of the picture; with both of them, actually. When she went into a gothic phase also, I became resigned to the idea that the dropped ball with my first three children wasn't going to be redeemed with Stew's children.

I even made a doomed effort to teach Rachel the secret language I had enjoyed as a child. Remember Gaidy? It is constructed by taking the vowel in each word and adding 'iggidy" to it. If you wanted to say, "she is stupid" (a typical girl's comment), it would sound like this . . . . shidighee—yidigi-is stidigu—pigidid. It looks a lot harder than it really is. Needless to say, my effort fell totally flat. Can't say I blame her. Who wants to have a secret language with your stepmom?

Another attempt to have a good family time was actually initiated by Emma. It was her idea to borrow canoes and kayaks and paddle down the Saco River. We had a great time which included swinging off a rope swing into the river. Even though I was over 60, I went off it also. I don't think it was a surprise for anyone in my family, but Emma's friends were flabbergasted. I got a big, "Yeah Mom" from them.

Unfortunately we bit off a bigger chunk of the river than we should have and Rachel and Mark got really tired and cranky. They couldn't wait to get off the river. It wasn't a success for them, but the rest of us had a grand time.

The one area that I did hit it off with Rachel was with the horses. I would help her in getting Arizona ready to be ridden. Pretty soon she was able to get him saddled up without my help. The only trouble was my English saddle disappeared, and by the time I noticed it missing, she and her father were long gone.

Unhappily, my stewardship was not a success in regard to them. However, the awareness of the purpose of my life began to grow on me. The purpose of life was the management, responsibility, and joy of stewardship.

Once I realized that, I found the answer to the question I had asked as a teenager: the question being, "Why did God create us?" The answer was staring me right in the face. It was to enjoy our companionship, variety, and beauty—as I did with my domain.

That is the gift, and task God has given us.

14 HARVEST

While I was growing up, I took on the nurturing of my youngest sisters by default. I didn't realize it at the time, and it seemed only an occasional moment here or there. What were these moments? Reading a story; or, showing another one how to draw. Or, having a sister sit in my lap while I put a Band-Aid on; Very minor moments, but apparently that small amount of attention was 'forever felt'.

The middle sister Elissa was not the recipient of my nurturing. She, actually, was the worst pain-in-the-neck to me.

Once my older sister Barbara and I had left the family to get married, things went from bad to worse. Dad continued his molestation with Steph and Elissa. He made a play for Margo but she had the sense to turn him down.

Why didn't that occur to the rest of us? Beats me!

I remember someone jokingly commenting to Dad about "his harem," and how uncomfortable that concept made me feel. How many people knew or suspected?

Elissa apparently went off the deep end. She was stubborn and rebellious. Dad committed her to a mental institution even though she was no longer a minor, and he had no right to do that. The story was she was suicidal but in later years Elissa said that wasn't true.

What they did to her was dreadful. Shock treatments, heavy duty drugs and I don't know what else. She began to do something we called "digging," but there was another fancy word for it. She would dig at the skin of her face to pull out a hair she saw. It wasn't like cutting, but rather hate of hair. She pulled all her eyebrow hair out and got these huge sores that eventually became ugly scars. Her face was so badly scarred it looked like she had been in a fire. The end result was mutilation. I asked if it was because she hated herself. She said no. It put her in a zone where she didn't feel anything. I didn't understand that, but she didn't seem able to explain it any better, so I let it go.

She got married and had a son. And, although she was a good mother when he was young, their relationship became very stormy in his teens. He eventually went to live with his father.

She had been so messed up chemically when she was hospitalized as a teenager, she had a difficult time holding down a job. Additionally, she was diagnosed as a manic/depressive; bi-polar I guess they now call it. The only difference between Elissa and the rest of us girls seemed to be that she was exhibiting externally the damage the rest of us kept hidden inside.

My heart went out to her. But come any closer to her?

Didn't happen.

Besides all Elissa's other medical problems she had advanced emphysema, and something called 'hording disease'. She had a very hard time getting rid of things and she also needed at least five of everything (it might break, you know). Shopping was a daily occurrence.

Previously, she lived in low-income housing. The owners had fire safety rules which did not permit the hazardous accumulation of 'all that stuff' she had. Because she couldn't clean it up, they threw her out. She put her many belongings in storage and lived out of her car for about a year and a half, in spite of the frigid New England weather. I kept asking her to come live with me, but she was even more stubborn than I was.

The second winter living in her car was much colder than the first, so in February she finally surrendered. I rented the biggest U-Haul truck that was available and went to pick her stuff up, three hours away. Packing that truck floor-to-ceiling still allowed us to bring only half of her things back with us. I converted the area over the ceiling to give her additional storage area for her stuff.

We got off to a rocky start at first. It began with my sharing food I had cooked when I had some time, which wasn't all that often since my work schedule was packed. I thought she would return the favor, but it was all one way. All take and no give, I thought to myself.

The next bump in the road was when she was bragging about how knowledgeable she was about tools. When she said she thought she knew more about tools than I did, I rose to the challenge. "Let's go down cellar and see who can name the most tools and describe what they are for."

"It's a bet,"

I held up my goat de-horning iron.

"What's this?"

"It's a soldering iron."

"Nope. It's for taking the horns off goats."

"How about this one?" Long pause.

I filled in the silence with the answer. "It's called an elastrator, and it's used to castrate buckling goats by stretching the elastic so you can roll it off onto the testicle."

"How about that box over there with the lid and collar?"

"I don't know."

"That's the dehorning box I made to hold the baby goats when I de-horn them."

"That's not fair. These are all specialty farm tools. I would have no reason to be familiar with them."

"How about electrical tools?"

"Yeah, I would know those."

"What's this?"

Silence again.

"It's called a ratcheting cable cutter, and it's for cutting cable in tight spots."

I held up a pad with a wire coming out of it.

"What's this?"

"I don't know."

"It's a blanket for heating up PVC conduit so you can bend it."

That led me to go get my metal emt bender.

"Do you know what this is?"

Silence again.

Next, I held up my set of knockout punches.

"What about this?"

"This isn't fair either. Of course you'd know more about electrical tools."

"All right, I'll just pick general tools."

I picked up a riveter. "What's this do?"

No response.

"What's this?"

"It's a drill bit."

"Yes, but what kind?"

No answer.

"It's an 'easy-out' for drilling out broken off bits."

By this time I was starting to feel bad. I held up a glass cutter.

"Oh, I know it, I know it—it's a glass cutter!"
"You're right"
I let it end with one she knew.
I said, "I'm getting tired of this. Let's go upstairs."

That was the last confrontation Elissa and I had. I was ashamed that my pride had risen up so strongly to the challenge. The old habits of competition and dominance were so ingrained they were almost reflexive. Letting someone win is harder than you think.

For awhile she pretty much kept to her apartment and I kept to mine.

Eventually, I bridged the gap by inviting her to come to church to hear our choir sing. With her musical background, I knew she would enjoy it.

Next, I asked her to sing Duets with me at the church service. Her soprano and my alto made a pleasnt blend. She even sang with the choir one year.

I think it was the music that drew her, but her interest grew to the point she was going to Bible studies with me.

When Elissa first came to Maine, she was an Agnostic. She doubted the existence of God, and she had actual certainty that Satan was just a myth.

I overcame my doubt by amassing enough years to know by experience that chance doesn't favor successful combination. Applying that thought to the complexity of the natural world, led to the realization that there had to be an intelligent designer. I found evidence of His power, goodness, and love, all over.

So, where does evil come from, if God is good?

There is only one true explanation. There is a counter force in opposition to God, and that is in the person of the fallen angel, Lucifer, more commonly referred to as Satan. As Elissa grew in her spiritual understanding, she came to accept the existence of Satan as an actual entity.

She also learned that just being a good person wasn't going to be enough. The Bible has much to say on this subject, Isaiah 64:6 "all OUR rightousness is as filthy rags." She learned that it was not possible to be good enough without Jesus. It was only through our connection to Him that we will be saved.

Her personality softened. No longer was she stubborn and inflexible. Her most dominant personality characteristic became overflowing joy that lightened all those she touched.

Elissa's driving gave her several opportunities to experience God's watch care over her. The first was when she hit a patch of black ice and completely spun around, ending up broadside in the road. As she sat there recovering her wits, a logging truck came barreling over the hill the way they do, and there would have been no stopping it. Elissa just barely got her car going and out of the way.

The second narrowly averted disaster was when she heard a clunking and couldn't quite tell where it was coming from. As she continued, the noise got louder so she stopped to see if she was getting a flat tire. All the tires were fine so she continued until she pulled into a gas station. There she discovered, three of her four tires only had two lug nuts holding the tires on. How she could have traveled as far as she had was a veritable miracle. It was then she finally realized God had His hand of protection over her life, and this brought her great assurance.

For some strange reason Elissa had never had any pets. She had a very strong nurturing drive with no way to express it except with her grandson. Because she didn't get along with her daughter-in-law, she didn't see her grandson as much as she wished. It was a source of deep pain to her. Plus she was a nuisance to her son.

One of my tenants had moved out and left a decrepit cat behind. I was able to persuade Elissa to adopt her and both their lives were improved tremendously. I cut a cat door in her apartment, so her new friend, Corrina (the cat) could come and go as she pleased. Elissa thought the sun rose and set on that cat.

Surprisingly, Elissa enjoyed going out on the four wheelers with Stew and I. She was much more cautious in her driving than we were, so we moderated our trips for her. She absolutely believed us when we said you couldn't tip a four wheeler over.

Wouldn't you know, she did exactly that!

We were going up a hill on a slant. It never occurred to us to tell Elissa to lean on the up-hill side. Both Stew and I watched in horror as she slowly tipped over sitting up straight in a locked position still on the machine. Somehow it rolled away from her so she didn't get hurt. My irrepressible sister still wanted to go with us the next time we went out four wheeling. I was proud of her.

Because of Elissa's many medical and personal problems, she didn't have much of a work history. She needed something to do so I suggested she apply at Community Concepts. This was a community service that provided transportation for poor people that needed to get to doctors' appointments. The program was funded by the state and the drivers were paid a good mileage allotment, rather than a salary. This volunteer driving turned out to be a perfect place for her. It gave her a reason to get going in the morning. It got her out to meet people and she was an outspoken witness for giving up smoking. She had no reservations and would approach anyone, sometimes saying the most outrageous things. But because of her positive outlook people would warm right up to her. She viewed her job as a service, which it was, but it also gave her enough money from the mileage allotment to buy a more dependable car. She even had enough money available to fly down to Florida to visit a friend. This self-reliance gave her great happiness.

Her camera was another joy. I cleared a spot by her driveway and gave her some dahlia bulbs to plant. She was so proud of them she took pictures, along with the chickens, turkeys, horses, sunsets etc. One of her favorite expressions was, "Get the camera." I also planted some cherry tomatoes on the other side of her driveway, so she could pick her own and not have to go into my garden. Sun-warm ripe Sweet 100's (the specialty of Young's Greenhouse) are the ultimate of garden delights.

My relationship to her made a complete turnaround. I began to enjoy being with her. We would play Scrabble and Boggle until the wee hours. It gave us a focus to the time we spent together. To establish that the score was meaningless, we would help each other. That way competition didn't rear its ugly head. I did have to bring a book to read when we were playing Scrabble though. She would take an interminable amount of time. Because of that, I much preferred Boggle which only takes three to five minutes, depending on what you set up.

We began to operate on the same wavelength and had some wonderful laughs together. I actually grew to love her more than Stew, (sad to say).

About two years after she came here, the x-ray of her lungs revealed her cancer had advanced. Because of her severe emphysema, there didn't seem to be much point in chemotherapy or radiation.

She continued to get around even when she had to take an oxygen tank with her. However, she began to lose strength so eventually she couldn't drive anymore.

I took over the task of getting her to the doctor's office. It was important to her that she be completely color-coordinated, from her jewelry, to her watch, to her socks and shoes. Presentation of herself was the fabric of her being. That took time which resulted in our being late on a regular basis. At this point, there was a significant lesson for me to learn. I needed to let go of my determination to be on time, to yield to her and her timing.

Home health nurses came in to help bathe her and do some light housekeeping. She would keep them in stitches with her up-beat outlook. She also had very good rapport with her young physician, Dr Timothy Carnes. She thought so highly of him she talked me into having him as my doctor. I had just gone on social security so I qualified for Medicare. I hadn't had a physical for many years. The doctor gave me a thorough exam but there was something more there behind his eyes that spoke of his sincere compassion.

On one of her visits Elissa spoke to him of her fear, of how hard her end would be. He was on a stool to be on her level in the wheelchair. He pulled in close so their knees were touching. He took her hands and looked her in the eyes. He reassured Elissa that they would do all that was necessary to make sure she was comfortable. Elissa trusted him and she met her last days with courage because of that.

It became apparent that Elissa didn't have much time left so I organized the first reunion of all five sisters since Mom had died almost thirty years ago. It was not a great success but it was a start and at least a crack in the walls—before there were no longer five of us.

A good example of the reconnection that happened as a result of that gathering was the understanding I shared with my older sister Barbara. When I was younger her conservative life style and values were a mystery to me. Now that I had become more conservative myself, there was more resonance between us.

Also there was a healing between the younger sisters, Steph and Margo. Unfortunately my older sister still had a hard time accepting their chosen lifestyles, very different from her own. We do have a long way to go to cover the distance we put between ourselves, but hopefully, that process has finally begun. We are still family, after all.

Does that label apply to the family I walked away from; the three children from my first marriage?

I would answer, that the wound I inflicted on my children did have a negative impact on my relationship to them. My oldest had built a very high barrier around herself, although, her young son has helped us to partially bridge that. The middle child has less of a barrier. And the youngest one has definitely distanced himself.

Are we still a family? Tenuously.

Family relationships can be highly charged which is what happened when Steph came north to Vermont to help her ex-husband, Robert Swaney. He had just gotten out of the hospital from prostate surgery. Steph was in a pretty poor medical condition herself so she wasn't much help to him. Both of them were so far off in their expectations of each other, they got mad at each other for their disappointment. Robert decided to drive her over and drop her off with us. Steph was seething with her fury. It bubbled over onto Robert and the rest of us were appalled with the malevolence in her. She said Robert had been treating her badly but he wasn't showing that when he got to us—not to say that he hadn't.

I was an emotional wreck myself, coping with Elissa's sickness and undercurrents of trouble with Stew and his children. I completely snapped and told Steph she couldn't stay with me either. Steph was flabbergasted that I would throw her out so soon after she had arrived there. We were all at an impasse. At 10:00 at night Elissa came over from her apartment, in her dirty old bathrobe and even without her teeth. This was not like Elissa at all. She was always very careful with her appearance, but she wasn't thinking about herself at all. She became the peacemaker. With a calm soothing voice she brought sanity back into the group. Arrangements were made for Steph to get on a flight the next morning.

The irony of this whole episode was she was the sickest one of us all, and she was the one to walk us out of the mess.

On Elissa's last day of life, she had an appointment to see the doctor, which she very much wanted to do. She mobilized her two home health nurses to help her get ready, so when I came to pick her up, there was no typical waiting. I should have known this was a different day because I saw she didn't have her jewelry on. I asked her if she wanted me to get her jewelry box but she said, "Not today."

We got to the doctor's and he asked, "How are you doing?"

She answered with the first negative I heard her use. She said, "Not too good."

I jumped in and told the doctor she hadn't been eating for weeks.

He asked, "No appetite, Elissa?"

She answered with another question, "Do you have a pill for that?"

He said, "Yes," and wrote her a prescription to take to the pharmacy.

While we were waiting at the drive-up window, she said "Could you please turn the heat up."

I told her I had the heat already blasting, and I was dying because I had long underwear on (working outdoors in February).

She said, "Feel my hands."

They were stone cold, so I started to rub them to warm them up.

I said, "It's a good thing it's dark outside, otherwise people might get the wrong idea."

She chuckled saying, "Not only would we be lesbians, but we would be incestuous lesbians."

To be able to joke about our awful past, as poorly as she felt, released a dam inside me and we both hooped with laughter to the point of almost crying.

I also respect how she had the courage to choose her own death that same night by removing her oxygen tube and ending her battle. Her love for me was demonstrated by waiting until I had gone to bed. She wanted to spare me the pain of her last moments. I deeply hope God spared her the worst of it in those last moments.

When I found her the next morning, Corrina, was curled around her head. That cat spent weeks on her pillow, leaving only for necessities. It has taken two years for Corrina to leave Elissa's apartment and turn to me for love. I will bury Corrina next to Elissa's ashes under the Pines. That is where I will go, when my time comes. (Steph and Margo both want to have their ashes there, also)

The memorial service for Elissa was a demonstration of family love. Many of the cousins made the long trip to attend, even flying in from far away. For some with reduced circumstances, it was actually a hardship. I felt enfolded in their love.

There was no way I was going to wear black, but wore my very brightest clothes in honor of Elissa's vivid sense of color. I think I startled quite a few people who were accustomed to the earth colors I usually chose. My cousin Molly, knowing Elissa's fondness for outrageous colors, also dressed in a dramatic orange-red outfit.

I wanted to sing one of Elissa's favorite hymns with someone that I often sang duets with, but she didn't show up because her voice was all frogged up with a terrible cold. Molly offered to sing it with me, and with essentially no practice, and never having sung together before, we pulled it off. Our voices had what is called the "familial blend", which is unusual since we weren't sisters, only cousins. That was a memory I will treasure for a long time.

When everyone came to the house afterward there must have been twenty of us crowded in, shoulder—to shoulder. It wasn't oppressive; rather it was comfortably intimate. I had Elissa's vast collection of jewelry laid out for family members to pick out what they might want of hers. I also duplicated some of the old family pictures with my copier for those who were interested. There were lots of interaction and exclamations of, "I've never seen that picture. Could you make a copy for me?" Getting together with the family was a wonderful experience, in spite of the pain of the reason for the gathering.

Someone there commented to me how much Elissa learned since she began to live with me. What people don't realize is that I learned a great deal from her. She taught me that it is possible to have great joy and a light heart, even in the midst of the most trying of circumstances. My life attitude improved because of her impact on it.

Later, my thoughts turned to the gathering after our own mother's death. I wondered why my sisters and I had split apart so thoroughly. It was difficult to understand. Granted, we all lived quite a distance from each other, but that was more a symptom of the problem, rather than a cause of the problem. I do know when Mom died, dividing up the stuff caused some ugliness to surface, but that was really not the root, either.

I don't think that failure to love each other is the problem, because not one of us would own up to that concept. We do love each other. So where is the breakdown? I think it has to do with lack of forgiveness and stewardship.

What is there to forgive?

Perhaps our differences in values, choices, and life styles.

Where is the failure in stewardship?

It lies in the renouncing of our connection and responsibility to each other; in the lack of attention and nurture and respect.

Failure can teach you a lot about what is missing in order to achieve success. My life thrust has been to expand my responsibility for myself and others, so starting up a food pantry in my community was a natural outgrowth. In one year it has grown from servicing twenty families to more than one hundred and sixty five families. The great thing is that all the hard work involved in getting and distributing the food isn't an onerous duty but a joy.

So how about some of the dead-ends I went down?

As a child my goals were to be tough, competitive, successful, and a good provider; very masculine qualities which I admired. As I matured I learned that female qualities could embody strength without toughness. Sometimes flexibility, softness, and gentleness can spring from great strength.

Competition was a harder quality to surrender. I had actually taken that attribute and pushed it further into combativeness. But, did I really want to fight?

The answer was no. That character trait could be mellowed out. Another way of putting it would be to say that you "esteem another more than yourself." That's actually a good definition for love.

How about the goal of success? That was an easy objective to surrender, because I was more interested in the quality of life, than the pursuit of lots of money, or whatever your definition of success is.

The last goal was the ability to be a good provider. This is an aspect that fits equally well with either gender: After all, who supplies the first milk to a child?

The way I see it, God said He created mankind in His image. He therefore, contained within Himself both male and female qualities. So, a balance of both male and female in one person would be ideal. In addition, the union of a man and woman in the intimacy of one flesh would also exemplify this balance.

I began the story of my life with the death of my brother, because of the formative effect his absence had. I learned that the conclusion I made when I was younger was wrong. There is no more value in being male than there is in being female.

This collection of events in my life seems to be a story of problem-solving and the overcoming of obstacles. In retrospect, it turns out that the biggest hurdle I had to overcome was myself. My independence hindered my ability to yield and connect to God

My tendency to charge into life, like a mare with the bit between her teeth, obliterated God's influence and connection to me. This connection is vitally important in the fulfilling of the responsibility and management of His property. I have learned that the more I empty out my own self-sufficiency, the more God can fill me with His sufficiency.

What has been God's purpose in my life? Perhaps it has been to write this book. Even though it may contain some really difficult details from the past, there is no virtue in glossing them over, or in ignoring them, just for the sake of appearance. Hiding bad choices and behaviors is the same as Adam and Eve using fig leaves to cover their shame.

So, the whole point of this book is, I am proud, not of my life certainly, but of my God, who helped me to climb out of the worldly pit I was in, and guide me into the light of His love. Because of that, I have received the bountiful harvest of his blessings for me.